jocks

Also available from Alyson Books
by Dan Woog

*School's Out: The Impact of Gay and Lesbian
Issues on America's Schools*

jocks

True stories of America's gay male athletes

by Dan Woog

alyson
books

LOS ANGELES • NEW YORK

Manufactured in the United States of America.

This trade paperback original is published by Alyson Publications Inc.,
P.O. Box 4371, Los Angeles, California 90078-4371.
Distribution in the United Kingdom by Turnaround Publisher Services Ltd.,
Unit 3 Olympia Trading Estate, Coburg Road, Wood Green,
London N22 6TZ England.

First edition: January 1998

02 01 00 99 98   10 9 8 7 6 5 4 3

ISBN 1-55583-399-3

Library of Congress Cataloging-in-Publication Data
    Woog, Dan, 1953–
        Jocks : true stories of America's gay male athletes / by Dan Woog. — 1st ed.
        1. Gay athletes — United States — Biography. 2. Homosexuality,
    Male — United States — Case studies. 3. Sports — Social aspects —
    United States. 4. Sports — United States — Psychological aspects.
    I. Title.
    GV697.A1W687 1998
    796'.086'6420922—dc21   97-30488 CIP
    [B]

Cover design by R. Goins
Cover photographs by Johnathan Black and Mark Harvey

This book is dedicated to every gay athlete, coach,
and sports fan in America. We are indeed everywhere.

Contents

Acknowledgments

WE ARE EVERYWHERE. I JUST HAVE TO FIND US.

That was the message I sent out when I began researching *Jocks*. I knew there were plenty of gay male athletes and coaches around; I just was not sure how to ferret them out.

The Internet helped. So did a number of people, including, in no particular order, Tom Radko, Michael Collins, Mike Paulson, Derek Billings, Calvin Burwell, John Nathan, Brian Burns, George Robbins, Andy Collins, Chris Fray, Chip Reed, Dan Kelly, Doug Nissing, Keith Sweet, Joe Clark, Molly O'Neil, Wayne Pawlowski, Grant Petersen, Dann Hazel, Todd Jennings, J. C. Cummings, Bob Parlin, Eric Rofes, Jeff Perrotti, Jim Torres, Kathy Henderson, Jean Pendleton, Chris Dodge, Sandy Berman, Karen Ocamb, and a sportswoman whose writing and insight I particularly admire, Mariah Burton Nelson. To my editor, Gerry Kroll, I am truly indebted; though not a jock, he is a true champion.

I owe special thanks to four people in the soccer world who have been particularly supportive of me — Albert Loeffler, my high school coach and mentor; Jeff Lea, former coach and current esteemed colleague; Lynn Berling-Manuel and Mike Woitalla, editors and friends at *Soccer America* magazine — as well as to the many young men I have coached who started out as players and ended up as friends.

To every athlete, coach, and "athletic supporter" who agreed to be interviewed and quoted, either by name or anonymously, I owe a tremendous debt. Without your willingness to tell your tales, this book would never have been written.

Dan Woog
Westport, Connecticut
September 1997

Introduction

"JOCKS" MAY NOT BE the world's most elegant book title. And at first glance gay male athletes and coaches may not be a particularly elegant subject. At second glance it may not even seem like an appropriate subject. After all, don't jocks and gay men inhabit parallel universes?

So much for stereotypes.

From the very beginning the worlds of athletics and homosexuality have intersected more often than many people realize (or at least admit). Ancient Greek men, according to *National Geographic* magazine, used sports as an opportunity to meet boys. The root word for *gymnasium* — *gymnos* — has nothing to do with athletics; it means *nude*. And, of course, Greek Olympians competed naked, in front of an audience limited to males (and the priestess of Demeter).

Civilization has moved a long way in 2,800 years, though not always forward. While several major male sports figures have publicly disclosed their homosexuality — among them football running back Dave Kopay and tight end Jerry Smith, baseball outfielder Glenn Burke, and diving champion Greg Louganis, to name a few — only two have done so during their playing careers: figure-skating star Rudy Galindo and soccer player Justin Fashanu. Far more common are the heated denials whenever a pro athlete's homosexuality is so much as hinted at, as happened with Dallas Cowboys quarterback Troy Aikman in 1996.

But for all its press, prestige, and power, professional sports occupies only one planet in the vast athletic universe. The total number of pro athletes and coaches is infinitesimal; far more numerous are the boys and young men competing at lower levels. In rural towns, faceless suburbs, and large cities across America, teenagers and twenty-something males shoot hoops, kick soccer balls, handle hockey and lacrosse sticks, run, swim, and cycle. They are working hard and working out. Every day they sweat and shower, train and compete in the most macho of all environments: high school and college sports.

And just as in any other endeavor that brings people together, some of them are gay.

Gay athletes and coaches are nowhere near as visible as, say, gay actors, musicians, or even student government leaders. The reason has less to do with percentages than with reality: The sports world does not exactly high-five them or grasp them in a winner's hug. In fact, recent news stories make it seem as if athletes and coaches are caught in a queer time warp. In 1996, for example, in California, two University of La Verne baseball players were charged with battery and civil rights violations after beating the president of the school's gay student union. Three members of the University of Miami football team entered another student's apartment, accused him of spreading rumors that a star wide receiver was gay, and assaulted him. A high school runner in Orange County, California, was attacked solely because his track coach had come out as gay.

Young athletes — gay and straight — often receive subtle messages that homosexuality is something to be mocked, avoided, or feared. A high school soccer coach designed this trick play: His players hoped to catch their opponents off-guard by arguing over who would strike the ball for a free kick. As both approached it, one called the other a "stupid homo." With the other team presumably distracted, one of them then put the ball into play. In another example of homophobia's insidious reach, a high school baseball coach chided two players sitting close to each other with, "You guys sleeping together or what?" And a high school sports magazine publisher reacted to my request that she include an item about this book by saying, "At the tender young age of this publication, I am not in a position to print [anything] that is controversial to the point of possibly offending potential subscribers or advertisers."

Clearly there is a reason for gay athletes and coaches to cower in their locker-room closet long after friends and peers involved in other activities have emerged from their own.

But this is the Gay '90s, and fortunately the situation is not **xiii** as bleak as it once was.

Patricia Nell Warren is part of the reason gay athletes today are as visible as they are. Warren was a long-distance runner as a youth, and her groundbreaking 1974 novel *The Front Runner* chronicled the running career, love life — and murder — of Billy Sive, a gay competitor in the then-future 1976 Olympics. It marked the first time a mainstream sports novel dealt so openly with homosexuality. Though it ends in anguish — the hero gets killed because he is gay — the mere existence of such a book kindled hope in untold thousands of athletes. For the first time, they realized that they were not alone.

In the two decades since *The Front Runner* appeared, Warren has received countless letters from gay and bisexual athletes. Runners write; so do football players and equestrians. Several correspondents have been members of U.S. Olympic teams. (Greg Louganis said that reading the book was a factor in his own coming-out.) Many who write — especially today — are in high school or college.

Warren has watched in wonder as acceptance of gay athletes has grown — both by the media and the public. For instance, she says, "While I was watching the farewell performance of figure skater Robin Cousins, I suddenly realized his sound-track song lyrics were a love song from one man to another. It was the most openly gay thing I've seen in figure skating, and I've watched skating for years. Yet the crowd gave him a standing ovation, and the commentators were full of praise."

However, she notes, old attitudes and traditions die hard — especially in team sports. Figure skating is not football. At the college level, coaches and athletes feel antigay pressure from alumni, trustees, and administrators. These pressures are especially intense — and effective — in times such as these, when money for athletics is dwindling and an openly gay athlete may provide a reason for an antigay alumnus to withhold a large donation.

In high schools the religious right exerts a painful squeeze on gay coaches and athletes through the school board. The story of coach Gumby Anderson — told in this book — is a good example. So are the tales of the boy who, as punishment for coming out as gay, was sent to train with the girls' track team and of another boy, who, after coming out at a Catholic high school, was "persuaded" to quit the football team.

Warren has noticed differences between athletes who compete in individual sports and those who play team games. She believes — and the stories in this book bear her out — that the people involved in sports based on individual performance are more tolerant of individuals who may be controversial in some way, as long as they are top performers.

Openly gay runners, tennis players, golfers, gymnasts, swimmers, wrestlers — all have easier times than openly gay football, basketball, or baseball players. The individual athlete stands alone; he has teammates but is not required to rely on them (or they on him) to the extent of team-sport athletes. "Team-sport athletes are less tolerant of individual quirks," Warren says, "because they get caught in a web of group attitude and social pressures." Locker-room squeamishness is only one problem. Another is the distaste felt by some straight people about having any physical contact or emotional connection with gays. Add to that the worry over "guilt by association" plus the normal anxieties most young people have concerning who and what they are, and it becomes clear that even one gay teammate can upset the entire athletic apple cart.

In addition, a closet of long standing encloses same-sex horseplay, hazing, and "fooling around" that many straight men enjoy — and have always attempted to keep secret. It is found in many all-male institutions, including military and prep schools, and is certainly present in sports. Having gay men — openly gay men, that is — involved changes all the dynamics, terrifying straight males who are not secure in their sexuality (in other words, most of them).

Pat Griffin, associate professor of social justice at the University of Massachusetts—Amherst, former coach, and current Masters athlete, also invokes the idea of "culture" when discussing young gay athletes. She sees a cultural difference between gay youth who participate in sports, and those who do not. "It's difficult for a gay male to find other gay males who share an interest in sports," she says. "It's easier for writers and actors to find other gay writers and actors because they've already been branded a bit 'different.' To be an athlete is not only not to be different; it's to be part of what is perceived as the mainstream."

Griffin notes that many people incorrectly assume that gay men are effeminate or at least "womanlike." It is not easy for them to adjust to the idea that "manly" athletes can also be gay — in part, she said, because that would force straight men to also examine the parts of their own selves that may be womanlike.

In addition, she says, bonding among athletes is clearly erotic: It involves physical intimacy on the field and nakedness in the locker room. Griffin adds that many men fear the resultant eroticism and project their fears onto those they perceive to be weaker than themselves: gays. "The physicality of sports makes these feelings very confusing for everyone," she explains.

"Sports is really important in our culture," she continues. "It is the place where men learn to be tough, to take their place in our patriarchal society. Sports plays an important role in the socialization of young men. There is a real link between homophobia and sexism. Little boys hear things like 'You throw like a girl' or 'You don't play football. What are you, a faggot?' " Some boys — including many excellent athletes — survive that socialization process by dropping out of sports; some buy into it as a way of becoming accepted or shoring up their own fragile self-esteem. But whether a boy is gay, bisexual, straight, or uncertain, the socialization process of sports leaves its mark.

That is one reason role models are so important. The generation of gays who are today teenagers and twenty-somethings are, for the most part, more comfortable with homosexuality than their elders. However, while gays who aspire to careers in politics, computers, architecture, law enforcement, or dozens of other fields now have many openly gay role models, those who dream of becoming athletes or coaches do not. The ranks of gay professional athletes are, as noted before, thin; their stories, for the most part, hardly inspire. (For example, Dave Kopay, the ex-NFL player, searched for years but never found a coaching job after coming out. Today, he sells linoleum in Los Angeles.)

So young gay athletes must look for role models among their peers or men just a few years older. Happily, they are finding them. This book tells some of their stories.

The tales are not always upbeat; in sports parlance, not everyone hits a home run. But that does not diminish them.

Fortunately, my research turned up far more happy stories than sad — a great winning percentage, to use another sports metaphor. For every youth who has been teased, tormented, or forced off a team, there are more who have found tolerance — even acceptance — among teammates and coaches. For every young athlete who felt ostracized during practice, there are far more who used athletics to develop self-esteem. (In fact, many athletes are now coming out for the very reason that they had good experiences while playing sports.) For every coach who has gone to enormous lengths to hide his homosexuality, more and more are showing their athletes, through words and deeds, that whom these coaches love has nothing to do with how well they teach skills or plan strategy.

Jeff Z. Klein, editor of *The Village Voice* sports section until 1995, is an astute observer of the emergence of gay sports issues. The New York weekly was the first alternative newspaper ever to treat any kind of athletics seriously; under his leadership the paper ran a number of groundbreaking stories on gay athletes, playing on gay and straight teams. "Even gay publications hardly ever covered sports in the late 1980s," he says — except for "the Dave Kopay–type anomalies."

But in the '90s, Klein notes, the Gay Games — the quadrennial athletic festival featuring competition in over two dozen team and individual sports — grew in visibility, and the straight world became more comfortable with the idea of gay athletes and coaches. The Troy Aikman story, for instance, received scant attention. Five years ago, the reaction would have been very different.

Yet today the story of gay athletes and coaches is not really about the pros — or even about the Gay Games, as open and celebrated as that event has become. The tale of gay sports is truly about the young men in high school and college and their coaches. They are the real champions. These men and boys are winners in every sense of the word because they are inching, trotting, even exploding out of the largest, dingiest, smelliest closet left in America: the locker room.

And whatever lies outside might be the toughest foe they'll ever face.

The Cross-country Coach and His Runners

It takes tremendous courage to come out as an openly gay high school coach. It also takes guts for athletes to stand in support of that coach. But it takes an overwhelming amount of bravery — not to mention great dignity, class, and self-esteem — to do so in the face of constant harassment, physical as well as verbal, from competitors and even classmates.

Yet that is exactly what has happened on the cross-country and distance track teams at Huntington Beach High School, in California's infamously conservative Orange County. When Coach Eric "Gumby" Anderson came out, some of his athletes turned and ran. Yet many more raced to his side. And that is exactly where they have remained, standing tall through taunts, intimidation, thrown bottles, and fistfights.

This is a story of the ugly side of coming out. It is also a tale about the pains and pleasures of growing up. And it gives true inspiration to anyone who doubts that, even in Orange County, most young people today want to do the right thing.

TWO DAYS BEFORE SCHOOL ENDED in June 1996, Huntington Beach cross-country runner Jerryme Negrete and a fellow senior drove away from graduation practice. A car with a sixteen-year-old football player and two other teenagers drove alongside. Words were exchanged.

The football player and his friends soon showed up at Jerryme's friend's home. A fight ensued, with the sixteen-year-old repeatedly calling Jerryme a faggot and making crude sexual remarks. Jerryme, trapped on the ground, said, "No, I'm not gay." It did not matter; the punches continued. Both sides of his jaw were fractured; he suffered head contusions, a damaged eardrum, multiple bruises, and blood in both eyes. For the rest of his life, he will have a steel plate screwed to his jaw.

The incident was not the first between the two boys. A few months earlier they had gone at it in a locker room.

Nor was the incident the first involving a member of the Huntington Beach cross-country team. In fact, runners had been harassed ever since 1993. That was when Gumby, the great cross-country and distance coach, became known as Gumby, the gay coach.

Coming out was Gumby's idea. Professionally, he stood at the top of his field. He was coaching one of his best track teams ever, a leading contender for the Orange County title. One of his runners was ranked in the top ten nationally. His book *Training Games* was about to be published.

Yet physically he was a mess. First came migraines; then stomach pains and sciatica. Each day was agony.

It would be hard to demonstrate a clearer connection between mind and body. Gumby — the nickname dates back to sixth grade, when a classmate belted him, then said he looked like the cartoon character flying through the air — had known he was gay as far back as age eight. He also knew it was socially unacceptable, something to keep quiet about, so all through high school he dated girls. As a Huntington Beach student himself in the mid '80s, he was surrounded by two phobias: homo and AIDS. He took comfort from his plan, devised back in sixth grade: He would marry, have children, and carry the pain of living a lie until he was twenty-five. At that point, he figured, he would decide what to do with the rest of his life.

At twenty-four, however, his body began sending physical signals to his head, stomach, and hips. Gumby recognized them for the warnings they were. One day at California State University, Long Beach, where he was earning a master's degree in sports psychology, he walked by the gay resource center, furtively grabbed a pamphlet, and left — but not before noticing someone attractive answering the phones. What Gumby calls "that little taste, so sweet, so feared," was enough to make

him return. Like an addict, he secretly craved that high of freedom. The good-looking man was there again. They talked. He
took Gumby to a gay bar. Gumby met his first boyfriend, had his
first enjoyable sexual experience, went to his first gay pride festival. The sight of 30,000 gay, friendly people, ambling openly
and happily in Long Beach, elated him.

But his boyfriend ran into one ex, then another. And another. Gumby felt he was no more than a prostitute. Heartbroken
for the first time — he had always found a reason to dump girls,
if they did not drop him first — he finally understood the pain
of puppy love. He felt hurt by his loss, ashamed of his ignorance,
but most of all devastated that he had no one to talk to about it.

Of course, Gumby had plenty of friends. A warm, outgoing
man, he had spent his life building a network of support. At the
heart of those friends were his runners, present and past.

Gumby was the consummate coach. He started while still an
undergraduate at Long Beach, commuting to his alma mater
Huntington Beach just ten miles south. He discovered a passion for
coaching, and when he could not land a full-time job at the school,
he became its resident substitute teacher. Daily contact with his athletes paid off. In addition to running techniques and tactics, he
taught them about physiology, nutrition, and goal setting.

More important, he taught them about life itself. "Some of
these runners I'd had since they were freshmen," he says. "We
were more than a coach and his athletes; we were friends. Long-
distance running develops that. We train together, go on runs
for eight, ten, twelve miles. While we're running we talk. When
we go to meets or drive five hours to running camp, we talk. I've
got an open-door policy at my home, twenty-four hours a day;
kids come, and we talk."

Those discussions had always been wide-ranging and challenging, Gumby notes. "I'd ask hypotheticals: What's the
biggest problem facing the world today? What would you do if
you were a parent and your kid stole something? What would
happen if your kid came out to you as gay? I'd probe and probe,

4 make them think and think. My athletes were open, liberal, loving thinkers."

And when Gumby needed them, they were there.

As he realized that the mental pressures of the closet were causing his physical ailments, then enjoyed the first sweet taste of being out and realized that true happiness would come only by being completely open, Gumby's method was typically well-organized and methodical. Within forty-eight hours he contacted everyone in his address book: seventy-two people. The only ones he did not tell were his current runners.

The first time was the hardest. He sat in his best friend's car and cried for an hour — without ever saying the *G* word. When he finally spilled the news, the friend said, "Is that all? It's a nonissue."

Other friends were equally accepting. He kept count. After reaching thirty yeses and no nos, he tossed the tally sheet out. Even Gumby's brother — who when they were growing up had said, "All fags should be shot" — told him it was no big deal.

Of course, certain people cautioned that while they liked and respected him no matter what, he should tread carefully in school. His mentor, the man he replaced as coach, warned him that coming out would probably mean the end of his career. His principal's initial reaction was that coming out was Gumby's decision, but he advised him not to make a public announcement about it. Later his warning became stronger.

After telling all his friends, including many former runners, Gumby was ready for the next step. It was time, he knew, to inform the current Huntington Beach athletes. He decided to start with the seniors. His "test case" was Ben Flamm, whom Gumby calls "my most respected runner. He was an incredible leader, a dedicated athlete, a 4.0 student, and very, very liberal. He always talked about how cool his father's gay friends were."

"At the time, the spring of 1993, I was running better than I ever had," Ben, a miler and two-miler recalls. "We saw each other

every day for long periods — Gumby puts so much into coaching. 5
During the time I'd known him, we'd talked about lots of issues,
including homosexuality. I'm liberal, open-minded, and I come
from a tolerant household in all respects. I guess that's why he told
me first. Plus, I think he would have felt funny or hurt if I'd found
out from someone else. We were very good friends."

For four years one of the places Gumby, Ben, and their
teammates had talked was the training room, as they stretched
down and iced after runs. It was an appropriate place for Gumby
to say, "Ben, I have something to tell you."

"I was 100 percent focused on running, because the state
meet was coming up," Ben says. "I got worried that maybe I
wasn't going to be allowed to compete or something. Instead he
said, 'Ben, I'm gay' — very straightforward. We talked awhile. I
told him it was cool. He told me the reasons I was the first athlete he told. That made me feel good." Ben hugged Gumby,
which made them both feel good.

Nevertheless, the revelation came as a shock. "I'd known
Gumby for four years," Ben says. "I thought I knew everything
about him. It was sort of like whiplash. I thought about all the
times I'd talked about women with him."

Ben soon got over the surprise. "He was the first person
close to me who'd come out," Ben says. "It was the first practical application I had of what I felt, a test of my own beliefs. I
hoped for myself and for Gumby's sake that I passed the test.
Still, there *was* that momentary comfort-zone problem, when
the past four years flashed by me."

Gradually, one at a time, Gumby told the rest of his seniors.
Most reacted well. One responded to the lunchtime news by
saying, "Is that all? Now can we eat?"

The next recipients were the most trusted parents. Again the
reaction was overwhelmingly positive. Ben's mother said,
"You've done more for Ben than anyone," then massaged his
shoulder. Each time he spoke Gumby asked the parents not tell
anyone else. He wanted to be the one, he said. Eventually, how-

6   ever, he realized that it sounded as if he were asking them to join
a conspiracy, so he dropped that part of the speech.

By the end of the summer, everyone who had been on
Gumby's team — and all their parents — knew he was gay.

Of course, one coming-out problem unique to educators is
that every year a new group of students arrives. While some may
already have heard the news through the grapevine, most have
no clue. By the end of the fall 1993 cross-country season, however, the upperclassmen had told the freshmen; word had also
filtered through Huntington Beach High. Slowly, the number of
runners on Gumby's teams dropped. Where he once coached
thirty to forty cross-country runners, he now had twenty-five.
The following fall his squad was down to nine.

In the spring of 1994, Gumby addressed the issue openly. In
case anyone did not yet know, he told all his distance runners he
was gay, then added, "I'm telling you because you need to know.
You may be harassed."

They already were. Throughout school the runners were
known as the "fag team." In addition to verbally taunting cross-
country athletes as they ran on campus, football players physically ejected them from the locker room. One boy's grandmoth-
er complained to the principal about Gumby's revelation to his
team. When the administrator asked why the coach had come
out publicly, Gumby replied that his squad had to know the reason behind the harassment. The principal deemed that answer
not good enough and asked for a formal meeting. Gumby —
whose mother was a judge — said he'd be bringing a lawyer; the
principal backed off. Gumby believes the administration feared
a gay-related controversy; at the time one was brewing over the
formation of a gay-straight alliance at Fountain Valley High
School, four miles away.

Ironically, Huntington Beach soon had its own group.
Senior Erich Phinizy helped start a gay-straight organization so

that other students would not have to go through what Gumby
did when he was a student there. Erich was one of Gumby's runners — and straight.

When his coach came out to him at the end of his junior
year, Erich admits, "It was a major shock. I was amazed. It was
not that I was homophobic, but I thought I knew him so well. I
had no idea he'd hidden such an important part of his life from
everyone for so long."

When Gumby casually suggested that Erich might want to
help form a gay-straight alliance like Fountain Valley's, the runner agreed. He contacted leaders at the nearby school, then
approached two teachers he felt comfortable with. They offered
immediate support. The word spread, and soon there were
twenty members.

To avoid the controversy that dogged Fountain Valley, the
Huntington Beach students called themselves the Student
Alliance. Though the word *gay* was not in the name and the
group did not face the depth of opposition its Fountain Valley
counterpart did, the road was not always smooth. Erich's car was
vandalized, with FAG written across the hood. Objects were
thrown at him. He received death threats. Yet through it all he
persevered, keeping Gumby's personal example in mind.

"A lot of people assumed that because I was one of his athletes and I was involved in this, I was gay," Erich says. "There
were plenty of people who just assumed the entire cross-country team was gay. I didn't say anything. I knew I wasn't gay, but
I also knew I was seen as gay."

Many times Erich felt isolated and overwhelmed. He often
thought of quitting, but, he says, "Gumby made things easy." So
did support from the gay community. Alliance members were
invited to Southern California gay functions. Seeing the inspiration his group brought to other people kept Erich going. One day
a Huntington Beach alumnus told him how proud he was of the
alliance, adding that he wished a similar group had been around
for him. "That made me realize that these little things happening

to me were really insignificant," Erich says. "I saw that the Student Alliance was a lot stronger than its critics. I also realized that being part of the alliance was just the right thing to do."

Meanwhile, Gumby's discussions with his principal continued. When the administrator wanted to know why Gumby thought he had the right to discuss his sexuality with students, the coach replied simply, "The First Amendment." He noted that he had told his athletes that if they could not handle the harassment, they should not be on his team — and that stopping the harassment was the principal's job, not his.

Gumby was bringing the problem on himself, the principal retorted. When he said he'd be examining Gumby's "clarity of judgment" to determine his fitness to continue as coach, Gumby's attorney asked whether the first seven years counted.

Shortly after a new vice-principal arrived at Huntington Beach, he jokingly handed teachers three-dollar bills bearing the likeness of President Clinton. The "queer" reference was unmistakable. Gumby's lawyer inquired whether that administrator would now be fired, based on his own lack of "clarity of judgment."

"The school was at war," the coach says. "On one side people were talking about 'the fag coach of the fag team and his fag runner starting the fag gay-straight alliance.' On the other side kids started coming out." By the end of the year, twelve openly gay students walked the halls of Huntington Beach High School.

"I'd gone from being intimidated by kids to being intimidated by the administration, and finally one day I realized I wasn't scared of anyone anymore," Gumby says. "I was confident I had legal and moral backing for what I was doing. My heart didn't pound all the time. When I heard bad things, instead of panicking I'd say, 'So?' I wasn't the same little kid I used to be. The principal realized I would fight."

The principal stood his ground too. Though Gumby had offered for three years to coach the girls' cross-country team —

the athletes, who had had a different coach every year, desperately wanted him — the principal would not allow it. "He didn't want to give me any more power than I already had," Gumby explains.

In the fall of 1995, the number of cross-country runners began inching up, to fifteen. That was the same semester a top-notch athlete from another school transferred in, solely because he wanted to run for Gumby. The fact that the coach was gay did not matter at all.

As a freshman and sophomore, Jacob Childs had competed against Gumby's runners. "They were the best, and he seemed really enthusiastic and into what he was doing," he recalls. "I had an older coach who wasn't really into it anymore. That all made me want to switch."

Jacob knew Gumby was gay. During his freshman year he and a friend were working out with a coach and one of his friends. When the discussion turned to Huntington Beach, the coach's buddy made a disparaging remark about Gumby. "We thought, *Whoa!*" Jacob says. "I was surprised, but it was not something I couldn't deal with."

When Jacob decided to transfer, Gumby's sexuality did not enter into the decision. "He's a good person and a really good coach," the runner says. "I came to learn…" All of a sudden, the articulate athlete stumbles. "It's hard to explain — I don't know — I don't think much about it. It's just there. Gumby is attracted to people of the same sex; I'm attracted to the opposite sex — it's different, but we're both normal."

No one tried to talk Jacob out of transferring; his parents were fully supportive. As expected, he became a better runner. But to his surprise he grew in other, less measurable ways as well. "I've learned a lot more about homosexuality and have come to accept it a lot more," Jacob says. "I wasn't homophobic before, but I wasn't sure I'd feel comfortable being around someone gay. But when he makes jokes or someone else does and we all laugh, it seems pretty natural. If guys are talking about girls, he'll add something about guys, and that seems natural too. Being around Gumby, I've learned that if something doesn't hurt anyone, who cares? And that goes for a lot of things in life, not just sexuality."

Jacob called his decision to transfer "the best thing I've done. I've experienced so much more. Gumby considers all of us his kids and his important friends. He's there to listen to any problem, in any area of life. He's like another father figure to me. Not many coaches are like that."

Of course, he learned plenty about running too. In 1995 Jacob did his part to help the cross-country team win the Orange County championship. But just as rewarding as his medal was the feeling of team cohesion — a feeling fostered by and shared with his gay coach.

With Jacob's success and the transfers of two other athletes (all of whom entered Huntington Beach knowing they might be harassed in school and during races, because Gumby warned them about it up front), the tide began shifting. The principal stayed away from the coach. Parents of older athletes "broke in" parents of newcomers, telling them they had nothing to fear; their sons were in good hands. Gumby took harassers to the office, then checked to make sure administrators followed through with appropriate punishment. They did.

Slowly the school — primarily middle- to upper-class; half white, a quarter Hispanic, a quarter Asian; largely conservative, with a few liberals and surfers sprinkled in — changed. "One class took a survey," Gumby says. "Twenty-nine kids said they had no problem with homosexuality; only one said he did. The eyes of the school were opening up."

Yet Gumby still had to douse small brushfires. For example, one runner transferred to Huntington Beach against his mother's wishes. That was a special victory for Gumby. "I've got the greatest kids in the world," he says. "It takes an extra-special kid to take the ridicule of being called something you're not. It makes me feel so good that kids stand up for something they don't have to stand up for. Straight sixteen-year-old kids have taught me a lot!"

The zen of distance running is something Gumby has pondered for years. "I don't know how to describe the quality of the human beings who are attracted to running," he says. "Are people of a certain mentality drawn to it, or does running breed introspection? I do think parents who encourage their kids to go into distance running are of a high mentality. I don't get the kind of parents and athletes who go into sports that end in the word *ball*."

Gumby does not deny that, after attracting a certain type of athlete, he tries to mold them a certain way. "I don't run down the field yelling at them," he says. "I run on the beach with them, and we talk about life." But, he notes, "I'm not preaching to kids about a preferred lifestyle, I'm *teaching* what life simply is. There are no logical arguments against homosexuality or for hatred based on sexual orientation. So if someone accuses me of preaching, I say I'm *teaching* a humanitarian viewpoint. And ultimately that's what a coach should be: an educator."

One young man knows particularly well just how excellent a coach and educator Gumby is. His perspective is different from most Huntington Beach runners. For him, Gumby serves as a special role model, because he too is gay.

Jeff Garland (not his real name) was a chubby child who always knew he was attracted to boys. His favorite pastime was eating. Then, in second grade, he realized he was not only fat but also fast. His life began to get better.

Jeff met Gumby during freshman year at Huntington Beach, but because he was a sprinter and the coach worked with distance runners, their paths seldom crossed. In the spring of his junior year, when both were still closeted, he got to know Gumby a bit better. Still, the runner thought the coach was "dorky" because he worked with distance runners. But senior year a distance runner bet Jeff that he could not cover a certain distance in a certain time; to win the bet he went out for cross-country and began hanging out with the runners and their coach.

The premeet spaghetti dinners were fun. Gumby and his runners enjoyed a close, easy relationship. Conversation ranged widely, covering not just running techniques and strategies but also politics, social life, the ways of the world.

"People had always joked about me since freshman year, 'Oh, yeah, that guy's a fag,' " Jeff remembers. "I didn't have a lot of girlfriends. Some people might have suspected, but no one knew for sure. I'm not sure whether Gumby suspected."

The older he got, the further Jeff edged out of the closet. As a senior he talked with an openly gay student at school, who replied to Jeff's tentative questions, "Closets are for clothes." One day the boy mentioned that he'd seen "that distance coach" at a gay pride event. Jeff was surprised. He knew Gumby never dated women — team members laughed about it — but for the first time he realized it was possible his coach was gay. "I felt something I'd never felt before," he exults. "Another gay person! Someone else who knew what I felt!" At the same time Jeff felt strange. He did not know what, if anything, to say.

Meanwhile, a friend's brother suspected that Jeff might be gay. When the brother mentioned a gay person he knew, Jeff asked, "Is it Gumby?" The brother said no, but told Gumby — whom he also knew — that Jeff suspected. It was early in the coach's coming-out process. Gumby talked to Jeff, telling the runner, "I know you have privileged information." The longer Gumby spoke, the more nervous Jeff grew. "I almost passed out," he says. "Then Gumby said he had to go, so I blurted out that I was gay too."

That hasty confession opened up a different world for Jeff. He saw life through new eyes. His lingering depression lifted; he found a boyfriend. He came out to his mother, an event he had never dreamed possible.

"If it hadn't been for Gumby, I don't know where I'd be today," Jeff says. "We went to meetings and gay pride events.

We learned things together. If I'd come out like that to someone my age, I would've been out partying, seeing who could pick up who. With an older person it was different. It was quieter, calmer. Somehow that was better."

Jeff graduated in the spring of 1993, the same time Gumby came out. Over the next few months, more and more people heard the news about both the coach and the runner. "Of course, there were rumors we were together," Jeff says. "In fact, two other runners and I moved into his house. But nothing happened. We all had separate rooms. There were two gay guys and two straight guys, all living together having a good time."

Today, Jeff attends community college. He dances and manages a store. "My personality has changed," he recounts. "I used to be introverted and shy. I didn't want anyone to know who I was, so I just didn't talk. I'm different now, and a lot of that has to do with Gumby. Because he wasn't afraid to be who he was, that made me more comfortable being myself."

Gumby's decision to come out has influenced more than that one gay runner. "It taught me the importance of being honest about how I feel and of acting on my feelings," says Ben Flamm, the first athlete Gumby told. "The strength he provided got me through hard times, even when I was no longer running for him."

He explains, "After graduation I got a scholarship to the University of Wisconsin, one of the top running programs in the country. I thought my choice was 100 percent right, but when I got there things were much different than I expected. I was ready for a new place where I didn't know anyone, a team with a lot of tradition, but I wasn't ready for two stress fractures. It was my first major injury. I stagnated. For the first time I had to face up to how I truly felt."

He called Gumby. They talked; the coach made Ben say out loud what he was feeling inside. Through their conversations, Ben realized he had to follow his instincts. He transferred to the

University of California, Santa Barbara, and began running faster than ever.

Gumby's influence is at least as strong on Erich Phinizy. "He's *the* most involved coach I've ever seen, and I've seen a lot," says the straight athlete who started Huntington Beach's gay-straight alliance. "His impact on my life has been tremendous. Gumby is such a role model. He was like a big brother to me. Whenever I had a problem — dealing with my family, divorce, whatever — he was there. He was exactly what I needed, exactly when I needed it."

Today, Erich attends California State University, Long Beach — Gumby's alma mater — and dreams of being a high school English teacher. "Teachers and coaches have quite an impact on students' lives," he explains simply.

Coach Eric Anderson — Gumby — has endured many hardships since coming out in 1993. His home and car have been vandalized. He's been spat at, threatened, accused of illegal recruiting and training. His permanent substitute-teaching position became less permanent. He has been insulted by administrators, colleagues, even another coach at his own school.

Gumby's team members have been harassed verbally and physically, by classmates as well as opponents. As long as three years after the coach came out, the attacks continue. Yet, drawing strength from one another, Gumby and his athletes have faced those challenges and overcome them all. By standing tall and strong — without moving an inch — these runners and their coach have won the biggest race of their lives.

The Tennis Player

When they discover — or finally confront the fact — that they are gay, some athletes scurry into the closet. It is impossible, they believe, to reconcile two such disparate parts of their lives. They see no way to be open about who they are in an environment filled with fag jokes, locker-room put-downs, and more-than-occasional go-get- 'em-guy butt pats. Because sports are so important to them — and so "normal" as well — the gay component must go. It is relegated to the fringes of their existence. Nighttime forays to bars or cruising spots and hidden liaisons become shadowy, fearful counterpoints to the wide-open, fully accepted (if not always admired) life of the modern male athlete.

The compromise seldom works. Few men can maintain such a facade. The resulting physical and emotional distance from teammates robs the gay athlete of many of sports' most tangible rewards (cama- raderie, kinship, even love for other men forged in the heat of train- ing and competition) and denies him the joys of full participation in the gay community (camaraderie, kinship, love for other men forged in the heat of isolation and societal disapproval).

Happily, not all athletes are so closeted. As the stories in this book illustrate, many have grappled with the question of whether gay ath- lete *is an oxymoron or a proud label. Ultimately these fortunate young men have discovered that they* can *stand, even thrive, with their feet planted solidly in two worlds.*

Every once in a while, in fact, sports drives the coming-out process, rather than delays it. No one exemplifies that more than Jason Cox, a proud gay man and varsity athlete.

"A TENNIS COURT IS AN ABSOLUTELY BEAUTIFUL PLACE," says Jason Cox without a trace of embarrassment. "It's so neat and ordered, with straight white lines. Whenever I see a court, I'm amazed how perfect it looks." On a trip to France, while his friends took pictures of the Eiffel Tower, and Louvre, Jason photographed red clay courts.

He waxes just as rhapsodic about the game itself. "Tennis is structured, with lots of rules and regulations, but within those confines you can be very artistic, creative, and aggressive. With a racquet in your hand, you can be whoever you really are. Tennis is my passion."

Tennis also impelled Jason's coming-out. It gave him self-esteem and power, both critical elements for a successful emergence. In fact, coming out was so important to him, he not only remembers the date — January 23, 1993 — he also celebrates it as his "rebirthday." At the time of our interview, the 21-year-old Jason considered himself four.

Like his social development, tennis came relatively late to Jason's life. He started playing seriously as a teenager. Before that his life was like many (though by no means all) gay males': more girl friends than boy; a sense of differentness, alienation, and isolation; lots of vaguely defined, unexpressed pain. Athletics was not even on the map.

That was somewhat surprising because Jason's father had been a gym teacher (he later became a school principal and superintendent), and his younger brother Mike was an excellent athlete. Jason spent his first twelve years in Danville, Illinois, a pleasant town on the Indiana border. In fact, the Cox family was so normal, his friends compared it to Beaver Cleaver's. "No one could believe we always ate together," he recalls.

But Jason was not an athlete. He could dribble a basketball only while standing still, he found football too rough, and after being hit by a ball at a professional game, he became (in his words) "baseball-phobic." He made no secret of his distaste for sports and hung out most often with girls. They talked on the phone for hours. He and his brother did spend time together, especially after the family moved to a house far from town, but Jason was just as content to be by himself. He read, played board

games, watched TV, and explored nearby woods and streams. A
special joy was just sitting on a log, thinking.

One thing he did not think about was being gay. He felt attracted to boys for as long as he could remember — in first grade he and a friend kissed and donned dresses, which their mothers found cute; in sixth grade he started experimenting with same-sex friends; by ninth grade it got much more serious, and he continued to mess around for the next two years — but Jason did not admit to himself what was happening. "Looking back, I think, *How could I not have known?*" he says. "But at the time I just thought it was a stage."

At the time he also had a girlfriend. Slowly he gained confidence — not easy for a boy who was so shunned in fifth grade that, for an assignment on life after high school, he wrote, "Will people still call me gay?" "I didn't remember that the kids did that until my old teacher mailed me the essay after graduation," Jason says, "and looking back, I don't think it had a homosexual aspect to it. But it shows how much of an outcast I was, even among gifted kids who were themselves outcasts in school."

Then came tennis.

Jason did not pick up a racquet until he was sixteen and his brother, Mike, three years younger but already an accomplished player, asked him to hit some balls. He borrowed his mother's old racquet, a heavy metal model, and enjoyed the experience. Then he saw the French Open on television, played a bit more, and was hooked.

"When I was younger I was tall, skinny, awkward, and left-handed, which made learning sports pretty difficult," he recalls. "But all of a sudden, at sixteen, I realized this was a sport I could *do*. When I walked on the court, I could hit the ball! Suddenly I felt things were okay." As Jason played more, he noticed physical changes. His legs grew muscular, and his body filled out. His long gawky phase was finally over.

18 Then came January 23, 1993. "I remember it so well because it hit just like a lightning bolt," Jason says. "It was 7 A.M., an early-bird gym class, and this guy walked in. I'd never seen him before, but instantly I could tell he was gay. I was so attracted to him. I know it sounds cheesy, but it was love at first sight. It was like, *Jason, you're gay. Duh.* I knew then and there exactly who and what I was."

The dominant emotion was relief. Once he said the *G* word to himself, Jason felt like a new person. "All of a sudden a huge weight lifted off my shoulders," he says. "I finally realized why I'd been so hurt and why I felt the way I did. I knew who I was. Looking back, I consider myself incredibly lucky to never have gone through that drug or alcohol or suicide phase. That's a credit to my family, for giving me strength and will."

He credits tennis too. "I'd been playing for eight months before I came out, and all of a sudden I was feeling fit and athletic," he says. "Finally I had my sport. I was content. I think that helped prepare me for the realization that I was gay and for my immediate acceptance of it."

Tennis also provided him with the strength to weather the difficulties that followed. Coming out to oneself is eventually followed by coming out to others, and Jason's process raced along. Within a week he told the first person, a friend he considered "cool, liberal, and accepting." He was bursting to share his discovery, and this girl had the advantage of not being friendly with his girlfriend. Her reaction was surprise: not at his revelation but at the fact that he had chosen her as the first one to hear the news.

Coming out to himself had been much harder than telling his friend, but after that things snowballed. He came out to one of the boys he'd fooled around with, who freaked out. The boy told Jason's girlfriend, omitting the information that he himself had been intimate with Jason at the same time. "She took it very, very badly," Jason recalls. "That was hard because she was such a good friend. She felt betrayed and lied to. It sounds like a lame excuse now, but I actually didn't feel like I had been cheating on her, because I was doing it with a guy. I know all this sounds like a bad TV talk show. It was just a weird, fast, terrible time." The girl, who was a year older than Jason, did not talk to him again until she left for college in June.

Soon after, he came out to his mother. She was surprised, though on one level she had also suspected his secret. Jason asked his mother to tell his father. She told her son that he had to be the one to do it. He could not bring himself to raise the subject until spring break two years later, only to find out that his mother had told his father the day after she found out. "I got all stressed out, with stomach pains," he recalls. "During all that time my mother and I had never mentioned it again." His parents' reactions have been mixed. His father wishes Jason were not so open ("I'm not," Jason protests. "My dad thinks having a subscription to *Out* magazine is being 'blatant,' even when it comes in a brown wrapper"), while his mother, who lost two relatives to AIDS, worries her son will contract the virus too.

Danville High School was a fine experience for openly gay Jason Cox. The gym class student who prompted the lightning-bolt revelation turned out to be a jerk (though gay), but from the second semester of his junior year through the end of twelfth grade, Jason dated a younger boy. The wonderful relationship eased all feelings of loneliness. Jason and his girl friends talked openly about boyfriends, including his own. His close friends told their good friends, then their acquaintances; soon everyone knew. Besides being called "faggot" several times a day and getting elbowed once, he suffered no recriminations. He and his boyfriend did not go to the prom, because Jason wanted to protect him from possible abuse after Jason graduated. However, he says, "I realize now that I blazed a path. There's a real queer contingent at Danville these days. And just last week I got a letter from someone thanking me for making it easier for him."

Through it all tennis remained a constant. Jason, who had always been involved in drama productions and music ("After graduation, everyone in the show choir came out!" he laughs), felt the urge to try something different. He joined the tennis team ("There were no tryouts, thank God"), and though Jason called himself "terrible," the coach was understanding and made room for beginners. That eleventh-grade year, Jason played junior varsity and practice matches, luxuriating in his new physical and mental fitness.

He played every day that summer, hitting with Mike for hours. Jason loved tennis, wanted to improve, and was undaunted by the fact that his younger brother was much better.

As a senior Jason was the top player on junior varsity; Mike played varsity sixth singles. Jason enjoyed moderate success on the court but major victories off it. "I realized I had the right to do anything anyone else did, including sports," he says. "That was a big, driving part of my decision to play on the team. It was something I really wanted to do, and I wasn't scared anymore. I was still awkward and different, but I could handle it. Coming out gave me strength, and playing tennis helped me come out."

For the first time in his life, Jason felt like a normal human being. Though he did not particularly like his teammates, he could talk to them without being mocked (while laughing to himself at their "cluelessness"). He could look at cute boys on other teams and enjoy the feeling. "I felt good and healthy," he says. "I had gotten past all of life's mysteries. I could do things! What a feeling!"

That senior year he and a friend visited Beloit College in Wisconsin, just over the Illinois border. He fell in love with the school and its small, liberal student body. He had always known he wanted to be more than a number in college and was pleased that his questions about gay issues on campus were answered intelligently. When he was accepted, and then received a financial-aid package, Jason was thrilled.

As soon as he arrived on campus in 1994, he was out. The second night of orientation, he talked with a resident assistant, the head of the campus gay group. She was the first out lesbian he knew. That fall semester was an incredible high: He was learning new things every day, had openly gay friends, and was dating a guy across the hall.

Jason, a biology major and women's studies minor, delved into a variety of political issues. He discovered connections among the politics of race, gender, and sexuality. Through his friendship with a gay African-American, he earned a "token white person" spot in a show put on by the black student group. He joined the campus's gay-straight alliance and ran the registration and workshop committees when Beloit hosted the 400-person Midwest Bisexual, Lesbian, and Gay College Conference. Then he was elected chair of the alliance.

One thing he did not do his first year was play tennis. Though he calls it "the lowest-key sport on campus," he had several concerns. He was worried about the time commitment, did not know if he was good enough, and once again felt intimidated by athletes' stereotypes. "I was anti football frat-boy assholes," he says. "Any racist, sexist, homophobic crap on campus can be traced back to the football-baseball fraternity. I didn't want any part of that."

However, as a sophomore he realized he missed the game. He had played only twice the previous year; that felt horrible because tennis had meant so much to him. He asked to join the squad; however, there was one problem. Practice began the week before the Midwest Gay College Conference. He was busy, stressed out, and apprehensive.

No problem, tennis coach Tim Schmiechen said. He told Jason not to worry; he could begin training when the conference was over.

Though rusty from a year layoff, Jason slowly improved. By the end of the spring, he was playing number four singles. Despite a 102-degree fever, he reached the consolation finals of the Association of Colleges of the Midwest League tournament. "I know it isn't the Big Ten, but to me it was a big deal," he says.

"What a great way to end the season! I had always lettered in academics, but to get a varsity letter in college absolutely blew my mind."

He enjoyed a good relationship with his teammates too. They were a different type of group than his other college friends, but no one ever made an issue of his sexuality. The number five and six singles players were like Jason — they considered tennis fun, not overly important — while the top three players were much more competitive. "They were jocks," he says. "They might even have come to Beloit to play tennis. In the past I was uncomfortable around high-level athletes like that, with the 'We're real men, we compete' kind of attitude. It's a mentality I'm not very fond of, but we got along fine."

Jason takes a friendly view of competition. He talks to opponents before matches and during changeovers, not common in college tennis. "I just like to meet people," he explains. "I don't know if it's because of who I am or if it has some connection to being gay. It's interesting: My gay friends think I'm really competitive, even when we play Ping-Pong. But I'm in the top division of a gay-lesbian tennis league in Milwaukee, and that's not competitive at all. I'm seen as the most competitive player there."

His gay friends respect him as a varsity athlete. "Some of them laugh and tell me I'm a big queen doing jock drag, but most of them think it's cool," he says. "They think it's nice to have an openly gay athlete at Beloit, because there aren't a lot anywhere." Jason and the number one player are the only two with cheering sections at home matches.

Clearly, he cannot separate his gay activities from his athletic endeavors. He took an interdisciplinary course, Sports in America, which focuses on the relationship between sports and societal values. Jason appreciated learning about — and watching his classmates learn — the roles gay men and lesbians play in athletics and the resultant effects on society.

However, a bit of high school fear still lingered. The very first day of class, when the discussion turned to gay issues, he

was intimidated. "I worried about looking stupid," he recalls.
"My hand shook when I raised it. The class was full of these huge football and baseball players."

Yet midway through the semester he began talking with classmates. He realized most were not homophobic — including the president of "the asshole football fraternity." In fact, Jason says, "I found out he's a nice guy. That helped destroy some of my own stereotypes." By the end of the course, when he received a high grade on his final paper on the Gay Games, he truly felt he belonged.

"I'm an athlete," he says. "I'm in sports. I may not be able to rattle off statistics, but I've learned a lot about racism, homophobia, and other social issues in sports. That's probably a lot more important than RBIs or whatever."

Today, Jason Cox is truly content. Tennis has given him the power to come out and be himself, and coming out has given him permission to enjoy tennis fully. He is ready for anything, including trying a new sport. He even knows which one it is.

His new goal is to dribble a basketball for more than two steps.

The Addicted Athlete

Joni Mitchell sang, "You don't know what you've got till it's gone," and that's as true for athletes as it is for people who pave over paradise and put up a parking lot. If the allure of athletics is training, competing, taking care of one's body, and reveling in the good, healthy feelings that flow from those pursuits, then it is safe to assume that most athletes scorn those who do not train, compete, take care of — or even care about — their bodies.

Yet many good athletes fall into patterns of destructive behavior. They abuse tobacco, alcohol, and other drugs; they sleep too little or too much; and they engage in risky behavior. They eventually stop looking, acting, and feeling like athletes. The more they lose the "elite" status that athletics provides, the less highly they think of themselves; the lower their self-esteem, the greater the chance that they will continue their self-abuse. Just as sports participation provides so much positive reinforcement — everything from external crowd adulation to the inner satisfaction of achieving a goal — dropping out for the wrong reasons can send an athlete sliding down a slippery slope, with each negative choice skittering into the next.

There are many reasons a successful athlete stops competing: burnout, disillusionment, academic pressures, financial woes. Most of those stresses do not lead to destructive behavior, however; the cause is often a personal crisis. In that category stress related to sexuality issues ranks near the top.

IT WAS ALMOST GRADUATION TIME, and Noah's life was looking up. The boy who since first grade had been bullied relentlessly and since fifth grade was labeled the "class fag" had moved at the beginning of his senior year to a new school elsewhere in Wisconsin, where he finally found his niche. As a runner he blazed to personal records — 48.5 seconds in the 400-meter run,

51.5 in the 400-meter hurdles — and won races for his new team. His group of friends included a girl who told him she was a lesbian. He also was growing closer to Brad, the first person he had met in his new town. They ran together on the mile relay team.

Noah (who asked that his last name not be used) and Brad (a pseudonym) spent more and more time talking during practice, in cafés and coffee shops, and at each other's homes. They covered some heavy topics, including gender roles and homosexuality.

One day a friend presented Brad with a graduation gift: a beautiful homemade quilt. Noah, getting ready to spend the night at Brad's house, wanted to sleep under the quilt. They decided to share it. Lying underneath, a foot apart, they stared at the ceiling and pretended to try to fall asleep.

Noah's feet were cold. He and Brad played footsie. Brad looked over and said, "It's really a shame men can't express affection and hold each other."

"Yeah, it sucks," replied Noah.

"Can you hold me?" asked Brad.

At that moment Noah flashed to a situation a few months earlier. On the night of her eighteenth birthday, his girlfriend cooked him dinner in his old town. For the first time he confided to her that he might be gay. She said that was impossible: He had no such mannerisms, he was not interested in art, he was an athlete, and he was a Christian. Two hours later she was sitting next him naked; she kissed him quickly and suddenly. Soon — also for the first time — they had intercourse. The next morning Noah knew for sure he was gay.

So, just as his girlfriend had done to him, Noah kissed Brad — hard, deep, and fast. As soon as he pulled away, Brad lunged back for another kiss.

"It was the most electric experience," Noah recalls. "It was nothing like kissing girls. This was with a boy I really loved. It was so much fun! We were both runners, and we had really great bodies. Of course, we both came."

The state track meet was scheduled for the next week. Both agreed they would not touch each other there. But the weather was poor, so with time on their hands, they went to a mall and bought matching hats. "Looking back, it's so obvious we were together," Noah says. "We sat with each other, we did everything together." They even slept in the same bed, in a hotel room they shared with the two other members of the mile relay team. Ironically, Noah later learned that those boys were also gay. They had been a couple for several years, though no one knew it at the time.

The mile relay team broke the school record and took seventh place in the state. However, the relay was not Noah's main passion. That was the hurdles, and for years he had looked forward to competing at the state meet. But in the final qualifying event Noah hit a hurdle and fell. He crawled, bleeding and crying, across the finish line.

He was devastated. "I'd put so much emphasis on the hurdles," he says. "I couldn't cope with something like that. It was essentially the end of my running career."

That experience was not the only reason he felt "fragile" the summer before entering Cornell College, a small Iowa school. Though he and Brad spent time together after graduation, camping and going to water parks, Brad became increasingly distraught. He thought gay sex was morally wrong. Noah thought it was wonderful; he had finally found the missing link in his life.

The relationship could not last. One afternoon, as they were breaking up in Brad's bedroom — giving each other one final hug — Brad's mother walked in. The next day she confronted Brad and told him that his brother had had a long same-sex relationship in high school but then became a born-again Christian, married, had children, and inherited part of the family farm. She sent Brad to a therapist.

The next time he saw Noah, he was angry. Brad told him what they had done was wrong. Noah replied, "Well, I'm happy, and I hope you are too." That was the end of their relationship, though a few years later they candidly discussed homosexuality. At that time Brad still worried about losing his family's love, about offending God, and about being gay in his job as a construction engineer. They played footsie again, and they again had sex. "He was my first love," Noah says wistfully. "I'll never forget it or lose my feelings about it."

But all that lay ahead. That summer, with his running career over and college looming, Noah felt at loose ends. He was eager to meet, for the first time, many gay people he expected would be just like him. At the same time, as an athlete he needed something to keep him going. He became more deeply involved in swimming, something he had done all year long, every morning before school. "That became my spiritual time," he says. "It was very important for me to do every day." As fall neared he decided to become a college swimmer.

Attending a small liberal arts school in Iowa would be in keeping with Noah's background. He was born in a tiny Wisconsin town "out in the woods." That's where the harassment — physical as well as verbal — began and escalated. Whenever Noah struck back — by picking on someone he perceived to be even lower on the social ladder, for example — it backfired, and the abuse grew worse than ever. "Some of those guys are now in jail, in dead-end jobs, or dead," he says with a bit of satisfaction.

His feelings about other boys were often accompanied by terror, particularly during gym class. However, he discovered one athletic pursuit he enjoyed: running. He excelled at it, and his tormentors could not keep up. Soon the high jump and hurdles hooked him as well; those activities and running were the only things that got him through each day. But one sophomore morning, fed up with the constant heckling, he made plans to hang himself in the locker room. Suddenly between classes the girls' track coach told him she had just received some new high-jump videos. For three solid hours he watched them. She told him she would help integrate those techniques into his training program. "I was definitely going to kill myself, and she was definitely there for me that day," he says. Later he found out that the school rumor mill was true: The track coach was a lesbian.

Noah even played basketball with some of the boys who picked on him. Though taller than they were and with a better jump shot, he seldom got the ball. "Every halftime the coach would say, 'Noah's wide open, why aren't you guys getting it to him?' " he recalls. No one said a word, but Noah knew why. Eventually he quit.

Moving to a new town before senior year was a milestone in Noah's life, and not just because he met Brad and the semi-open lesbian friend. A gay couple lived together in what locals called the "Gay Chalet." "I always wanted to knock on their door and say, 'I'm gay. What do I do?' " Noah says. "I never had the guts. But every time I got near their house, I felt that it was this great symbol of fidelity. It was good for me just to know they were there."

Noah's journalism class engaged in intense debates over how to cover the topic of gay teenagers. Nothing ever got written — "We couldn't interview anybody, because no one knew anyone," he says wryly — but he was heartened by the impassioned classroom defenses of gay people he heard from many people, including the teacher. Their advocacy meant more to him than they will ever know.

Of course, other incidents rankled. When his Baptist Bible study group discussed homosexuality, Noah listened in silence to a chorus of disapproving remarks. Comments like those convinced him that leaving the tiny towns he'd known all his life and attending a liberal arts college in a liberal state like Iowa would be a turning point.

It was — but in ways Noah never could have imagined.

For the first time ever, the young man met many gay people his own age. He expected them to be like him and was stunned that they were not. At meetings of the Ten Percent Society, he sat among students he had nothing in common with. "They were smoking cigarettes, talking about the theater, bashing athletes," he says. "Here I was, Mr. Fellowship of Christian Athletes. I'd so looked forward to meeting gay people I could relate to. This was such a letdown. I can't express how depressed I was."

A straight friend — a well-intentioned woman he calls the "quintessential fag hag" — lent a sympathetic ear. "During this whole coming-out process, I wasn't very sure of myself," Noah says. "This woman struck me as someone who would be affirming, someone I could talk to. She'd say, 'Have a beer with me. Have a cigarette with me.' I'd say, 'I don't drink. I don't smoke.' She'd say, 'Sit with me while I do.' One day I had a cigarette, and I was hooked."

She offered to take Noah to a gay bar, to help him meet other gay people. At first he was uncomfortable, but the more he drank, the more relaxed he grew. The beer and comfortable feelings fed on each other.

Noah and the woman had a falling-out, but he soon met another female who also sucked him into the gay bar scene. That's where he had his first one-night stand. He soon had another, then another. And another. Very quickly he was hooked not only on cigarettes and alcohol but also on sex.

"I wanted desperately to be around gay people," Noah says. "The only place I could find them was in the bar. I still had this image of myself as this athletic Christian, when in reality I was no longer taking care of myself and not being very Christian. I was so afraid of getting to know people. The only way I could relate to anyone was through sex."

On campus he hung out with women who were dating wrestlers. They all became friends, and those athletes were the first people at school he came out to.

"I don't really know why it was the wrestlers," he says. "They were just nice people. There was this one huge guy dating one of my female friends, and one day I said to him, 'You know, I'm a fag.' He said, 'That's cool.' So then I asked if I could touch his chest. He said, 'Sure.' He was grinning because he knew he had a beautiful body. I just said, 'Thank you,' and he said, 'Anytime.' "

Noah told several other wrestlers too, and their responses were similar: He was no different than they were except for whom he liked.

Soon Noah was coming out to other people. "I got off on telling people I was gay," he recalls. "It was liberating, especially telling people who were big and looked scary and could crumple me into a little ball. Getting good reactions from those people was very empowering."

One group of people he did not tell was his swim teammates. They were very homophobic, he says. They did not even want to set foot in the Grinnell College locker room because of that rival school's reputation for homosexuality.

He explains the difference between the wrestlers' and swimmers' reactions by saying, "People like wrestlers don't take any shit from anybody, but they also don't give it. But also, the wrestlers were good in their sport — conference champions, tournament winners — and the swimmers were mediocre to poor. The swim team had less self-esteem, and that might have had something to do with their lack of acceptance of others. Successful athletes take care of themselves mentally as well as physically; they're highly developed as people because they're highly developed as athletes. The wrestlers were just more developed than the swimmers, I guess."

When Noah switched from running to swimming, he lost much of the self-worth he enjoyed as a successful athlete. As that sense of confidence eroded, he tried to compensate by finding gay friends. The more involved he became in the local gay community, the more things that were once important to him — abstaining from tobacco, alcohol, and marijuana; believing in Christ — crumbled. When his few gay-bar attempts at friendships were rebuffed, he turned to the comfort of anonymous sex.

He dropped out of college for a while and lived with his parents. His destructive behavior escalated. By the time he transferred to the University of Wisconsin—Madison, he was no longer an athlete. He tried out for the crew team and was cut. His self-esteem plummeted even further.

His journal reveals the extent of his anguish. "I drink too much," he wrote. "I smoke too much. All this anonymous sex can't be good for me."

"I was desperate for gay friends," Noah explains. "I saw people doing all these things, and I just did what they did." A friend showed him how to get blow jobs in public bathrooms. He did that two or three times a day and also had regular "fuck buddies" on the side. There was constant sex but never an emotional connection. Incredibly, Noah graduated from Wisconsin with a 3.98 grade point average and was accepted into the graduate program in sociology at Stanford University.

In the summer of 1994, just days before he was to leave Madison for California, he met someone in a bar. Within minutes the man was groping Noah all over, sticking his hands down his pants. When he asked what Noah liked, Noah burst into tears. He told a woman friend at the bar, "I have to do something." They walked to the capitol steps, and under the stars he cried again. His life was in shambles, and he had no idea what to do.

Driving a U-Haul west, he resolved to make a clean break. He knew no one in California and was ready to start fresh. He pledged to himself to stop having anonymous sex; of his many destructive behaviors, that bothered him most.

Graduate school is often stressful, and piled atop Noah's many problems was a new one: He was unsure of his own worthiness to be at Stanford.

Within his first two weeks, a man cruised him a hundred feet from the sociology building. Noah followed him, and they had sex in a bathroom next door. He went home, sat in his living room, and sobbed. He called a female friend in Madison and told her what happened. She and others had worried for a long time about his many encounters but like everyone else had no clear answers.

Filled with anxiety, Noah sought bathroom sex every day. But Stanford is much smaller than Madison, and he often ran into his "anonymous" partners at the pool, in the library, and even in class.

Then Noah met a man he liked, and they explored a relationship. When Noah told him about the bathrooms, the man said he did not want to be Noah's therapist. For his sake, Noah made an effort to stop — he went only five times during their seven months together and felt horrible after each — and also cut way down on his drinking. "It was the longest relationship I'd ever had," Noah recalls. "For the first time I experienced a type of love I'd never had with another human being."

Despite his many anonymous encounters, Noah felt relatively safe from AIDS. Virtually all of his activity involved oral sex. The few times he was unsafe, he freaked out, got tested, and remained safe for months. But in August of 1995 he admitted everything he had done for five years — and with whom. His lover (with whom Noah had had unprotected sex) grew enraged and hit him, bloodying his nose.

"It was a terrible day," Noah says. "I surrendered. I said I couldn't control myself. I decided to stop all my destructive behaviors."

He talked with a gay Lutheran minister from Germany. The man suggested a walking tour of the Castro district in San Francisco. "Fourteen beers and five margaritas later, he asked me if I liked to fuck or get fucked," Noah says. "We smoked a joint. He pulled me into an alley. I pushed back, and that got him excited. He raped me, right there in the alley. It was the worst experience of my life."

But he hurt so much he could not drive, so Noah spent the night at the man's flat. He told Noah, "Just because you had sex with a minister doesn't mean you can't come back to the church." The next day, back at Stanford, Noah saw the minister at the pool. The man told a mutual friend about their encounter. The friend called Noah and said, "A few beers and margaritas and you're a pretty good date, huh?" Later the minister came by to pray. Noah threw him out. Two hours later he returned; this time Noah's roommate sent him away. "I've fed on that anger for a long, long time," Noah says.

He continued to drink every day until January 1996.

Suddenly one morning that winter Noah woke up and decided he no longer wanted to live as he had for the past several years. He simply stopped. For months he had no sex at all. Then he met someone he liked. After they fooled around Noah felt "weird." The man asked whether he was addicted to sex. Noah said he thought he was. The man told him he did not have to handle it alone. He recommended a twelve-step program for sex addicts, and Noah went.

Today, he is reconstructing his life. He abstains from anonymous sex, drinking, drugs, even cigarettes. He swims and works out every day. He competes in road races. He is close to completing his master's degree.

Athletics once again anchors his life. Noah has found sports to be "spiritually nourishing" in a cosmic, rather than Christian, sense. Nothing, he realizes, compares with the feeling of running the hurdles. ("Sex is close," he admits, "but I don't feel guilty after a race.") Winning — or simply running well — is life-affirming; swimming, competing, and trying to reach a personal record all feel "good and clean and fun." He needs athletics in his life. Without it he does not know what he would be or where.

Noah looks back with deep sorrow on his desperate half-decade-long search for acceptance in what he thought was "the" gay community. He remembers longingly that brief six-month period when he was a senior in high school, had just kissed Brad, and life felt so sweet. He knew then — and knows again now — what is right for him and what is not. In between he tried doing what he thought all gay people his age had to do — only to discover that those were not things he had to do at all. At last he is meeting gay people his age with wide ranges of interests, far beyond bars, booze, and random blow jobs.

Most of the gay men he knows now, people who are "more or less athletic," were not out in high school or college; in fact, many were active homophobes then. Others were not sports-minded at all; not until they entered recovery or burned out from going to bars or clubs did they discover the ability to hit a jump shot or a tennis ball, to run for miles, or swim for hours.

Noah realizes now that there is life outside the gay world. He joined a Masters swimming program, for competitive athletes no longer in college. Not long ago he watched a man set a Masters record for 88-year-olds. "I draw a lot of inspiration from him," Noah says. "I want to be an 88-year-old swimmer. I look back and regret the years that athletics were not a part of my life. But now I also know I can look forward to all the years when it will be."

Yet the gay community still holds strong appeal — in its healthiest, most positive sense. When told that the Masters program in the San Francisco Bay area is filled with gay swimmers, his eyes lit up. "Wow!" Noah says excitedly. "I've got to look into that! They sound like people I'd really like to meet."

The Hockey Referee

In the hierarchical world of athletics, referees rank well below athletes and coaches on the glamour scale — above statisticians and locker-room attendants, to be sure, but not by much. It takes a certain type of personality to voluntarily submit to near-constant abuse from players, coaches, sportswriters, and, of course, unknowledgeable fans. An official must be as physically fit as the competitors (there are, after all, no substitutions for refs) and willing to forgo one of the prime benefits of sports: camaraderie. Referees travel, sleep, and eat isolated from the athletes whose games they officiate; in fact, fraternization is strictly prohibited.

The pressures are even greater on gay referees. In a job where success depends in large part on earning respect and keeping it — often through a combination of self-confidence and machismo, both greatly exaggerated — gay officials are virtually unheard of. No matter how difficult it is to come out as a gay athlete or coach, those are the athletic equivalents of hairdressing and interior design compared with sports officiating.

Yet as in every other area of sports, there are gay football, basketball, and baseball officials. There is even at least one gay ice-hockey referee.

BRETT PARSON REMEMBERS THE INCIDENT WELL. It was the winter of the gays-in-the-military debate, and he was deep in conversation with a fellow National Hockey League referee. The other man had a family member in the service whom he suspected was gay; the official was enraged that his relative could lose his job over something as irrelevant as sexual orientation. Brett was struck by the depth of his colleague's sensitivity, awareness, and concern.

The next day, with no game scheduled, they went for a keep-in-shape workout at the rink of the city they were in. While lacing up, they chatted with the trainer of the home team. Reading a headline about President Clinton's first controversy, the trainer said, "Fuckin' faggots want to get in everywhere."

Brett's fellow official, the man who hours earlier had expressed such compassion for his possibly gay relative — in fact all gays everywhere — replied, "Yeah, it's fuckin' disgusting."

Brett looked over in surprise; the man never met his gaze. Later Brett asked about his hypocritical response. "I don't need the grief," the man said. "All this gay stuff isn't as important to me as my job."

In a sport like hockey, where the perception of being a tough guy is important — toughness being measured primarily in terms of penalty minutes, broken bones, and missing teeth — a referee must be at least as tough as the players he controls. Any hockey official perceived as weak will never last. And standing up for gay rights is one of the surest ways to be considered weak.

Brett Parson is anything but weak. A native of Washington, D.C., who caught the hockey bug when the NHL Capitals came to town, he checked and slashed his way up the youth-league ladder, from Mini-Mite and Bantam all the way to Midget, at age seventeen. "I was not the most prolific scorer," he admits. "I was more of what you'd call a physical player. I didn't finish many games." In other words, he was thrown out of them.

During one of his suspensions — perhaps for fighting or overzealous contact; ten years later he cannot remember — Brett was sentenced to officiate younger-league games. To his surprise, he loved it. A few Friday nights later, he was tossed out of yet another contest. The next morning he called the official who had ejected him, told him he liked refereeing more than playing, and asked for help getting assignments.

Not long after, during a blinding snowstorm, Brett received a phone call. Could he officiate a pro game in Roanoke, Virginia, 230 miles away? You bet. He was not yet eighteen.

Though he never viewed hockey officiating as a career, within eight years he was whistling NHL games. He knew if he did not grab the brass ring at the top of the profession, he would always regret turning down an opportunity few men get. He did league games for a year, then walked out of the next referees training camp. The reason he gave was that he was fed up with the attitudes of pro players: They made too much money and gave too little back to the game and their communities. Brett told people he felt he could contribute more to hockey as a volunteer and turned his energies toward referee education. Since leaving the NHL in 1993, he has run training clinics across the country. (His full-time job is in law enforcement.)

But he kept his underlying reason for retiring secret. The life of a gay official, he had come to understand, is incredibly difficult. Because any professional league's survival depends on the honesty of its games — and that integrity rests largely in the hands of referees — those refs are scrutinized relentlessly. Any lapse can end a career. A closeted gay official risks blackmail; an openly gay one, no matter how competent, would probably never be accorded enough respect by athletes, coaches, and colleagues to succeed. (That, of course, is purely theoretical. No official in any professional American sport has ever come out of the closet during his career. There was, however, one openly gay Brazilian soccer official, who defiantly declared, "I am a pro on the field, a pansy off it.")

"I wasn't promiscuous or stupid," Brett says, "but I did have relationships with men. Anyone I broke up with could easily have dropped a dime to the NHL. Or if I had been pulled over one night in front of a gay bar and recognized as a referee, that would have been the end too." During his year in the NHL, he still was not out to his parents; that added to his pressures. He did not want them finding out he was gay by hearing the news on CNN.

In addition, he says, "I'm the type of person who fights battles on principle. I knew that if I stuck with the league, I'd end up in a union-leadership position and would probably end up working on some domestic-partner benefits issue. The NHL isn't ready for that, so it was better not to get involved."

Yet it was not just the top rung of professional hockey that wasn't ready for a gay referee. Throughout his college days Brett had officiated minor-league hockey. It was a double life: As a graduate student he was an openly gay resident adviser living on campus with his partner, but he also spent several days a week on the hockey road, where no one knew his secret. (But they might have suspected, he admits: "I moved three times. And every time I lived with the same guy.")

Despite retiring from officiating, Brett remains passionate about hockey. "I can't think of any other game that incorporates so much skill," he says. "You really have to be an athlete to play; there's no way around it. A hockey player has to be able to skate, pass, shoot, score, and body-check; do it all under pressure and with tight teamwork; and be in great cardiovascular condition too. Hockey puts together everything I like in sports."

It is, he adds, as macho a sport as it seems to outsiders. Brett has made lifelong friends in hockey, men who respect him as a masculine man for all he has accomplished. Yet he is unsure how they would respond if they learned he is gay. "I don't say that lightly," Brett notes. "People in most other areas of my life react well, even those I don't expect to. But hockey…that's another story."

While unwilling to discuss with certainty hockey's uneasiness about homosexuality, Brett hazards some guesses. There is, for instance, the team aspect: Players spend hours in locker rooms and hotel rooms with other men. "On a team you very much depend on each other," he says. "And it's a very physical dependence." Homosexuality throws a new, uncertain element into those fragile relationships.

Though most athletes love their sports, hockey players blast beyond the normal bounds of commitment into near fanaticism. From an early age they keep bizarre hours; 5 A.M. practice sessions are not uncommon, while youth and amateur games might not start until midnight. They pay exorbitant fees — for ice time, skates, pads, and travel — and do it all in rinks that are frigid in winter, steamy the rest of the year, and seldom down the next

street. "I just don't think other athletes are as loyal to their sport
as hockey players are to ours," Brett says. Homosexuality introduces an alien, untraditional component into the clearly defined,
traditional world hockey players inhabit.

Too, hockey more than most sports is insensitive to minorities, Brett notes: "It's a white man's game. There are very few
African-Americans, Asian-Americans, Native Americans. And
those are just the *visible* minorities. I've even seen players with
hearing impairments be given a tough time."

It is also a Darwinian sport. "Survival of the fittest, plain and
simple," Brett says. "Players and coaches take whatever advantage they can. If someone has a weakness, they seize on it." Had
they known Brett was gay, players and coaches would have made
comments to get under his skin or undermine his authority,
while general managers, even team owners, might have suggested that certain calls were in some way connected to his sexual
orientation.

Brett knows these theories cannot fully explain the depth of
hockey's almost visceral dislike of anything gay. However, it is
something he has experienced many times and in many ways.
Pejoratives are routinely tossed around the ice: "Faggot" and
"cocksucker" are the worst names any hockey player can call
another. The mere mention of the *G* word in idle conversation
brings hoots of derision.

Yet Brett insists that hockey referees are among the best people he knows. He is amazed at their intellect, buoyed by the
insights they offer away from the rink. Some of his best conversations have been with fellow officials, in hotels, restaurants, and
airports. "You know what 'NHL' stands for, don't you?" he asks.
"No Home Life. When you're away from your family for three
weeks at a time, rotating different refereeing crews every two or
three days, you see through the bullshit. You have plenty of time
to think about things."

At the same time, he adds, the rink is no place for introspection. A referee cannot be an objective thinker; he is an authority

40 figure. "When you're a ref, you're in charge of that building — and everyone in it," he says. "You put on a facade; you have to in order to get respect. You say and do things that totally contradict how you really feel."

It takes incredible self-confidence to officiate, he notes. A referee must be cocky enough to make a decision in front of 20,000 people, be the only one in the entire building who believes it's right, then carry on amid thunderous criticism as if nothing happened.

Feeling alone, receiving little outside support, developing a thick skin — those are traits referees share with other groups of persecuted minorities. Like, for example, gay people.

Brett agrees that there are parallels, and though he is used to standing outside society's boundaries, he is hesitant to categorize himself. "I'm a Russian Jew hockey ref who speaks Spanish," he jokes. "How many of them are there in this world? I consider myself a part of all those groups. When I'm in each group, I identify with that one. I'm proud of being gay, but I also don't fit with a lot of gay stereotypes — and I know they are stereotypes because people like me *don't* fit into them. I move easily in the athletic world because I'm still in shape and compete, but I also know there are a lot of athletes who are not like me."

Which identity is most important to him? "It may seem corny, but 'human being,' " he replies firmly. "I identify with the human race. I don't go around telling everyone I was an NHL ref, the same way I'm not hell-bent on proclaiming, 'I'm gay, hear me roar.' I'm content to live in my little house in the suburbs with my partner, go to my job, see my friends, and help train referees."

One of whom may one day wind up in the NHL too. Perhaps that man will do what Brett Parson could not. His one regret is that he never achieved his professional dream. "If I spent fifteen years in the league and got assigned to the Stanley Cup finals, then I would have come out to everyone and said, 'See, a gay man did hockey's biggest game, and nothing bad happened,' " he concludes. "That would have been my great swan song."

The Football Player and His Father

It is not easy being a gay athlete; the stories here prove that beyond any doubt. But they are not the only ones to bear a gay burden. Whenever a gay jock comes out to his family, those loved ones must suddenly grapple with many important questions. Why did our athletic-minded son turn out that way? Whom should we tell — whom can we tell? What does this mean for the rest of his life — and ours?

Those questions are magnified whenever a father is deeply involved himself in athletics. A man who felt he shared a common bond with his son suddenly discovers that their experiences and ideas are not as similar as he always thought. As a result, fathers who inhabit the sports world on a regular basis (as opposed to those who visit it only casually) may react differently from those who are in professions where machismo is less celebrated — or homosexuality more tolerated.

Then again, dads with jock genes may not react one bit differently; these stories, after all, are about debunking stereotypes. Consider, for example, Mike Henigan.

UNTIL HE WAS A JUNIOR IN COLLEGE — Harvard — Patrick Henigan did not really know the word *gay*. Sure, he had always been attracted to men, and growing up in the 1980s, he could not escape hearing the all-purpose put-down. But because of his athletic background — his grandfather was an Illinois legend in several sports, and his father, Mike, earned small college All-America honors as a Northern Illinois University football linebacker — Patrick never connected homosexuality with himself. "I wasn't what I considered to be a stereotypical gay man, feminine and unathletic," he explains. "Maybe I was just dumb. But as I grew up and lost my stereotypes, I realized those didn't matter. I was gay."

Perhaps his pedigree had more to do with it than he realized. For Mike Henigan was not only Patrick's athletic gene–contributing father, he was also a football coach. More to the point, he was *Patrick's* football coach.

Mike coached his son at Fountain Valley High, in that sunny, sports-minded Orange County, California, community. He was an assistant, not the head coach — his primary job was as the school's athletic director — but his passion for the game was undeniable. "From the time we were real little, my younger brother, David, and I were around sports," Patrick recalls. "We were water boys and ball boys at my dad's games. I excelled at a lot of sports, not just football. I liked soccer and baseball very much."

He emphasizes that his father applied very little direct sports pressure. "He was very good about making clear that I didn't have to do anything," Patrick says forcefully. "If I had trouble batting, he made sure I knew I didn't have to hit .350. I just had to try my best." At the same time Patrick felt indirect, subtle pressure to emulate his dad. "Sports was what we did," he says simply. "On Saturdays we went to games."

Mike considered himself and his wife, Adrienne — a woman he had dated since they were high school freshmen and married when they were college seniors — to be well-rounded people. They wanted their children (besides Patrick and David, there were two older girls) to do well in school and become involved in a variety of activities. When Patrick proved to be more academically motivated than David, his father pronounced himself "thrilled." Patrick was doing things that Mike, in retrospect, would love to have done as a child. But athletics had always come first for him.

Athletics brought father and son close together at Fountain Valley, where Patrick transferred in order to play football. "My dad made it very clear that I didn't have to go to his high school *or* play football," Patrick says. "I could have stayed at Marina (in nearby Huntington Beach) to be with my friends. Because of the transfer rules, I had to sit out a year, so freshman year was a pretty tough adjustment."

Mike's football experience at Fountain Valley was both good and bad. Playing for his father was awkward. Not only did

Patrick receive no special treatment, but he felt his father was   **43**
harder on him than on other players. But Patrick was big — six
foot two and 250 pounds by his senior year — and his teammates soon recognized his talents as an offensive guard.

Playing football senior year, he realized he had made a good
decision. "It was a fantastic experience: meeting new friends,
being with my father out of the context of my family, doing
well," he says. "It was great for my self-esteem, because at that
time I was going through so much."

College recruiters called, including Ivy League–level teams
and the service academies. Patrick was not sure he wanted to
play football in college but recognized sports as a means to an
education. He took recruiting trips and was especially enamored
of West Point. "I mean, how can you not like having meals with
generals?" he asks. He received an appointment to the military
academy and was ready to go, but two weeks before heading out,
he was accepted by Harvard. "My parents initially said no
because the Ivies don't give out athletic scholarships, but my
mom was so excited, they came up with a way to pay," Patrick
says. In retrospect this was another fortuitous decision. "I probably would have been very uncomfortable at West Point. And I
probably would not have been able to come out the way I did."

Patrick played two years of football at Harvard before stopping
for two reasons. His heart was no longer in it; at the same time, finally coming out to himself, he saw no way to reconcile homosexuality
with athletics. He thought there was no way to be strong, masculine,
and gay. He had heard locker-room chatter about an openly gay Yale
football player. The comments had a "get him" edge, and Patrick
made a mental note never to come out while on the team.

At liberal, tolerant Harvard, where had those ideas taken
root? "There are a lot of bad things about athletics everywhere,"
Patrick says. "Starting with Little League or Pop Warner, there's
this concept that to be a man is to be an athlete, to be an athlete
is to be strong, and to be strong you have to have a certain atti-

tude. Unfortunately, coaches engender this in their players, from a very young age on up to the pros. It's a stereotype, sure, because lots of coaches and athletes get beyond it, but it's also true that a large part of athletics gets wrapped up in it."

All summer before junior year, he grappled with the decision of whether to play. Finally, two weeks before preseason camp began, he told his coaches, family, and friends: He was giving up football. Their comments shocked him: "Well, okay, you're an adult, that's your decision to make." "Face it, you were never going to be a pro!" His father added, "You had to give it up at some point." Looking back, Patrick likened those reactions to what he heard when at last he came out. In both situations his fears bore little connection to reality.

At Harvard, Patrick retreated deep into the closet. He did well academically and athletically ("That was probably an unconscious overcompensation to try to be 'normal,'" he says) and made a conscious decision to be "a macho frat man type with athletic friends." He lived in Kirkland House with many other athletes and joined the Flannel Club, the closest thing at Harvard to a fraternity with a bad reputation.

"I dated a few women, but when things got to the point of serious physical interaction, it didn't work," Patrick says. Still, he played the jock role; he walked the walk and talked the talk of a stud. His daily life was filled with homophobic and sexist attitudes.

All the while Patrick was having a few random same-sex experiences with fraternity men, which he and his partners "blamed" on alcohol. But at the same time he was enjoying emotionally satisfying gay experiences. Harvard has several visible and active gay groups; through their newspaper articles, movie nights, and awareness programs, Patrick was discovering people with a very different view of the world than his. Slowly his awareness of homosexuality grew.

"It might've crossed people's minds at the end of college," Patrick says when asked whether anyone knew his secret. "But no one *really* suspected until the year after graduation." Living in New York with friends, he grew very depressed. "People wanted to ask me but didn't," he recalls. "Later a few people told me they thought I was just asexual."

New York in 1990 was a defining moment in Patrick's life. After graduating as an American history major, he and three friends received temporary teaching certificates. He was assigned to sixth grade; the students, discipline problems all, could read only at a second-grade level. "I got the job because I was a big guy who'd played football, but these five-foot-one women could command a classroom better than I could. It was the toughest thing I'd ever done."

Though despondent about work, he saw another side of life: men holding hands with men, rainbow flags flying from apartments, gay people feeling pride in who they were. Patrick confided in no one but devoured books about gay life. His favorites had sports themes: the novel *The Front Runner*, the biography of Martina Navratilova, the autobiographies of baseball umpire Dave Pallone and football player Dave Kopay. He identified most closely with Kopay's tale. As he realized that gay people could be anyone — including athletes — he came alive. On every page he highlighted key ideas; in the margins he wrote his thoughts.

"We had no inklings whatsoever," Mike Henigan says of his son's sexuality and subsequent turmoil. "As a young child he was always different from his brother and sisters, cousins, and kids of our friends. He wasn't interested in watching sports on TV. He'd play a bit of baseball, then go inside to talk. He was always extremely interested in academics, in school leadership. He was always the sensitive one, the one who remembered to send cards to his grandparents and loved to read. But we never suspected anything like that."

After a year in New York, Patrick — who still had not set foot inside a gay bar — decided to come out to his family and friends. The occasion was his five-year high school reunion. He finished *The David Kopay Story* on the plane. After arriving in California, he headed to the beach, where he wrote a twenty-page letter to friends and relatives. "As I reread it now, it's very angry," he says. "I talked about every fear I ever had. But I copied it, gave it out, and was the hit of the reunion. There was plenty of gossip. I did not hear one negative thing, at least not to my face. Everyone's been supportive. Here's something I was so worried about for so long, and it ended up enriching my life so much."

He handed the letter to his parents, one sister, and her husband after asking to talk and telling them to sit down. "In our family that's the signal for a bomb," Mike Henigan recalls. "He told us he's gay, then gave us a long letter to read. It was very powerful; Patrick's an excellent writer. It was filled with a lot of anger at society, but it was not blaming us. It was very challenging. He said, 'Here's who I am. You can like me for who I am, or our relationship can end.' "

Mike and Adrienne cried, then hugged. Patrick presented them with several books on homosexuality. The Henigans told their son they loved him but needed time to deal with the news. They stayed up all night talking.

"Despite being a health teacher, I fell into the stereotype that all gays will die of AIDS," Mike says. "Where Adrienne was really worried that his siblings might not accept him, I worried he might be destroyed."

Adrienne bought more books and fed what she learned to Mike. "It was good for me that Patrick went back to New York, so I could work through it that way," he says. It did not take him long.

"Adrienne's brother had come out in 1978 at their mother's seventieth birthday, back in De Kalb," Mike explains. "We were the only members of the family to stand by him. Still, the news hits a lot different when it's your son."

"Because of our relationship and backgrounds, I knew it would be hard," Patrick says. "I knew he'd still love me and wouldn't disown me, but because of my father's base of friends and colleagues, it wouldn't be easy for him. That was my worry, but I realize now that that was very unfair. My father has always gone beyond that stereotype of a coach; the things that are important to him are beyond athletics. It was unfair of me to stereotype him. My mom and dad cried for an hour, but after that they were fine. I mean, they had an awkward six months or so, when they were closeted with friends and peers, but that was part of their coming-out process, which is natural. Overall they've been very good, and it's been very good for them."

For two years the Henigans went on with their lives. Mike worked through his guilt — not that they had caused their son's homosexuality but that they had been insensitive to his terrible loneliness while growing up. Mike moved from shock and tolerance through acceptance, eventually reaching the stage of cherishing and relishing Patrick's uniqueness.

But something was missing. The couple felt a restlessness to do something, a yearning to act whenever they heard or saw bigotry. They watched gay people die, including Adrienne's brother's friends. Then, in 1993, a student approached Adrienne at Fountain Valley High School, where she works as a career technician. The boy showed her his college application essay; it was his coming-out piece. Adrienne told him it was strong and well-written. Then the boy and his twin came forward in school and asked to start a student alliance group for gays and lesbians. Two teachers supported them publicly. Adrienne approached the teachers — one a close friend, the other not — and said she and her husband would support the alliance too. The pair were stunned and wondered why.

Within days the school blew apart. A group of students calling themselves the Future Good Boys of America tried to stop the alliance. There were pickets, news stories, television interviews. Every time Adrienne heard gay people described negatively, she thought, *That's not who Patrick is.* She came out to the

48 two alliance advisers as the mother of a gay son. They both knew Patrick; after all, he had been student body president just a few years earlier. The teachers asked Adrienne and Mike to speak at the first alliance meeting. That was a big step for them; the only other person at school who knew about Patrick was the head football coach.

The lunchtime meeting was packed with a hundred students, some of whom came just to gawk at the attendees. "You could have heard a pin drop," Mike describes. "Most people knew Adrienne; not too many knew me, except as the macho athletic director. And there I was, saying I loved my gay son."

The controversy escalated. Patrick addressed the issue in a letter to the *Los Angeles Times, The Orange County Register,* and the *Huntington Beach/Fountain Valley Independent.* The Henigans addressed the school board twice. Their photos appeared in the paper. The *Times* ran a page-one Metro section article. Television and radio talk shows called. "The media loved it," Mike says. "I was the stereotypical football coach, expected to be macho, he-man, intolerant, and here I was reacting in a way that might be considered unusual."

The national support group known as Parents, Families, and Friends of Lesbians and Gays rode to the rescue. They sent speakers to board meetings. Through the federal Equal Access Act — the same law under which schools must permit Bible clubs to meet on campus — the alliance was allowed to form. The controversy died down. For four years now the group has met; there have been no further problems. Dozens of students attend meetings — yet in all that time only one athlete has come. He is straight.

Galvanized by their experience, the Henigans continued their activism. Today they serve as copresidents of PFLAG's Orange County chapter.

Mike Henigan maintains that he and his wife have always been open-minded and that he never fit the stereotype of either a foot-

ball coach or athletic director. "Professionally, Patrick's homosexuality — and my coming-out as the father of a gay son — has not
affected me one bit," he says. "Before I or anyone else knew about
Patrick, I was respected as someone who was not one-dimension-
al, and Patrick was respected and liked by a lot of different people
on our campus." Only one teacher made a negative comment, in
the form of a Christmas-card condemnation of homosexuality
placed in every faculty mailbox. Mike responded in writing. Now,
he says, both men know and understand where the other is coming from.

The athletic director was approached privately by a number
of other coaches and athletic directors, all of whom said the
same thing: "Thanks. Now I know someone else in my position." He describes many as "macho people I didn't get along
with from rival schools." One who stands out was a man at a
Catholic school whom, Mike says, "I never would have expected a kind word from."

His coming-out process has helped professionally in other
ways too, Mike says. Though always an advocate for racial and
religious fairness at Fountain Valley, he has become even more
outspoken because he is defending his own son. For instance, he
takes extra steps to make sure health students receive accurate, up-
to-date information on AIDS and homosexuality. He wears a
PFLAG lapel pin — a heart intertwined with a pink triangle —
every day. "I can't tell you the number of times someone asks what
it means, and that opens up a great discussion," he says. "I'm a
firm believer that true change comes from one-on-one contact."

He meets often, one-on-one, with the coaches he supervises.
A booklet he compiled on successful coaching included a section
on tolerance. But he believes the most important action he takes
with his coaches is "to live who I am and who my son is all the
time. They hear me talk about him and his lover going to the
Gay Games. They hear about my involvement with PFLAG.
More than any documents or formal training programs, they see
how we live our lives."

On a personal level, he describes the past several years as "phenomenally, tremendously enriching." Through his son he has met wonderful men and women; by sharing his family's story with colleagues, he has deepened and broadened his professional relationships as well.

Since 1978 Mike has eaten lunch at the same table every day. The group — virtually all male — is extremely conservative, with coaches, religious fundamentalists, and solid Orange County Republicans well-represented. From the time Mike came out to them during the initial alliance controversy, he has raised issues about homosexuality and encouraged his friends to ask questions. Some say they like Patrick very much but do not understand his "choice." Realizing that education is a lifelong process, Mike takes that in stride. He is buoyed by the reaction of one group member, who told Mike that their lunchtime discussions have changed him as a person and made him think about many other social issues as well.

When Mike spoke for this book, there were no openly gay athletes at Fountain Valley High. (In fact, despite the presence of the alliance, there are very few openly gay students in any other clique at the school either.) For that reason, says Mike, it is important for coaches and athletic directors to address sexual orientation in the context of "total tolerance." Whether the issue is race, religion, or sexuality, coaches and administrators must be careful how they talk to and about people and how they treat them on and off the field. "It's an issue of basic human dignity," Mike notes. "Athletes of every race, religion, and orientation have the civil right to participate in sports without feeling uncomfortable. No longer can a coach or a teammate say, 'You throw like a girl' or 'You block like a faggot.' That's demeaning not only to gay kids but to every other athlete, every other human being. The good thing is, I think more and more people are starting to realize that."

Patrick's perspective on athletics has been changed by his coming-out too. "I thought there were no gay athletes, that you couldn't be gay and also be dedicated to training and competition. Now I play in gay volleyball and softball leagues, and I have a whole new impression of sports. I used to think I was the best gay athlete in the world; now I know that's just not true. There are so many great players out there — incredible, amazing athletes. It's a shame so few people know about them."

His father does. "We've talked about the male aspect of being an athlete," Patrick says. "He recognizes how hard it is, even today, for any athlete to come out. The macho image permeates all athletics. You know, I took my father to the Gay Games in 1994. It was very important for him to see all that. He was extremely impressed. And I'm impressed that he's been able to convince a few coaches to alter their approach a little, to understand that every athlete is an individual, that you *can* be gay and also an athlete."

While volleyball and softball have replaced football in Patrick Henigan's life, sports in general have taken a backseat. He spent his final months at Brooklyn Law School looking for a job. Ideally he would like to work at Lambda Legal Defense and Education Fund, a gay rights organization where he interned previously.

"And if I could work on issues of athletics," he says, "that would be incredible!"

The Wrestlers

Of all the sports in the world, it's hard to imagine one more asso-ciated with homosexuality than wrestling. Though modern athletes do not follow the ancient Greek practice of grappling nude, the close body contact endures. Every element, from the strip-down weigh-in to the starting position (both wrestlers kneel, one behind the other; one of the back man's arms rests lightly on his opponent's elbow, with the other draped across the abdomen) to various pinning combinations, makes it a difficult sport for many boys to accept. Students, male and female, consider it "gross," mocking it with a ferocity accorded no other sport; more than a few physical education teachers and coaches hold it at arm's length as well. Add to that the occasional sensational stories with homosexual undertones — such as the weird behavior of the Du Pont heir who built an entire wrestling complex on his estate, paid men to live there, and ended up being arrested in connection with the death of one — and it's easy to see why some people call it "the gay sport."

Wrestling is no more gay, of course, than football, basketball, golf, or badminton. But it takes a special breed of athlete to overcome the stereotypes — especially if that athlete is indeed gay.

"WRESTLING'S NOT GAY," says Jay, a grappler from New England who asked that his last name not be used but who — like most wrestlers — is passionate when discussing his favorite pastime. "Look at football, where the quarterback has his hand on the center's butt, and then everybody tackles each other. Or any other sport in which people pile on each other after a big win. Wrestling is no different. There's the same number of gay peo-ple in wrestling as any other sport: 10 percent."

He is able to say that now; it is not something he allowed himself to think about while he was in high school. He no longer competes; after a solid scholastic career, including finishing third in his state as a 103-pound junior and fifth in New England as a postgraduate at 112, Jay's hopes for a college career fell victim to the National Collegiate Athletic Association's Proposition 48, which prohibits students with low high school grades and SAT scores from competing as intercollegiate athletes during freshman year. Wrestlers, more than athletes in most other sports, find it difficult to miss that first season; Jay never tried out for the team again. But he is coaching at a high school near his hometown, where his mother still lives, and that is why despite his self-acceptance and relative renown in the gay community, he is reluctant to come out to his athletes or coaching colleagues.

He started coaching while still in high school, as soon as he understood the importance of technique. Wrestling is a sport that, more than most others, must be *taught*. While strength, quickness, balance, and pure instinct can take an athlete far, one can truly succeed only by learning a variety of moves (many not particularly natural), then drilling them over and over under the supervision of someone more experienced. Wrestlers are a tight-knit breed; they share secrets about technique with each other, are willing to teach their most successful moves to opponents, and take seriously the idea of passing their knowledge on to younger grapplers.

So as a senior Jay began working with middle school athletes. He enjoyed the twin satisfactions of any teacher: imparting knowledge and being looked up to. When his own career ended, coaching became a natural progression.

Occasionally, especially from high school students, he hears the word "fag." Sometimes it is just part of common adolescent dialogue; other times it does have homosexual undertones. It always makes him uneasy, but he says nothing. He does not want to out himself.

His feelings are complex, and he did not crystallize them himself until a girl tried out for the high school team he was working with. Whenever he taught her a move or drilled with her, he was nervous; that's the case when most male athletes wrestle females, but his anxiety had a different root.

"If I accidentally hit her breast, I worried that people would see it and say I was a scumbag, just trying to cop a feel," he says. "Then what could I say: 'I'm gay, I don't give a shit about her'?"

That experience made him wonder what it would be like for his male wrestlers if they knew he was gay. "Seeing as a coach how uncomfortable I was around this girl, I wouldn't ever want to put any guy in that position with me," he says. "I just wouldn't want anyone to feel that way when they wrestle me. So it's better if they just don't know."

That was not the only disconcerting experience Jay had with the girl. At the end of the season, she asked him privately whether he was gay or straight. That was the first time anyone had even suspected.

"Of course I told her I was straight," he recalls. Her instincts were right: There was someone on the team Jay had been attracted to. "As much as I tried to hide it, she saw through my act. She noticed my expression whenever I saw him, because she was attracted to him too."

His attraction to the grappler had nothing to do with wrestling, Jay insists. "Sexual preference has no place on the mat," he says. "Gay or straight, you go out to win. There's too much going on competition-wise to even think about sex. There is no arousal whatsoever. It just doesn't happen."

The intimacy of the locker room never bothered Jay — in fact, he loved the ritual of showering because "that's where you can talk the most amount of shit" — and though occasionally he noticed someone cute during weigh-ins, he knew enough to keep his thoughts to himself. "It's hard to be aroused by seeing a bunch of people jump on a scale," he says.

The sport's homoerotic image is never far from his mind, however. During one of his first practices as a high school freshman, the captain joked, "You know, on average, one out of every thirteen wrestlers is gay." That stuck in his mind: Thirteen is the

number of grapplers on a varsity team. He vowed never to let 55
anyone know that on his team, he was the one.

He also does not want to provide ammunition to those who, on discovering that he is gay, might remark, "See, it *is* a gay sport." He knows what happens in bars when strangers learn he is a wrestler: They say things like "Boy, I'd love to wrestle *you*" or "I bet you can show me some moves!" "That's offensive," Jay says. "It's clear to me that it's not about wrestling at all. They're saying something derogatory about the sport I love. My sexual preference has nothing to do with sports. I'm proud to be gay, I'm proud to be a wrestler, and I wouldn't want to do anything to make either one look bad."

Wrestling has been as important a part of Jay's life as anything else. Growing up with his mother and brother (he saw his divorced father only occasionally), Jay attended six different schools. Dyslexia compounded his difficulties. In retrospect he thinks his isolation was caused more by his learning disability than his sexual orientation. "They sent the LD kids off to different classrooms for part of every day," he recalls. "We really felt different."

Jay tried soccer in third grade, but after spending much of the season on the bench, he never went back. In middle school he attempted football but was too small to do well. He tried lacrosse too, but the practices were infrequent and disorganized.

His eighth-grade teacher, the high school wrestling coach, talked Jay into attending the youth program he ran on the side. For the first time Jay tasted athletic success. He placed third in a small wrestling tournament, and suddenly he could hardly wait for high school to begin.

"I loved wrestling for the experience of competing on an even level," he explains. "In most sports the bigger you are, the better you are. With wrestling, seniors who never talked to underclassmen would compliment me in the halls. It made me feel like a good person, that other people could see me and notice me."

56 Gradually the self-esteem he gained from the sport — for the fact that a wrestler competes one-on-one, wearing just a singlet and headgear, in front of a crowd, with no one to blame if he loses, no one to share credit with if he wins, instills confidence in even the most uncertain boy — helped ease his way in other areas of life. He came out to himself in high school, to his family and nonwrestling friends in college. He smiles more often than before and looks more people in the eye.

Though he does not think he will come out soon as a coach, he expects that with time things will become easier. "Pretty soon I'll be coaching kids I did not go to school with," Jay notes. "As I get older it won't be a situation where I'm twenty-two and they're eighteen. There'll be more of a barrier between us, and I won't have to worry so much." He looks forward to establishing himself in one school system, so if the word does get out, he will have a solid reputation to fall back on.

As much as he does not expect it, he sees one scenario in which he might out himself. "If there was a kid on my team who was gay or was getting harassed about it whether he was gay or not, that might be the time for me to say something. The time usually comes when a coach has to take a stand. That might be it."

Jay smiles after saying that. He knows that some of wrestling's most important lessons are learned off the mat.

Gene Dermody — short, squat, and heavily muscled — understands the unique relationship between wrestling and life too. His favorite hangout is the Eureka Valley Recreation Center's second floor, where the Golden Gate Wrestling Club trains. That room, with its heavy mats and stale air, is much more familiar to Gene than the bars, restaurants, and clothing stores of Castro Street, San Francisco's gay district, just one block east.

Gene Dermody is a wrestler, plain and simple. Little else matters to him — not his job as a "computer nerd/consultant" or his former work as a lounge singer; not the late-night–early-morning club life that is San Francisco's primary draw for some gay men; not even the fact that Golden Gate is a gay wrestling club. For Gene, the operative word is *wrestling*, not *gay*.

"Voyeurs, spectators, people that see homoeroticism every-where project it naturally onto wrestling," he says. "But any wrestler, gay or straight, knows you can't have two focuses while you compete. People wrestle for the competition, not for any sexual component."

In fact, Gene notes, in San Francisco's gay community his wrestling club has a reputation of being too mainstream. "We're not a sex club, and we're not a self-help group," he insists. "We allow gay men to relate to each other on a nonsexual level. You know, a lot of gay men have trouble relating in nonsexual ways. Wrestling lets you do that. There's a bond on the mat that is not transient. Wrestlers aren't criticized for being weaker or less tal-ented, only for not trying. Dedication and commitment to the sport have nothing to do with getting laid or how you look. The more you wrestle, the more you realize how unimportant the rest of that stuff really is."

Gene admits that many factors can influence someone to try a sport, and the opportunity to roll around on a mat with anoth-er male may indeed be uppermost in some men's minds — at the beginning. For him wrestling's appeal was what it was not: It was not basketball, for which he was too small, and not gymnastics, for which he was too heavy. It was a perfect way to release his aggression; to prove that he was strong, solid, *in command*.

Besides, he always loved to roughhouse.

Most wrestlers, he adds, are loners. "We get very few foot-ball stars, guys who love the team spirit and the limelight," he says. "Wrestling attracts guys who sort of have a chip on their shoulder about something. That's true whether they're gay or straight."

There was no wrestling team at Gene's academically orient-ed all-boys Jesuit school, St. Peter's in Jersey City, New Jersey, so his first exposure to the sport came on the Bronx campus of

58   New York University, where he majored in chemistry. A 123-
pound walk-on, he called himself "not very good," but he picked
it up quickly; with so many moves based on principles of
mechanics and physics, wrestling holds particular appeal for science types. Because he was in a low weight class, where good
grapplers are hard to find, he received opportunities he otherwise might not have had. However, the one-two punch of a
demanding academic load and sudden physical growth ended his
varsity hopes.

Through that whole period Gene thought he was straight. "I
was totally unaware of sexuality," he says. "I took some courses
down in Greenwich Village, and I thought all the hippies were
friendly. Well, some were more friendly than others." He dated
women, nearly became engaged, and could never understand
why everyone got so excited about sex.

A year after graduation, "a little blond" cruised him and
picked him up on the 42nd Street subway shuttle. "To this day I
can't understand how stupid and ignorant I was," Gene recalls.
"But he seduced me, and the gates opened. I thought, *So that's
what sex is about!*"

At that point Gene realized that sex had been subjugated by
wrestling; that part of wrestling's attraction for him was the
attraction of being around men. However, he insisted, there was
no sexual component; competition was competition, and on the
mat that was all he cared about.

His first job was as a chemistry, physics, and general science
teacher in the Fort Dix, New Jersey, public school system. He
also served as assistant coach for the high school wrestling team.
That's when he realized he had a talent for analyzing and breaking down the many complex wrestling moves, then putting them
back together in ways appropriate to the various ways young
athletes learn — visually, physically, or verbally.

Gene spent two years as a teacher and head coach at a
Catholic school in Paramus, then moved on to other, better-
paying districts closer to New York. At each school he was also

head wrestling coach. He never felt conflicted about his homosexuality.

"People think it's glamorous to deal with hundreds of young kids," he says. "Well, sex is the furthest thing from your mind. In fact, it's enough to cure you of any thoughts! Intellectually, kids are just not there. They don't learn as fast as when they're older, so you have to spend s-o-o-o much time explaining things over and over. Physically too they don't develop skill and strength until they're older. I dealt with them from a business point of view. I didn't bother with all that psychological-profile stuff. I went on gut reactions." However, he was not all rough, tough, and gruff. He enjoyed the rewards any coach feels when young athletes listen, learn, and succeed.

Gene coached high school wrestling for twelve years; in his free time he wrestled for a YMCA team. During that entire period he lived in a condominium on Manhattan's Upper West Side. Wrestling was a core part of his life; he realizes now that it also kept him alive. New York in the '70s and early '80s was a hedonistic, destructive place for gay men, but Gene did not participate. "I guess with my Jesuit upbringing I felt a need to be in control," he explains. "I had lots of boyfriends. Most of them were dancers, and many of them are now dead. I saw all the drugs and other stuff, but I just never did it. I never had sex with two or three people in one day. Maybe I was undersexed, but, knock on wood, it saved me."

After Gene realized he was gay, he came to understand that a number of his college teammates were too. They told him they always knew he was — even if he had not — but did not want to push the issue until he was ready.

As a teacher and coach, he did not announce his homosexuality, yet neither did he hide it. "I was single, I lived in the city, I wore Levi's 501 jeans," he chuckles. "It was pretty much common knowledge, but I was never accused or blacklisted. The principals knew, the boards of education knew. I think the kids knew more about me than I knew about myself. I brought wrestling buddies to social functions. But I never wore an arm-band, I never waved a flag. That just wasn't me."

In 1982 Gene saw a flyer for the first Gay Games. He called up and registered. He arrived in San Francisco not knowing what to expect and found an entire contingent of New Yorkers. He wound up carrying the state flag during opening ceremonies and discovering a community of gay athletes he never dreamed existed.

"There was so much camaraderie," he marvels. "There was this whole crowd of guys just like me — people with real jobs, people who didn't abuse their bodies. And to top it off, it was extremely competitive."

Gay Games founder Dr. Tom Waddell presented Gene with the third-place medal ("I was pissed I only got a bronze!" he says), and that week changed his life. He quit his teaching job, moved to San Francisco, and studied computer technology. He zoomed up the corporate ladder while luxuriating in meeting mirror images of himself.

The Golden Gate Wrestling Club was founded by several people who organized the first Gay Games. When their leader died of AIDS complications the day after the second Gay Games ended (Gene earned a silver medal), he took over. Today it is a bona fide city program with a core membership of thirty-five (including ten women). It's run like any other sports club and is fully sanctioned by U.S. Amateur Wrestling, a branch of the U.S. Olympic Committee. The club passed a rule prohibiting anyone under eighteen from joining, but that has not deterred several parents from pleading with Gene to accept their sons anyway. They know, as he does, that the sport can give a gay person physical and emotional strength, confidence, discipline, and the self-esteem to deal intelligently with an often hostile heterosexual world.

However, wrestling does not attract more gay men than other sports, Gene emphasizes. "It's so intimidating as a twelve-

or thirteen-year-old to walk into a wrestling room in the first
place, with all those sweaty people rolling around," he says. "If
you're gay or think you might be, it can be almost impossible.
From what I've seen, I think track and swimming might have a
lot of gay people — but not wrestling."

But gay wrestlers do exist, and enough of them find their way
to the Eureka Valley Recreation Center to make the Golden
Gate Wrestling Club a force to be reckoned with. Gene
Dermody is proud of his team but prouder still of the individuals on it. "We've got guys who had drug and alcohol problems
and sex addictions," he says. "Now they're wrestling, and maybe
for the first time in their lives, they feel good about themselves.
They meet people and form a bond that goes beyond sex. It's
about dedication and commitment and competition, not about
who looks best or who can get who. All that sexual stuff is unimportant. But this — wrestling — is real."

The Roommates

Sports are a cornerstone of many adolescent boys' lives. Their rooms are wallpapered with posters of athletic heroes, and they practice moves and skills and fritter away hours perfecting their autographs for that magical day when they're actually besieged by fans. They dream of a future filled with sporting success and adulation.

Many parents share or at least support those fantasies. Fathers, mothers, and assorted stepparents sacrifice to pay for equipment, camps, and travel; they move meetings or change work schedules to attend games and even practices; and they are always there to savor the latest triumph, commiserate over the most recent setback, or pop in the video they've just taped.

Of course, all teenage athletes do not enjoy such high levels of familial involvement. Some parents cannot afford the money or time; others are uninterested or do not understand their child's choice of activity. Some are unable to reconcile their son's athletic career with the fact that he is gay. For those youngsters, sports take second place to simply existing.

HUNTER ALLEN AND DAN HARRIS are a pair of California boys. Just a year out of high school, they are happy, healthy housemates in Hollywood. In various ways they are engaged in the most fundamental task of young adults everywhere: discovering who they are and figuring out what they want from life. They've got entry-level–type jobs, a good circle of friends, and the world ahead of them.

What they do not have are their families or the sports they loved. Their parents separated themselves from both boys' lives when they learned their sons were gay; in the turmoil of self-discovery, the athletes were forced to abandon the games they loved. Though Hunter's and Dan's backgrounds are dis-

similar, their lives ended up the same. Homosexuality changed 　　63
everything.

Hunter grew up in a Mormon family in the San Francisco
Bay area. Every Sunday his father took Hunter, his younger
brother, and two younger sisters to church. As a bishop Hunter's
father shared the church's traditional, antigay values.

From a young age Hunter knew he liked boys. He became
sexually active in his early teens but never attached the word *gay*
to that behavior until he was sixteen. That was about the same
time he stopped identifying with the church. Until then he figured he would follow the path of most Mormon youths: Go on
a mission, attend college, get married, raise a family.

When he came out to his parents, in 1995, they kicked him
out of the house. "You'll burn in hell," his father said. "You're
not my son anymore." (His mother has since reconciled with
Hunter and been supportive of him.)

Hunter stayed with friends, dropped out of school, and
moved to Los Angeles to live with a lesbian aunt. Recently his
father called and invited him back. But the call came too late:
Hunter now has his own apartment and a job with a production
company.

Before he quit school, Hunter was a good runner: He once
finished seventh out of 400 in the league cross-country championship. Though his teammates were surprised at his coming-out
news, they really did not care. Hunter had many friends; all supported him.

He liked running because of the concentration it required. He
enjoyed building himself up physically, mentally, even spiritually.
He marveled at the endurance it took and felt especially joyful
whenever he ran in a pretty place like the country. Hunter appreciated the lack of "in-your-face competitiveness"; running is not
like some ball sports, in which athletes who do not whip everyone
else's asses are considered losers. In fact, he theorizes, one of the
reasons athletic gay people may be attracted to running is that it is
not an intimidating, one-on-one sport like basketball or football.

At one time running actually took the place of religion for Hunter. He meditated not in church but on trails through the woods. The important difference was that running had no rules. "It was my own religion," he explains. "I was able to define things for myself instead of having to follow what other people believed."

He found it hard to stop running. Despite leaving school and moving to Los Angeles, he wanted to continue. But without a coach, teammates, and races, it was not the same. For all its solitude, running is also an interpersonal sport.

Eventually Hunter resumed his education at EAGLES Center, a Los Angeles Unified School District school for gay, lesbian, bisexual, and transgendered students. (The acronym stands for Emphasizing Adolescent Gay/Lesbian Education Services). As befits an alternative high school, there were no sports teams; in fact, there was no physical education program at all. "They completely ignored the physical aspect of education," Hunter says. "This was a school with lots of hookers, street kids, kids who do drugs. I thought sports would be healthy for them, but all they were interested in was going to clubs."

The teachers voiced a similar attitude, which Hunter describes as "We're gay here. We don't need to do that. We'd rather focus on artistic stuff."

"That made me mad," he says. "It's just putting stereotypes on ourselves. I was trying to figure out what it means to be gay and how running fit into that. Now I realize that being gay is just a very small part of my personality. I'm also a writer, a smart guy, and nice. But what they were saying to me was that *gay* means only certain things, like knowing all the dance music. That's stupid. I have gay pride, but I also have pride in myself as a human being. I like to think, I like to read, and I like to run."

In his two years in Los Angeles, Hunter has made many friends. He has consciously tried to meet people outside the gay community and involve himself in nongay activities. In 1996 he volunteered for the Clinton-Gore reelection campaign.

Right now he has what he calls "a stable, secure life" and is satisfied with it. He credits that — and his ability to overcome being thrown out of his house and giving up a tremendously pleasurable activity — with his overall attitude of self-acceptance. "If you come out poorly, people get the idea that you think you're bad," he says. "If you're okay with who you are, then other people see it and react accordingly. That's what my friends and teammates did. I loved myself when I came out, and other people treated me well. Not my parents, but other people I cared about. Now I'm moving on with my life."

Hunter's roommate, Dan Harris, is a native Southern Californian. He calls his hometown, Temple City, "a good suburban place for white-collar workers to raise kids." It was filled with culs-de-sac and Brady Bunch clones. He rode his bike to school and had plenty of friends.

When Dan was in sixth grade, his parents wanted to escape the encroaching problems of Los Angeles and moved out to the high desert town of Yucca Valley. That was "real redneck country," Dan says. "Lots of hicks."

Life got difficult. Around the time of the move, he realized he fit the definition of *gay*. That bothered him; he had heard his father characterize gay people as "psychopathic killer-rapists." "I knew I wasn't a crazy murderer," Dan says. "I just liked guys!"

When he moved to Yucca Valley, Dan was a baseball player. His father had introduced him to the sport; he considered it good masculine fun, and Dan enjoyed it too. "I wasn't effeminate," he notes. "I liked bombardment in gym and playing with my dad's guns."

But as he recognized he was gay, Dan became depressed. He gained a lot of weight during his junior high years but continued playing baseball. "I was good at it, so it became a self-esteem thing," he says. "I always played on good teams, and we were always high-fiving each other. Baseball was something I could do well. I knew it, and everyone else knew it."

Dan built a backstop in his yard and laid out a baseball field. Friends came over often. Home run derby was a favorite activity.

There were other games too. Between the ages of eleven and thirteen, Dan was a promiscuous sex partner. He describes a typical day: "We'd be trading baseball cards, and I'd ask my friend, 'What would you do if I told you I was gay?' We'd talk a little bit, and I'd tell him I was curious. He'd say he was too. So every weekend I'd have sex."

Dan and his partners never talked about it afterward. That made him feel bad; it still does, especially since he has learned that one of those buddies is bisexual and another "goes back and forth."

His many encounters changed his views on sex. The impersonality of what he was doing turned him off to any close contact. As he got older, he stopped having sex altogether. Now he is waiting for Mr. Right.

The less secure he became of his sexuality, the less confident he became of himself. His loss of self-esteem showed in his baseball; the more he worried, the poorer he played; the poorer he played, the more down he got. The cycle was vicious and endless.

The good feeling he once had from baseball now came from eating. His weight ballooned. While he ate he watched television.

One day he saw MTV's *The Real World*. Pedro Zamora, the gay roommate, inspired Dan. For the first time he understood that gay is good. The show turned his life around. He lost weight. He joined the school band, went to as many athletic events as possible, and made many friends. "Pedro Zamora saved my life," Dan says. A couple of days after the TV star died of AIDS complications, Dan came out.

He wrote IN MEMORY OF PEDRO ZAMORA on his backpack. A couple of students teased him about it, then challenged him: "Are you gay?" Without thinking, he answered yes. They peppered him with questions: "Do you have AIDS?" "Which one is the girl?" The news tore through school. Within a day he went from being one of the most popular students to one of the least.

In the coming weeks names and rocks were hurled at him.
He got in fights. His complaints to school administrators were met with a gruff, "Hang in there." His parents told him it was his own fault for coming out.

One afternoon at McDonald's a classmate threatened him, then returned with three truckloads of friends brandishing baseball bats. That was Dan's last day in Yucca Valley. He wanted to graduate with his friends, but after the incidents at school and McDonald's, he realized he did not have many.

He called a gay woman he knew, Patricia Nell Warren, the author of *The Front Runner*, a best-seller about a young gay runner yearning to be himself (Dan had met her when she signed books at a gay store in nearby Palm Springs). She discussed several options, including community colleges, high schools that offer general equivalency diplomas, and the EAGLES Center in Los Angeles; he decided to attend EAGLES.

Patricia also suggested he call another young man she knew, Hunter Allen. They moved in together as roommates and classmates at the EAGLES Center.

"I liked the school's support for being gay and the fact that there were no more hassles," Dan says. "But most of the kids there were flamboyant or eccentric. They couldn't fit in in their regular schools because they were too queeny. I went from one extreme — redneck — to the other. I didn't fit in there either. I wanted to be in sports, and there just wasn't anything like that there for me."

Today, Dan runs and works out in Los Angeles, but he misses baseball. "It kept me going," he explains. "Even when I was depressed, it was always there for me."

He works at a creative agency and is on the lookout for sports-oriented friends. "I want to find people with the same interests," he says. "I need to see people who look like me. I didn't think it would be so hard in the gay community, but it is."

The Boyfriend

Along with coaches, sportswriters, and fans, another group of people takes an avid interest in the daily lives of athletes: their lovers.

They are the ones who watch while others cheer their men on. They provide support when their mate comes home tired, sore, reeling from a bad performance or bitter loss. They serve as confidants, cheerleaders, and, occasionally, critics. To be an athlete's lover seems in many ways glamorous, but it is burdensome too.

The traditional image is that these roles are filled by girlfriends and wives. But of course gay jocks have boyfriends and husbands (spiritually, if not legally) — men who fill those same roles. Unlike opposite-gender lovers, gay athletes' companions do not step into the spotlight or receive public recognition. They do, however, carry the same burdens.

And they bear them alone.

FOR TONY MAURICE (a pseudonym), the worst part of loving a college basketball star was the games. Tony sat in the stands, watching his boyfriend perform while feeling as much possessive pride as nearby girlfriends felt for their straight lovers. But while the women around him eagerly shared their good fortune, reveling together in the excitement of the contest, the thrill of loving an athlete, and the jealousy of those around them, all Tony could do was stare.

It hurt even more that his boyfriend did not want to be seen with him in public.

A relationship with a male athlete was the last thing Tony expected in 1987, his first year at Florida A&M University. He enrolled in the black college in Tallahassee soaring with the all-things-are-possible optimism of most freshmen. While growing up in a small beach town on the west coast of Florida, he had gazed longingly at guys in thongs, not women in bikinis. But he also knew that that was not what his friends were doing, so he tried to block out those feelings. He had sex with as many women as he could and considered himself straight.

In his job on campus, he developed a "buddy-type friendship" with a coworker, Calvin (not his real name). Tony, a shy young man, was awed by Calvin, who though also only a freshman was already drawing notice as a varsity basketball player. On Martin Luther King weekend, Calvin celebrated his birthday at a club. On his way home he found himself caught in a downpour. He knew from their casual conversations that Tony lived nearby. At 2 A.M. Calvin knocked on the door and asked if he could come in out of the rain.

Though surprised — the two had never socialized outside of work — Tony replied, "Sure."

"Isn't it amazing I remembered you lived here?" Calvin said. Looking back, Tony realizes that the fateful knock on the door was more than coincidental.

Tony offered Calvin a robe but did not watch him undress. Calvin stretched across the bed, while Tony claimed a small corner of it. A few minutes later Calvin got up to go to the refrigerator. He no longer wore Tony's robe; in fact, all he had on were leopard-skin bikini briefs.

As Calvin bent over to get water, Tony was aroused but pretended to sleep. When Calvin climbed back onto the bed, their bodies touched. "I almost jumped into the next city!" Tony recalls. "The rest is history."

The rain finished the same time the two men did, a couple of hours later. Abruptly Calvin said, "See you later, man," and walked out the door.

For the next month Tony felt "paranoid" every time he was near Calvin. They said nothing to each other at work. With basketball season heating up, Calvin was often away.

But a month and a half later, again in the rain, Calvin initiated a conversation. He told Tony he liked him. Tony laughed, but Calvin persisted. "No, you don't understand," he said. "I really *like* you." Tony had never heard anyone say that to him before. In fact, he had never even considered the possibility.

They talked casually a few times after that. Three weeks later they had sex again, at Calvin's apartment. This time they went even further than before. "I was so naive, I had no idea a man could penetrate another guy," Tony says, remembering the event with wonderment. "When he put a condom on me, I had no idea why. 'There's no female here!' I said. But then he sat on my lap and took me to a land I'd never been in before."

That night Tony fell in love with Calvin.

Their relationship lasted four years. Tony felt slightly guilty about sleeping with another man and tried to hold on to his "last vestige of masculinity" by acting very straight around other people, but Calvin's reaction was even stronger. Throughout their entire four years together, he always had a girlfriend. He seldom appeared in public without a woman on his arm. He even fathered a child.

During sophomore year Calvin joined a fraternity. "His machoism was going through the roof, but he kept telling me it was all for show," Tony recalls. "He talked about going pro and said that meant there was a role he had to play. He went to bed with at least four or five females that I knew of, but he always said that was part of the image he was trying to project. It didn't even bother me when he fathered that child. I grew to a point where I was used to the setup."

Being young, nervous, and uncertain, Tony went along with the charade. "I had nothing to compare it to," he explains. "It was a hurting thing, but I loved this guy. We told each other we loved each other, and to see him with another person hurt me so much. He was extremely handsome — gorgeous, with dark green eyes and black, silky, curly hair. I think he knew he had a level of control, emotionally, because I was just accepting that he was with all these women."

At the beginning of their relationship, Tony did not mind sitting in the crowd during games. He would go just to watch Calvin play. Soon, however, that grew difficult. "I'd see him enjoying himself on the court, getting the press, being cheered on by cheerleaders, and meanwhile I was being swept under the rug in public," Tony says.

It was even worse afterward. Calvin would head off to fraternity parties while Tony, unable to watch as Calvin cavorted with his frat brothers and "little girls," trudged home. There he would tune in a replay of the just-completed game or watch Calvin being interviewed on the news.

Those lonely nights, he realizes now, were a big mistake. "I allowed him to steal my own joy and happiness," Tony says. "I should have let him go just so far and had fun myself."

Calvin's conflicted nature was overpowering Tony more and more. The basketball star did not want anyone to see them together in public beyond fleeting, casual conversations. Yet he became intensely jealous whenever Tony talked with anyone else — male or female, straight or gay. Calvin would phone from parties to assure himself that Tony was actually home. "And I would just sit there, waiting for his calls, alone," Tony says. "But of course he had no problem coming over on *his* free time to my apartment and hanging out the whole weekend."

During their four years at A&M, only one person knew they were a couple. One night a next-door neighbor heard their lovemaking through the apartment wall. The next morning she came over. "Wow! You must have had a great time last night!" she joked to Tony. Suddenly Calvin walked into the room, naked. The woman, realizing who Tony's partner had been, threw her hand over her mouth and rushed out, mumbling, "I'm sorry."

After Calvin left, Tony went next door to tell her he would not lie about what she heard and saw. However, no one else knew about the two men — not even Tony's gay friends. To this day, he believes, no one has a clue.

In 1992, a few minutes after graduation ceremonies ended, Tony approached Calvin. It was the first time he spoke honestly about their relationship, and a wave of relief surged through his body. "I loved him, but I was happy to see him out of my life," Tony recalls. "I felt it was time for me to get on with my stuff." They exchanged parents' addresses, promised to write, shook hands, and parted.

They stayed in touch for a year or two. Then one day a letter from Tony came back with a note saying Calvin's family had moved. That was the last Tony heard until recently, when he ran into a mutual acquaintance. She said that Calvin had recently asked about him. Tony felt elated and was glad to learn that Calvin was doing well.

In retrospect, despite Calvin's closeted possessiveness, Tony is happy that his first gay relationship was with him. "Even though it was super-undercover, there were good things about it," he says. "If my first time had been with a flamboyant person or someone a lot more experienced, it might not have been as positive. Even though it wasn't his first time, we stumbled through things together, and I learned a lot."

Tony learned about gay sex, of course, but also about relationships in general. "I gave him a bit of control over my life," he says. "That's something I've vowed never to relinquish again. I learned not to overly trust someone too. He never overtly lied to me, but he lied by omission." Their level of communication was weak, he understands now: "As far as putting our feelings on the table, well, he had a bib around his neck, a knife and fork in each hand, and he was cutting through me like I was liver."

Yet Tony also feels regret. "I'd love to talk to him again, because I don't think I brought things to proper closure," he explains. "This was my first experience. It lasted four years. We grew together. Not a week goes by without me thinking about him."

How much of their problem was related to Calvin's being an athlete? "That was a major motivating factor," Tony says. "I was trying to be a macho guy myself. I felt that by being with him, I was with a *real* man, not just a gay man. I bought into that whole concept that he was a sexual person, not a gay person — that he was hypersexual because he was an athlete. And I think he felt that way too."

Tony realizes that he was also attracted to Calvin because so many females were. "That turned me on," he admits. "I had access to him, and most of them did not. Even though nobody else knew I had access to him, he knew it, and I knew it. He wouldn't have had that aura around him if he hadn't been on the basketball team, and I probably wouldn't have been attracted to him the way I was."

Calvin seldom talked about his life as a basketball player, but from casual comments Tony understood that he was under tremendous pressure to keep his homosexuality secret. The only time Calvin ever spoke of something gay in the context of athletics was when he discussed a football player with a flamboyant look and walk, whom Calvin suspected "messed around." His description of the reactions of other athletes gave Tony the impression that to act in any way other than as a straight-appearing macho jock was to invite suspicion, distrust, and, ultimately, problems.

Today, Tony is more out than he was in college, though not at his job in the financial industry. He goes to clubs and socializes with gay friends. He thinks his sister knows, although homosexuality is not discussed in his family. He reflects often on his time at Florida A&M and has come to terms with those often stressful, seldom satisfying few years.

"You have to understand, all of this would not have happened in another environment," he says. "This was a predominantly black college, a small college, in the heart of the South. Tallahassee is a small city in the middle of the Panhandle. Every radio preacher for miles around was condemning gay people to hell. I was going out with an athlete, someone everyone looked up to and all the females admired. There were pressures all around. And I was young and naive and had no one to show me the way." Tony's regrets are tempered with reality: "If I could do it all over again, I probably would have the same relationship. I liked it; I got something out of it."

However, he notes, hindsight helps. His first gay relationship taught him a very important lesson. "If I'm sorry about one thing, I wish I could have approached it from a different angle," Tony concludes. "He laid out all the rules, and that's not what a relationship is about. It's not about one man standing in the bleachers watching another man perform and not being able to get any pats on the back himself."

The Swim Coaches

Gay men fight many battles. In addition to the general homophobia and ignorance about homosexuality that still pervade much of society today, there are specific internal conflicts: Whom do I tell? When? How? What if they flip out?

Because sexuality is so personal a concern, many gay people bear their burden alone. Growing up, they cannot develop the support system most straight people rely on to carry them through difficult times. For years gays hide the essence of their being from those closest to them; when the time comes to tell family members and good friends, the fear of negative reaction can be overwhelming, even paralyzing.

But their reactions are not the only ones gay people worry about (or, in some cases, obsess over). Americans now spend at least as much time in the workplace as with family members; whether to come out to coworkers is often another major issue, fraught with as much tension as telling anyone else. After all, we can always find new friends, and family we see only occasionally. It is the people at work with whom we interact at least a third of each day, five days a week. We share offices, phones, and bosses with them. Many straight workers tell colleagues intimate details of their lives. Can gay people trust them enough to do the same?

Gay coaches have an added worry: coming out to their teams. Coaches work not only with colleagues but also with athletes, some of whom may be quite young. How does a gay coach handle the thorny issue of coming out to his team?

Every coach has a different attitude and strategy about this. Yet no matter how they deal with it, all share one common bond: They understand that coming out is not one single act. It is a continuing, lifelong process.

FOR MOST OF THE FIRST TWENTY-SIX YEARS of his life, Keith did not have to confront coming-out issues. The reason was simple: He did not consider himself gay. Though he had had strong feelings for males ever since puberty, Keith (who asked that his last name not be used) denied them: "I looked at the stereotypes on TV and said, 'Gay people wear pink silk shirts, have limp wrists, and act feminine. I don't; I'm a jock. I'm not gay, so I must be straight.' "

He was so sure he was straight, he even got married. Again, Keith's reality clashed with his self-image: "I thought of myself as an independent person, not a follower — I didn't drink or do drugs — but in actuality I was the biggest follower there was. People kept asking when I'd get married and set me up on dates. So I ended up making them happy rather than making myself happy. I learned the hard way that I had to be truthful to myself."

That difficult lesson began just a few months after his wedding when a gay video was mistakenly placed in the wrong mailbox at the Vermont college where Keith worked as assistant swim coach and assistant dean. The person who received it, a wrestler, screened it for his teammates. The intended recipient was enrolled in the Reserve Officers' Training Corps, and he suffered dearly. Unlike members of the military who are paid to work, ROTC students are not protected under the "don't ask, don't tell" policy. The young man was booted out of the program, losing his all-important scholarship. The ensuing controversy triggered intense emotions inside Keith. For the first time he confronted the fact that he himself might be gay.

"I was so upset at what happened to that kid," he recalls. "As assistant dean I brought the wrestlers in. We talked about respect for privacy and whether they had the right to do what they did. The wrestling coach was helpful, but this is such a conservative place, the harm had already been done. All I could do was watch."

The incident caused Keith to realize that he was not living his life as the person he was meant to be. After intense soul-searching, he decided he had to come out.

The first person he told was his best friend. That was by far the hardest revelation, he says, because of their strong bond and the fact that Keith had never spoken the *G* word to anyone.

That began a "marathon week" of coming out. He told his wife he "might be, could be" gay; she handled it reasonably well, if quietly. Then came his parents, his father-in-law, the senior vice president of the college (who had served as a reader at his wedding), and the head swim coach. All took the news extremely well and supported him unconditionally — except his parents; they took a long time coming to terms with the news.

The head swim coach's reaction was perhaps the most important to Keith. He had swum for the man — a former Marine — during his own college days and feared him more than his own parents. "When I would get in trouble it was like, 'Call my dad or mom, but don't tell my coach.' Then I became his assistant, and I wanted his support so much. I'd known him for ten years, but I wasn't sure how he'd react."

Keith's worries proved groundless. "When I had the secretary make an appointment for me to see him, he was all worried and asked her what was wrong," Keith recalls. "I got to his office, sat down, and began bawling my eyes out. I told him I was getting divorced, and it was not because of my wife. I told him I was gay. His response was typical of everything I heard from my closest friends: 'Man, Keith, I thought something was wrong with you or something. You had me all worried!' " In retrospect Keith says, "He's seen a lot of athletes and students go through a lot of things. I guess this was not the biggest shock he's had in his life."

In the coming months the head coach supported Keith in small but meaningful ways. When they were together on the pool deck, the older man asked how things were going, how Keith's wife was doing. The coach also chose that time to reinforce, quite explicitly, his preseason speech to the team that he would never tolerate discriminatory comments about anyone. Having a man so close, in such an important area of his life, express those thoughts to him and the team helped Keith through several difficult months.

Keith decided not to out himself to the college swim team, however. With the season at its midway point, he did not want to distract them with news that could shock, confuse, or concern them. In addition, he says, "I don't necessarily think they need to know what goes on inside my house. That's personal. They are students, not colleagues." If anyone asked, he was prepared to tell; however, he had no plans to raise the subject himself.

Actually, Keith says, he had no reason to fear a negative reaction had he come out to the team. "Swimmers are unique," he says. "They're not the typical breed of big jockheads. Most swimmers are intelligent and independent. Swimming is a team sport, but when you hit the water, you're by yourself. You learn to think independently, not in a group mentality." He could not recall ever hearing a homophobic comment from a swimmer; in fact, he says, when the news broke that Greg Louganis was gay and infected with the virus that causes AIDS, "there were no bad feelings on our team. Everyone supported him and wished him well."

However, through his work as assistant dean, he knew that homophobia was well-entrenched in other areas of school life. One resident adviser refused to put up Safe Zone stickers, which indicate places on campus (such as the adviser's room) where students can feel comfortable talking about sexuality concerns. "He was a big football jock who didn't want anyone to think he had anything to do with gay people," Keith explains. "Unfortunately, I couldn't force him to put the stickers up."

The assistant dean notes that gay bashing is common among students. However, he adds, "they're starting to realize about differences. There is no gay organization here yet, but we try to educate them on a constant basis. I was talking to one kid who made homophobic comments, and he asked if I was gay. I said, 'What if I was?' That sort of stopped him. Most kids here don't think they know anyone gay. It probably won't be long until they know about me."

The coming-out process continues for Keith. He still hesitates for a second or two before entering a locker room, fearful that someone might think he is entering that male sanctuary for the wrong reasons. At the same time, he is sure the head coach is unconcerned. "I'm still very new at all this," Keith says.

Yet in the year after he told his friends, family, and the head swim coach, he has also taken major steps forward. He has discovered a gay community he never knew existed, a gay world that has lifted his spirits and energy. He has also noticed a clear change in his relationships, as a dean and coach, with his own students and swimmers. Though he always considered himself approachable and friendly, he now relates especially well with people he thinks might be gay.

Someone once told Keith that coming out would be harder than jumping out a skyscraper window. "I found out that's true," he laughs. But it is a leap he has survived. Turning serious, he says, "You know what I really look forward to? I think someday I'll be able to help a swimmer or student who was standing where I was just a year ago. That would be so gratifying."

Erik Scollon is a few years younger than Keith. He too is a pool rat, a man whose most identifiable characteristics while growing up were his goggles, Speedo, and chlorinated hair. He is just now embarking on his coaching career, and the in-or-out question haunts him nearly every day.

Life was good when Erik was young in Rochester Hills, an upper-middle-class suburb of Detroit. He joined his first swim team at nine and took to it like — well, like a fish to water. He felt lithe and agile in the pool in a way he never did on land. He did not mind the almost manic dedication competitive swimming required; if it took a year of training to slice a tenth of a second off his time, he'd do it. He swam for club and school teams all the way through twelfth grade. At Albion College he qualified for the NCAA Division III nationals all four years in his best events, the 200- and 400-yard individual medleys, and made All-America several times.

The realization at age sixteen that he was gay was not particularly bothersome, though he kept the knowledge to himself. "I wasn't antisocial, but part of swimming is that you don't have to work with or rely on someone else to do well," he says. "Being gay was my thing too, no one else's." (It was actually two team-mates' thing also, a fact he did not learn until after graduation.)

He came out to friends at nineteen. He told them being gay was something important about him that they needed to know. The worst reaction was "Let me think about this," followed by gradual understanding. He never felt uncomfortable around team-mates. However, Erik acknowledges, if he had been a team-sport player — with its deeper demands of trust and cooperation — things might have been different.

Sharing a locker room with a gay man was never an issue with his teammates, just as being in proximity to so many fit, well-toned bodies was nothing special for Erik. "When I'm at the pool, I'm there as a competitive athlete," he says. "Swimming is not a spectator sport for me."

In fact, he believes that surrounding himself for so long with naked men (and the rest who, in their skimpy swimsuits, might as well have been) perhaps eased his coming-out process. "Ever since I was nine, I've run around in a Speedo," he says. "I was always comfortable inside my skin; I was not body-conscious like so many other gay men. So that was one less thing to worry about."

Erik took his degree in visual arts to New York, where he hoped to balance the two most important components of his life: art and swimming. While trying to produce his own work, he found jobs as a swim instructor and lifeguard. But the city proved too expensive, his part-time employment encroached on time he needed for art, and he could not find a position doing the one thing he really loved: coaching.

So in 1995 he moved back to Michigan, and after only one month as an assistant, Erik was asked to be interim head coach of a swim club in Grand Rapids. Soon after, he was offered the permanent post.

Erik is out to his fellow coaches but not to his one hundred boy and girl swimmers, ages four to eighteen, or their parents. "Grand Rapids is a very family-oriented, conservative community," he explains. "The Christian Reform Church is very vocal here. I know there would be objections to it. Some people even complained about my two pierced ears." Other parents, he notes, would not care if his entire face were tattooed; they know that their children enjoy swimming for him, and that is all that matters.

The situation is frustrating. As he has bonded with his swimmers, they have taken an interest in his life beyond the pool. When they ask about a girlfriend, he would like to reply, "His name is..." But he understands it is a parent's prerogative to decide what his or her child is exposed to, and while it might be nice to be open with everyone over, say, fifteen, once the news is out to one swimmer, it will be out to all.

So he dances around the subject. When a twelve-year-old asked, in jest, if he was gay, Erik responded, "Why would you ask?" The boy, dumbfounded, could not answer.

Proudly, Erik says he has never lied; he just redirects the question. Yet he realizes there may come a time when he will be forced to confront the issue. One part of him hopes it will happen after enough time has elapsed that his credentials as a strong, effective coach overpower any criticism. But another voice in his head cautions him not to dream; it reminds him that at any moment he could be smacked hard in the face by ugly reality.

"It's so tricky working with kids," he says. "I'm with them two hours a day, six days a week. Anything I say, positive or negative, really affects them. Kids carry coaches' words with them the rest of their lives. I still remember things my coaches told me, whether I want to or not. I just try to be socially responsible and stop any bad comments — racist, sexist, homophobic, whatever — as soon as I hear them."

He handles his multifaceted role — surrogate parent, teacher, friend, confidant, disciplinarian — with care. He tempers his self-reproach about lacking the strength of his convictions to come out on the job with the knowledge that he has been coaching for little more than a year, with no proven track record. He keeps telling himself he needs to walk before he can run.

One of his first big steps was coming out to his fellow coaches. It took only a few weeks before their professional relationships blossomed into friendships; that's when he opened up. Two coaches have been particularly supportive. But all have cautioned him how conservative Grand Rapids is, reminding Erik that even a handful of parental complaints could cost him his job.

Coaching has grown increasingly important to him. During his year's stint he has invested a tremendous amount of energy and emotion in his young swimmers. His fifteen-year-olds are quite talented; he hopes to coach them until they enter college. Though he has long enjoyed both the physical act of swimming and the emotional charge of competing — one of the biggest rushes of his life was anchoring the last leg of the final relay, surging forward to touch the pad a few milliseconds before his opponent — he is finding the new challenges of coaching just as satisfying. He is still in his favorite arena, his beloved pool, but now he feels he is achieving even more by helping scores of boys and girls train hard, push themselves, and ultimately improve. "When they're successful, I'm successful," he says.

Having tasted that success, coach Erik Scollon wants more. He has made compromises today to ensure that he will continue to succeed tomorrow. But as any athlete knows, situations change rapidly and without warning. Conservative Grand Rapids may soon have its first openly gay swim coach.

The Straight Athletes

In the same way that the civil rights struggle of the '50s and '60s galvanized whites as well as blacks and that women in the '70s welcomed men's support in the fight to obtain economic and social equality, so too has the gay community enjoyed the backing of straight allies. The past decade has seen national organizations like Parents, Families, and Friends of Lesbians and Gays and the Gay, Lesbian, and Straight Education Network draw homosexuals and heterosexuals together; at the same time millions of individual straight men and women, with ties to no organized group but bound by a deep sense of social justice, have spoken up and acted out against homophobia and its evil twin, ignorance.

Rarely, however, has the battle been joined by straight high school athletes. Forces such as peer pressure, adolescent insecurity, time constraints, and silence about the problem have conspired to keep male jocks — even those who sincerely want to do the right thing — on the sidelines.

All of which makes Brookfield, Connecticut, such an interesting exception. In that tight-knit community, the courageous words and deeds of a few athletes prove that strength, hard work, and commitment need not be limited to the football field or basketball court.

BROOKFIELD, A SLEEPY TOWN of 15,000 nestled in the rolling hills of western Connecticut, is a place out of a rapidly fading America. Once rural, now making the uneasy transition to suburb, it still retains much of its Currier-and-Ives New England charm. There are more barns than Big Mac outlets; the roads bear names like Obtuse and Trailing Ridge, and even a visitor can sense the easy familiarity that settles over a place with but one elementary, middle, and high school. Brookfield's physical landscape is snowy white in winter, lush green in spring and summer, and brilliant red and gold in fall. All year long, however, the political landscape is conservative.

Brookfield is prosperous and pretty, the kind of place where residents think nothing of naming their homes. Just a few days after high school graduation, two newly minted alums sat in a comfortable house called Goose Hollow and talked about their town, their school, their teams — and homosexuality.

Both young men are built like athletes. Ryan McCaffrey is blond, tall, and solid; Jeff DaCunha is darker, more lithe. Whether together or alone, they exude the casual confidence so typical of youths who know they are strong and fit and feel secure about themselves. During a wide-ranging discussion that touched on the pain of gay youth, sexuality stereotypes, and other difficult-to-discuss subjects, neither Ryan nor Jeff — both practicing heterosexuals — ever once felt the need to declare, "Of course, I'm straight, but..." or casually mention the name of a girlfriend.

They have known each other since first grade, when Ryan's family (his father is a reinsurance broker, and his mother is the highest-producing real estate agent in the Danbury area) moved from Seattle. Since a basketball-related stress fracture in his spinal column ended his sports career, Ryan considers himself more a musician than an athlete — an All–New England trumpeter, he was looking forward to majoring in music at the University of Richmond — but his athletic pedigree is strong. From fifth grade through high school, he played the regional junior tennis circuit, earning a top 40 ranking. As a sophomore he helped his Brookfield High team capture the medium-size schools' state championship.

Jeff, born in nearby Danbury to an electrician father and social-worker mother, played soccer all the way until high school, then switched to football. It was a wise choice. The team went 13-0 and won the state championship; he earned All-State recognition as a receiver. He was also an All-State runner, blazing to a 51.6-second finish in the 400-meter run, and an All-

Conference swimmer (22.95 seconds in the fifty-meter freestyle). After high school he planned to concentrate on one sport, football, at Middlebury College.

However, both Ryan and Jeff downplay their athletic accomplishments. They do not want to be categorized as "jocks," insisting that at Brookfield High, unlike many other schools, students do not split into easily defined cliques.

"That's one of the benefits of growing up in a small town," Ryan says. "Everyone goes through school together, so you know each other inside and out. Athletes are friends with musicians and artists and actors. You respect everyone's abilities and individualism. People get along, and there aren't many clashes." Though at Brookfield football is king, with players respected by classmates and teachers alike, in such a small school, it is also easy for athletes to get involved in activities other than sports.

For Ryan and Jeff, that meant peer counseling. The school's program, fifteen years old, is one of the best in the country. It is not easy to become a peer counselor — students must fill out applications, be interviewed, then undergo six months of training — and the job is just as hard. Peer counselors attend weekly meetings and act as liaisons between students and faculty, but their most important task is to spend hours listening to other adolescents' problems, helping explore options. Topics include divorce, financial worries, low self-esteem, eating disorders, and much, much more.

Ryan became a peer counselor for two reasons: He likes helping people, and he remembered how thrilled he was as a freshman whenever a senior said hello. Jeff had a more personal reason: In ninth grade an upperclassman had helped him out. "I loved the way she took time out of her life to talk with me and drive me home," he recalls. "I wanted to do the same for other people."

During Ryan's first months as a peer counselor, a few students asked circumspect questions about homosexuality. When he mentioned that fact to the group's adviser, she told him about an upcoming conference. "Children of the Shadows," sponsored annually by the University of Connecticut Graduate School of Social Work and organized by youth advocate Robin Passariello, draws over 600 youth — primarily gay, some straight — and adult service providers for two days of panels, workshops, discussion groups, and networking opportunities. Among the attendees that year were Ryan, basketball player and honor student Tim Smyth, and five faculty members.

"I was always pretty secure about my sexuality, but I sure didn't run around telling people I was going to a gay and lesbian conference," Ryan recalls. Yet the day turned out to be a pivotal event in his life. Hearing about high suicide, drug abuse, and dropout rates and realizing that gay and lesbian youth were perhaps the biggest minority in his high school spurred Ryan into action. When the group got together back at Brookfield, they seized on an idea from the Massachusetts Department of Education: offering pink triangle Safe Zone stickers to interested teachers. They wrote a Statement of Purpose to be hung alongside; it explained that the stickers indicated that this was a safe classroom, where discrimination against any human being would not be tolerated, and that students could feel free to talk about anything with that teacher. Six faculty members out of the school's sixty took stickers.

For two years the Safe Zone program existed quietly and without controversy. Most of the 700 students did not even know what the stickers represented, Ryan says. But for those who did, it was a godsend.

Suddenly, in October 1995, everyone knew. The mother of a sophomore girl wrote a letter to school officials with copies to two local newspapers. The writer excoriated the Safe Zone program, claiming among other things that the stickers promoted sex with children and bestiality. (She also said she saw nothing wrong with her daughter's discriminating against gay people, just as it was all right to discriminate against drug users.)

When he first learned of the letter, Jeff figured it was simply
a piece of hate mail he'd never hear about again. Principal
Thomas Smyth — Tim's father — thought the same. After listening to the peer counselors describe the program, so did
superintendent of schools Dr. David Bristol.

They were wrong. The family pressured a board of education subcommittee to take up the issue. Ryan and the family
both addressed the group. They then spoke in public at a full
board meeting along with a number of staff and students,
including soccer captain Nick Ortner. The board voted five to
two to retain the Safe Zone stickers.

But the issue would not go away. In March the board held a
third meeting. One hundred people showed up to speak in favor
of the program; two dissented. It was televised on local cable
television; viewers saw Ryan and Nick make two more impassioned speeches. Once again the board voted five to two to keep
the stickers.

Most people at Brookfield High also strongly back the Safe
Zone program, Ryan says. It was a nonissue until the letter
writer created such a controversy. In fact, many members of the
school community did not even know it existed. Once they
found out, Ryan heard the same question over and over: What's
the big deal?

He, Jeff, Tim, and others used the opportunity to educate
their friends — and teachers — about the plight of gay youth.
Most people had no idea how much loneliness, alienation, and
pain gay teens endure. When the peer counselors told them,
they were stunned. There were no jokes or snide remarks; in
fact, there was no backlash of any kind.

"I think because we were so prominent in school, that made
it easier for people to see that it's all right to be gay and not all
right to make fun of anyone because of that," Ryan says. "The
fact that athletes — the captains, the leaders — stood up made
it the opposite of the way things usually are, when people speak
first and think later. All prejudice stems from ignorance. When

we got this topic out in the open and people heard about it, they opened their minds, listened, and got educated." Though Brookfield had not been particularly homophobic, Ryan noted a subtle attitudinal change after the controversy. "People now think twice about saying 'fag' or 'queer,' " he says. "If someone does, it echoes in the air, and there's silence. That's good to see."

Ryan emphasizes that he and his friends do not see themselves forcing a "gay agenda" on anyone. "We didn't say that everyone should think homosexuality is right," he stresses. "What we did say is that everyone should have the right to live however they want. Don't impose your morals on other people."

Attendance at three "Children of the Shadows" conferences reinforced what Ryan had learned at home. "I'm very liberal, and so are my parents," he says. "They've always tried to instill the idea of diversity in me."

Jeff describes himself as "conservative and old-fashioned but very open-minded. I love to listen to different points of view." He calls the two "Children of the Shadows" conferences he attended "awesome. My favorite workshop was 'Gay Men, Straight Men.' It was so cool. It was split fifty-fifty, but nobody knew who was who. It completely broke down stereotypes on both sides: mine about gay people and theirs about straight people — especially athletes."

Ryan considers the peer-counseling experience — particularly the Safe Zone controversy — the most important part of his career at Brookfield High, far more than his tennis championship or any academic class. "I learned so much about life and about accepting people," he says. "I saw people from all walks of life. It taught me about 'the system,' both good and bad, and that ultimately the system works."

He feels gratified that so many people, including friends like Jeff, Tim, and Nick, stood up for what they believed was right. He was amazed too by the response their actions got, especially when the story went national. One man heard Ryan quoted on the radio, then pulled off a California freeway to call Brookfield

High. His message was to keep up the fight. "My son committed suicide because he was gay," the caller said. "If there were Safe Zone stickers around then, maybe he'd be here today."

"Until then I never realized the effect this could have," Ryan says, clearly touched.

That realization is particularly important, given that there is no clear way to quantify the impact of the Safe Zone program. "The board of education wanted numbers, so they could see whether the stickers were doing their job," Ryan explains. "That's ridiculous. You can't measure something so confidential and personal. All I know is, I had three kids talk to me. Who knows how many others saw the stickers and realized they weren't alone? Anyway, who cares about numbers? Would it have been better to have a tragedy in this town to make the problem more real? If we averted one tragedy last year, this year, next year, that's great. But then, how do you find out about something that *doesn't* happen? It's silly to even talk about it. Just knowing the stickers are there should be enough."

Yet everyone likes rewards — especially athletes — and the peer counselors got theirs. The Brookfield Youth Commission presented its annual Humanitarian Award to Ryan, Nick, and student council president Aaron Walrath. And just before graduating, Ryan and Tim were honored in Hartford by the Connecticut chapter of the Gay, Lesbian, and Straight Education Network for their contributions to the fight against homophobia.

"It's so wonderful to see young gay people standing up for their rights!" one woman told Ryan during the reception.

He just smiled, making no move to correct her misassumption about his sexuality. As the straight student knows from his days on the tennis and basketball courts, actions speak louder than words.

The Suicidal Jock

For some males, the path toward accepting their homosexuality and reconciling it with their self-image as an athlete is quick and easy; for many others, it is long and torturous. Living two lives is never simple; when those lives are so disparate — one is hypermasculine to the point of misogyny; the other turns gender identity on its head — it can cause almost unbearable pain.

Gay athletes exist in two worlds that seldom meet but often intersect. The locker room, with its constant chatter and implied camaraderie a place of comfort for straight jocks, can turn into a den of horrors for gay men. The conversation and banter, while sounding light and easy on the surface, carries an undertone of hostility. Anyone who is in any way different is put down; sex roles are clearly defined, and woe be to he who deviates — or is believed to deviate — from those norms.

The gay world is no better. To a man struggling with his sexuality the gay community can seem just as rigid, intolerant, and stereotypical as any locker room, playing field, or sports arena.

If I'm an athlete, I can't be gay, a young man may argue with himself. But I think I am gay, so how can I be an athlete? If he has no role models to follow — no gay athletes or coaches, no athletic-minded gay friends or mentors — he is in a desperate situation. The result can be very unhealthy: paralyzing fear, overwhelming depression, and poor performance during games, in the classroom, or at work. No wonder suicide may seem the only way out.

NOT UNTIL GREG WAS A JUNIOR IN COLLEGE did he finally tell his parents why he had been so troubled for so many years. One winter night he blurted it out: "I'm gay."

"That's ridiculous," they replied. "You're an athlete. You're popular. You went to military school. You have normal parents. You've got girlfriends. Don't even think that you're gay." More confused than ever, Greg wrote a suicide note. He contemplated firing a shotgun at his head until a friend came over and talked him out of it.

That was not the first time Greg had tried to kill himself. In high school he slit his wrists. During freshman year in college, drunk, he planned to leap off a bridge. He was halfway there before friends stopped him. A few months after coming out to his parents, he swallowed antidepressants.

Other attempts at self-destruction were more subtle. He raced mopeds down narrow streets and "played" with a scuba knife. In a lacrosse match he bruised his spleen and was told not to return; the risk of serious damage was too great. Greg manipulated his way back onto the field, putting himself in situations that invited errant stick pokes or contact that could result in falls. "I was hoping I'd bleed to death," he says.

The inner tension and torment Greg had felt for as long as he could remember were too much to handle. Everywhere he turned he saw obstacles. The athletes he spent so much time with hated gays. The gay people he knew were either too interested in him as a sex object, too flamboyant or limp-wristed, or just too weird. His parents denied his problem; the girls he had always gone out with did not understand either. How, he wondered, had he gotten himself into such a mess? And what could he do to get out of it?

Greg's conflicts were apparent as soon as he asked that his full name not be used, explaining, "I'm not out now, but when I am I want to look back and see at least my first name in print." He had more than his sexuality to deal with while growing up in a small East Coast town. A severe learning disability also affected his coordination. In fifth grade he could not kick a ball and endured relentless teasing because of it. But something about soccer attracted him, and he persevered long and hard enough that it became his favorite sport. He eventually developed into an accomplished lacrosse player, swimmer, scuba diver, skier, and mountain biker, but soccer proved most rewarding.

In ninth grade he headed off to a private military academy, one with a good reputation for students with learning disabilities. Despite his problems — or perhaps because of them — he had developed a pleasant, easygoing personality, and his popularity soared even higher at prep school. On a campus that was 80 percent male, guys were lucky to find girlfriends. Greg always did.

He dated for four years and had plenty of sex with females. It was not particularly satisfying — he had had experiences with boys that were far more fulfilling — but Greg tried not to think about that. Everyone assumed he and the girl he dated for nearly four years would eventually get married and produce children as tall and good-looking as their parents.

On the outside life was wonderful. Greg played soccer and lacrosse, joined the school ski patrol and a church group, was named head prefect, and overcame his learning disability. He made the honor roll, earned an academic and fitness award from President Bush, and was nominated for *Who's Who Among American High School Students.*

On the inside, however, life was a mess. Incidents like watching a soccer player get "swirlied" — having his head stuffed into a flushing toilet because his teammates thought he was gay — terrified Greg. His confidence plummeted. Some days he could barely step on the field, so petrified was he that someone would discover his secret.

He knew very little about homosexuality. His devoutly Lutheran parents did not talk with him about sex, not even to mention condoms. The only time the *G* word arose was on their forays to Provincetown, during summer trips to Cape Cod. "Look at all those faggots," his parents would laugh.

Greg figured the more sex he had with women, the straighter he would become. He tried and tried, but that approach never seemed to work.

He chose a small Division III college primarily for its oceanside location and the chance to play soccer. It was a sport he had

always dreamed of excelling in, but as a freshman he was so 93
depressed, he could barely concentrate. The only gay people he
saw on campus were "flamey" or arrogant or used drugs. Greg
had no idea who or what he was. He began drinking, thinking
that would make him happy and/or help him get women.

Always interested in physiology and sports medicine, he volunteered in the athletic trainer's room. He got along well with
his fellow athletes but believed he could never make training his
career. Gay people aren't trainers, he told himself. Throughout
freshman year he found himself confused and unable to focus.

That summer he studied to become an emergency medical
technician. The coordinator's macho attitude intimidated Greg.
Halfway through the course the familiar feelings returned: Greg
knew he could never be an EMT because he had homosexual
thoughts. How could he ever deal with a naked person in a trauma room?

Finally he summoned the courage to attend a support group
for gay youth. There he learned that the coordinator of his
EMT course was gay. Greg panicked and for three months did
not say a word to the man. Eventually, though, Greg's desire to
become an EMT overcame his fear of anything gay, and he
spoke to the coordinator. The man wanted to become a better
soccer player, he told Greg, so a friendship based on mutual
interests was born.

But when he returned to campus for his sophomore year,
Greg was still depressed and suicidal. He faked happiness, while
inside his life was crumbling. During preseason practice, just
before classes began, he got up the nerve to talk to a member of
the school's lesbian, gay, and bisexual alliance. As Greg spilled
his guts, the student began hitting on him. The closer he tried
to get, the more Greg pulled away.

Greg's depression overwhelmed any interest in soccer or
school. He was playing poorly, and his grade point average sank
to 1.5. Finding the campus alliance "too gay," he started going
to local clubs and bars. Yet he could never enjoy them because

of his terror that he would see someone from his team. ("I know, I know, if they were there, it would be for the same reason I was," he says. "But I couldn't stop thinking that they'd tell everyone about me.") At the same time, to allay any suspicions about himself — suspicions no one had — Greg convinced a girl to give him oral sex on the soccer field one night and "arranged" for his teammates to catch him.

Before junior year a friend with whom Greg planned to room the following year came out to him. Greg told him he was okay with it, but he was unable to take the next step and come out himself.

That summer Greg found his first boyfriend, a man four years older. "I was as happy as a pig in shit," he says. "I was head over heels in love." His joy carried over into the fall soccer season. "I realized that even though soccer is a team sport, one individual can have a big effect," he explains. "I started to become more of an individual, and that made all the difference." When the captain was forced off the team for steroid use, Greg took over for the final two games. He took a gorgeous woman to the end-of-season banquet; all his teammates were jealous. That night Greg and his date had great sex.

At the same time, his relationship with his boyfriend was ending. Greg was crushed; his suicidal feelings returned. Finally, he came out to his gay roommate. At first the man did not believe him; then he wanted to have sex. Greg was not interested. He felt even worse after a week in Key West, Florida, with the man who had been his EMT coordinator. In addition to seeing so many "flamboyant" people, which turned Greg off, the man kept pressuring him to have sex. He too was not Greg's type. With so many conflicts swirling around athletics and sexuality, Greg felt more confused than ever.

Yet one thing always brought him joy. "When I play soccer, that's the only time I can totally be myself," he says. "It's the one time sexuality isn't on my mind. Soccer is like heaven. Heaven would be soccer goals and soccer balls all around."

Greg denies the suggestion that his devotion to soccer —
which entails an enormous amount of running, weight lifting,
and other training — is a way to avoid dealing with his homosexuality. He insists he works so hard because he wants to be the
best athlete he can. "I made such an ass of myself trying to kick
a ball when I was younger," he says. "Now I can launch it all the
way across the field, and I want to be even better than that."

His preconception was that college would be a place to meet
other gay jocks, people who were not "swishy" and with whom he
could talk openly about anything. They, in turn, would be con-
siderate and solicitous of him. It did not happen. Not only were
there no gay athletes, but the straight jocks were rabidly so. His
lacrosse teammates, for example, could not understand why he
chose to room with a "faggot"; the soccer players, though less
crude, nonetheless also showed low degrees of tolerance and
acceptance. The lacrosse team even had a ritual in which a player
who scored his first varsity goal must have sex with a woman while
teammates who had already done so watched. Points were awarded for creativity. Greg passed the test (though his point score was
low). None of that rampant heterosexism stopped Greg from
"fooling around" with athletes (he had more experiences with soccer teammates than lacrosse), but there was always an uneasy feeling that for them it was nothing more than a sexual release.

Things were no better at the youth group Greg attended in
a nearby city. He was the only jock there, and at his first meeting he got the distinct feeling that despite being gay, he was not
welcome. "Because I didn't 'act' gay, there were people who
didn't like me," he says. "What did they want me to do, flap my
arms and take off?" At the same time he was repelled by the
looks and attitudes of many young people there. "It was like
they were trying to draw attention to themselves," he explains.
"It's people like that who turn people like my parents against all
gay people."

Back on campus Greg resisted the entreaties of the gay
alliance student — the one who had hit on him during their first

meeting — to come out to the entire school. The activist believed that Greg's status as an athlete is important; Greg countered that the "dumb jock" atmosphere made coming out dangerous. He recalled a tennis player who tried to hang himself because of conflicts about sexuality; when the athlete returned to the locker room, hockey players abused him mercilessly. His own sport of lacrosse is not particularly friendly, Greg notes: "There's a 'beat 'em up, take 'em on' mentality with anyone who's different." He was not willing to announce how different he really is.

Still, he considers himself a jock and, in fact, wears the label proudly. To Greg, a jock is someone exceptionally devoted to sports. A year earlier, he says, that would not have been the case; his self-confidence was too low. By his junior year, however, he felt better. "I run, I work out, I practice every day," he says. "I love sports. I love to perform and watch other athletes perform. Any athlete with the guts to go on a field has my respect. Sports gives anyone self-confidence. It's almost a way of looking at life. I know it sounds weird, but it almost gives me a chance to live."

That is a chance he almost denied himself several times in the past. How does he reconcile being a jock with being gay?

"I don't know," he answers, genuinely puzzled. "I really wish I could be open, out, not have anyone care other than that we're all there for the same reason, to play. Unfortunately, in any locker room or shower, you hear people mumbling about 'faggots.' So many people think gay people are limp-wristed fruits. I'd like to be out on campus. If I were, I'd probably be running the gay group."

But he is not out. Even on the soccer team — playing the game he most loves — he feels completely alone. "People just wouldn't accept it," he insists. "They'd see a stereotypical gay person, not someone who's on the dean's list, who runs and works out and plays sports. They'd snicker. I know they would not accept me for who I am."

Such conflicts continue to buffet him. His parents still pester him about it; their questions lead to arguments. His mother is sure he is too young to know he is gay. He is racked by stomach pains. As it has done for so many years, Greg's sunny disposition masks a private hell.

"No one knows how much pain and suffering a gay male athlete goes through," he states. "I've spent hours crying in my room because people won't accept me for who I am. People say that being gay is only a part of you. I say, 'Then why does it hurt so much? Why is there so much pain?' "

He does look toward the future with a glimmer of hope. He would like to become a psychologist, working with gay men and women. In addition, he wants to find a lover. "Someone like me," he says, "someone who will accept me for who I am. I told my mother not to expect me to have a white picket fence, but I do want to settle down." He pauses. "And a dog. I really want a dog. I love dogs. A dog would be cool."

The Flirt

To many minds, the term gay jock *is an oxymoron. Gay men, these people believe, can be many things — musicians, actors, dancers, playwrights, florists, interior designers, social workers, even doctors and lawyers and such — but what they cannot be is athletic. It is a feeling held not only by straight people who just don't "get it" but also by gays who clearly should. Happily, through such events as the Gay Games and the coming out of diver Greg Louganis and baseball umpire Dave Pallone, those stereotypes are crumbling.*

But what happens when an athlete is also a singer and actor? While growing up, does he feel torn between these two seemingly dissimilar interests, just as he is tormented by his desire for males and his knowledge that much of society brands it a deviance? Does he seek comfort in the more welcoming world of the arts or try a "cure" by submerging himself in athletics?

Jon Arterton is founder, arranger, rehearsal director, manager, treasurer, and spiritual soul of the Flirtations, the politically active, unabashedly gay a cappella singing group that delighted and inspired audiences for nearly ten years before breaking up in 1997. He and his group stirred audiences at the 1993 gay and lesbian march on Washington, in the movie Philadelphia, *at the 1996 Olympics Gay and Lesbian Visitors Center, and on concert stages around the world. Whether performing anthems like "Something Inside So Strong" ("The higher you build your barriers / The taller I become"), lullabies like "Everything Possible" ("You can be anybody that you want to be / You can love whomever you will") or parodies like Mr. Sandman ("I want a man / No one psychotic or Republican"), the Flirtations inspired men, women, and teenagers — gay, straight, and everything in between — for almost a decade.*

But before he was a Flirtation, Jon was a jock. For complex reasons — some related to athletics and arts, some not — he did not come out until he was thirty-six. Today he is over fifty, and though he makes his living making music, he continues to feel strong ties to his athletic roots. This is his story.

AS A TRACK STAR at all-male St. Albans School in Washington, D.C., Jon Arterton was better known than a younger teammate named Al Gore. After all, as a freshman Jon ran the mile in four minutes, forty-five seconds; Al's father was only a U.S. senator, and at St. Albans those dads were a dime a dozen.

Jon loved athletics. In the spring he ran track, in the fall cross-country (in which he never finished lower than third and set many course records). Each winter he wrestled.

Sports served many purposes. They helped Jon feel good about himself. They provided acceptance from peers. They allowed him to measure himself against his talented elder brother, who preceded him by two years at St. Albans. They earned his parents' approval. Finally, athletics was a way to deflect attention that might otherwise have focused on Jon's sexuality. Though well-known on campus, Jon was also a loner. In those pre-Stonewall, white-bread, ivory-tower prep-school early-'60s days, homosexuality was simply not discussed.

At St. Albans, Jon was aware of his same-sex attractions; he'd had them for as long as he could recall. But he pushed them aside, dumping them in a corner of his mental closet behind many other less stressful issues. Besides, back then no one talked about such things. He realizes now that a few friends may have suspected, but they alluded to it only in passing or with humor. Reluctantly he took a girl to the prom. That event and others like it were conducted, he says, in a language he did not speak.

But besides athletics Jon knew another language: music. He sang at the Washington Cathedral, where his father served as minister. He played bells in the choir. His accomplishments as a musician matched those as an athlete.

For his all-around activities, he received a Morehead Scholarship to the University of North Carolina at Chapel Hill. The award was virtually a tradition among St. Albans track stars. Because Jon's times were even faster than some of those graduates who had gone before him to UNC, he felt an obligation to work hard and surpass their collegiate achievements. But he got injured and grew unhappy away from home, and his interest in running waned. He ran track and cross-country for a year and a half, then left the athletic program. However, his interest in sports never flagged. He competed on fraternity teams and enjoyed every minute of it.

The time he had once spent running was now taken up with singing. He entered graduate school at the New England Conservatory of Music, then landed his first job at the Williston-Northampton School in western Massachusetts. Private school educators are expected to throw themselves into campus life, and Jon did. In addition to teaching English and music, he conducted the chorus and coached wrestling and track. Interestingly, his greatest success came as wrestling coach, where in six years he helped develop numerous New England champions.

As at most prep schools, life at Williston revolved around sports. Good coaches, like good athletes, rose in the pecking order. Attendance at games and meets by those not competing was expected; colleagues and students alike saw the fruits of Jon's labor. Even vacations were spent playing tennis with fellow faculty members. As they had been at St. Albans, sports provided a cover for Jon. "It not only gave the outside world the idea I was 'normal,' not queer," he says, "it gave me that impression too."

Surrounded by energetic boys with budding sexual energy, Jon was aware at one level that he was, indeed, queer. But those feelings backed him further into the closet than he had been in high school and college. He could not admit even to himself what he was. He continued to believe that his thoughts would vanish if only he kept doing what he was doing: playing sports. Keeping active. Dating women.

One of the most moving parts of any Flirtations show was their spoken piece, "One of Us," conceived by Jon. Each member revealed facts about his life — though the speaker of any particular line was not necessarily discussing himself. "One of us was an MP in the U.S. Army," they would say. "One of us was fag-bashed with a two-by-four." "One of us smuggled AIDS drugs into the country."

A line that always elicited gasps was "One of us was in the closet until he was thirty-six." In the 1990s that fact alone is shocking. Audience members were even more stunned to learn it was Jon — this fiercely proud gay man — who spent so long hiding who he was.

The fact is, for many years he himself hardly realized he was gay. Today, he laughs, "I don't know how I missed it. I was a music major, I went into theater and antiques — and still I didn't know!"

His artistic side did not clue him in. It was traditional at both St. Albans and Williston for the best athletes to also act and sing, so he was never teased or taunted for those activities. In addition, years of listening to his father's views on homosexuality — "abnormal," he called it — made Jon feel too shameful to connect it consciously with his own life.

Jon left Williston to earn a master of fine arts degree in acting at Smith College. He moved to New York, but theater roles were hard to come by. He bought a Brooklyn brownstone for $25,000, renovated it, discovered a passion for antiques, and opened a store.

At thirty-six several events converged, and for the first time Jon was forced to examine his own life. A woman he loved and had lived with for four years left him; he was devastated. When he looked up from the wreckage, he realized his two best friends were gay: a woman who lived across the street and a man around the corner. Gazing further around his neighborhood, he discovered he was surrounded by gay people — and they put him at ease. One night at dinner, when his lesbian best friend made a general comment about having no time for untruthful people, Jon blurted out, "Marcy, I'm gay!"

After thirty-six years he had finally come out to someone. Over the next two months, he zoomed out of the closet to hundreds of others with wild abandon. He worked at the Gay Men's Health Crisis hot line and joined ACT UP. He went to gay bars, read gay magazines, and changed his wardrobe. "The first thing Marcy and her friends did was shave me," he chuckles. "I had spent so many years hiding behind dark glasses and a beard. All of a sudden I was bald."

A year later a friend, lesbian comedian Lea DeLaria, asked him to audition for a show called *10 Percent Revue*. After being out of music and the theater for half a decade, he suddenly found himself working in an openly gay musical.

Rapid politicization followed. The October 1987 march on Washington inspired him; after returning to New York, he talked with Elliot Pilshaw of the *10 Percent Revue* about putting their talents into musical action. Jon's idea was a one-man show; Elliot's was for a gay group similar to the sixteen-man Yale Whiffenpoofs. From those two visions and the inspiration of spiritually powerful singing groups such as Sweet Honey in the Rock sprang the Flirtations. Posters plastered around New York sought "politically active gay male singers" (later the group included a lesbian, Suede). "Fortunately the right people showed up," Jon says. Among the first Flirts was Michael Callen, a diva, songwriter, author, activist, and feminist with a soaring, thrilling falsetto voice who, among other things, lived with AIDS for twelve years while helping define and publicize the concept of safer sex.

The first rehearsal was held in early January 1988. One decade and several personnel changes later, the Flirtations finally stopped singing.

Touring nationally and internationally, recording and performing at benefits and schools (including, at last, an appearance at Williston-Northampton), Jon traveled in very different circles than he did as a runner and wrestler. Yet to this day he remains irresistibly drawn to athletics. The power of sports has stayed with him and continues to move him. At times those feelings set him apart from others in the gay community.

While watching the 1996 Olympics on television, the former athlete agonized as gymnast Kerri Strug heroically competed — and won a gold medal — despite a sprained ankle. He was deeply affected by her tenacity and courage. But, he learned later, at the same moment he was leaning forward in front of his television set, trying to will Kerri to victory, fellow Flirtation Jimmy Rutland was turning away, dismissing the entire Olympics bathos with the comment, "Oh, come on, Mary!"

Jon even admitted, ambivalently, to a certain attraction to boxing. "I know the world would be a better place if it didn't exist," he says. "It's a brutal, senseless exercise that reflects mankind's seamy side. But I watch it. There's something about the survival aspect, the raw competition, that compels me." He always roots for the underdog — and sees parallels with his own life. He finds himself hoping that the man being beaten up will suddenly reverse roles and destroy the oppressor. He acknowledges this as a microcosm of how he saw the world when he was young, standing both in his brother's shadow and the gay closet. He feels primevally satisfied when someone unrespected rises up and turns the tide.

"Certainly most people I'm in contact with don't share these interests," he says. Some, however, do — though many are lesbians. Author and activist Urvashi Vaid is the most rabid football fan he knows, while comedian Kate Clinton comes close. For his part, although he has not been to a professional football game since he was twelve, when Jon hears that the Washington Redskins have won, he gets "all warm and glowy" inside.

Why does he feel this way when most other gays do not? "At various stages in our lives, we're all exposed to athletics," he explains. "I think if we have a good experience when we are young, we are sent in one direction, while a bad experience sends us in another. Every person I've met, gay or straight, who has a disdainful view of athletics had an early shameful experience with it, whether it was in gym class with a mean, overbearing teacher or just playing kickball with the neighborhood kids.

The people who found recognition, support, friendship, and validation, whether they're gay or straight, seem to retain their affection for sports."

Yet all too often it is the gay child or the one who will turn out to be gay — not the straight boy — who has that all-important, life-affecting negative early experience with sports. Perhaps gay boys, already knowing they are different, shy away from games and gym class, thus incurring the wrath of classmates and phys ed teachers. Maybe they are simply not interested in playing or consider themselves uncoordinated; that comes first, and the feeling of isolation follows. Or good athletes with same-sex thoughts might nonetheless be shattered on hearing homophobic comments around the field or locker room; they're driven away at a young age and never regain the sense that sports can be healthy, wholesome, rewarding fun for anyone.

Ultimately, however, such questions are chicken-and-egg. The reasons many gay men feel uncomfortable playing sports or consider themselves unathletic is less important than the fact that it happens. "When you're young you tend to see everything in tightly defined categories," Jon says. "Something is either good or bad. Only later, when you're older, do you see shades of gray. Kids can be brutal in categorizing who is valued and who is not. And for kids, one of the biggest ways to be valued is through athletics. Either you're accepted or you're not. If you're athletically successful, you're accepted, and that's something positive no one can take away. You hear the applause, and you feel good."

Jon hears applause frequently as an adult, just as he did when he was young. Years ago it came on the track and in the wrestling room; now it comes onstage. He is living proof that the words he has sung so fervently, so many times, are true. You can indeed be anybody you want to be.

The Soccer Coaches

In the hierarchical world of American male sports, football reigns king, and basketball stands just below as prince (or perhaps pretender to the throne). Soccer, meanwhile, has suffered for decades down in the netherworld, just a rung or two above ice dancing or men's field hockey. It has always been hard for Americans to appreciate this "foreign" sport (though in fact the first college football game ever played more closely resembled soccer than the modern gridiron version), in which players use not their hands but their heads, a flimsy shin guard provides the only protection, and the center of attraction is a plain white ball.

Things are changing, of course. As soccer has moved into mainstream America — spurred by suburban youth leagues, the 1994 World Cup, and the realization that it is a rough, tough sport that demands both fitness and finesse and is best played by intelligent, analytical athletes — its image has undergone substantial improvement.

Nonetheless, the game still has a ways to go. Many Americans continue to view it as a poor substitute for "contact" sports (never mind that there is more banging and bruising in soccer than in virtually any other game). Football players and coaches — perhaps stung by the exodus of some of their best athletes to soccer — still deride it as a "pussy" sport, unworthy of real men. (They probably do not even know that the first active athlete in any sport to come out as gay was British soccer player Justin Fashanu.) Thousands of high school and college soccer athletes across the country are familiar with the epithet soccer fags.

Perhaps there is some truth to that. The sport has a long history of tolerance and acceptance of athletes who are "different." Homosexuality is often less of an issue with soccer players than it is with athletes in many other team sports. And straight or gay, most soccer players have learned to wear the "soccer fag" badge with pride.

106   IN THE SPRING OF 1992, Mark McGrath felt great. He was finishing his first year as a history and law teacher at Dwight-Englewood, a prestigious New Jersey private school. As junior varsity soccer coach and assistant to the head coach, he was considered an integral part of one of the school's most successful sports programs. Mark had long ago integrated his two major identities — jock and gay man — and as the academic year drew to a close, he sensed the time was right to begin coming out on the intellectually liberal, socially conservative campus.

Mark's history colleagues, while "wonderful people," were older than he was. Many had Ph.D.s; if they coached at all, it was individual sports like cross-country. He gravitated more to people like head soccer coach Chris Schmid. Both were jocks — more than that, Massachusetts-born jocks. They shared a passion for the Boston Red Sox, Celtics, and Bruins. And, of course, they both loved soccer.

It was only natural that the first person Mark came out to at Dwight-Englewood would be Chris. He admired him as an athlete and coach — Chris, after all, was the man who had raised the school's soccer program to such exalted heights and in his late thirties could still demonstrate skills and drills with pinpoint precision — so he brushed aside his mentor's few "intimidating" qualities. Chris was, Mark admits, "a stout, macho German, a physical education department chair at a school where phys ed is taken very seriously, and a man who married a pretty little blond tennis pro." With his mustache Chris resembles Kaiser Wilhelm. But Mark considered Chris one of his best friends on the faculty and believed the feeling was mutual.

So that May, Mark told Chris he was gay. He intended to use Chris's validation as a springboard for coming out to the entire school, but Mark found to his surprise that that step would have to wait. Chris's initial reaction was not one of acceptance or even tolerance. It was disbelief.

"I couldn't start on my action plan for the rest of Dwight-Englewood because I discovered Chris was starting at ground zero," Mark recalls. "Before I could move forward with everyone else, he had to work through his own feelings."

The first clue was Chris's body language: tense, taut, constricted. Then came his spoken and written words. For two or three weeks, he greeted his assistant like a stranger. He called him "Coach McGrath," not "Mark." He wrote memos about practice rather than communicating directly. Face-to-face discussion gave way to avoidance.

Mark likened Chris's reaction to the shock some parents feel when their child comes out. "It was almost like he felt betrayed," Mark says. "I wasn't ready for his level of surprise. I tried a few times to talk. He said, 'We will. I'm just not ready now.' "

But that summer Chris and Mark were forced to interact. There were soccer camps to run, the upcoming season to plan. In addition to that work, they arranged to meet for tennis matches and beers. Gradually they worked things out.

"Chris showed a sophistication that belied his limited exposure to gay people," Mark says. "He asked questions — Where did I find partners? Why hadn't I talked about it before? — that were better and more probing than I had gotten from my own parents. It wasn't just lip service; he really wanted to know and learn. I was surprised how much he wanted to 'get it.' " In retrospect, Mark notes, Chris got it very quickly.

As he got it he moved to where Mark had hoped he would be at the start: standing right beside his assistant coach as an ally. Chris's fifteen years at Dwight-Englewood had given him a deep knowledge of the school, its politics, and its personalities, so it was only natural that when Mark met with the headmaster to discuss coming out, Chris was there too.

Mark had two reasons for meeting with the headmaster that fall. One was to come out to him personally; the other was to discuss coming out to the school in a way that would benefit everyone. "I think the headmaster was surprised to see this odd couple together," Mark says, referring to the two coaches. "He cautioned against coming out to 'these students who adore you.'

He was worried about the conservative parents and the conservative board of trustees."

Chris's response delighted Mark. "Well, you tried," he told his assistant after the meeting. "Fuck it if he's not going to do anything." The head coach's reaction gave Mark the courage to move forward.

That fall was a magical time for Mark. Buoyed by his newly strengthened relationship with Chris and feeling ever more comfortable and respected as both a teacher and coach, he also exulted in the varsity team's successful drive to the Bergen County prep school soccer championship. This was a big deal in soccer-crazy New Jersey, and all of Dwight-Englewood was caught up in the excitement.

As part of the celebration, team members shaved the two coaches' heads. "I was as exposed and vulnerable as I'd ever been," Mark says. "I said to myself, *Well, this is the time!*" It was just before Thanksgiving.

A few days later Mark was asked to speak at the weekly school meeting about what the county championship meant to him. The request was impromptu; he had just ten minutes to prepare. *Bingo!* he thought. *Now I can come out!*

He scanned the sea of Dwight-Englewood faces — students, soccer players, colleagues — and drew a deep breath. "I was asked to talk about what this season meant to me," he began. "I have a lot of feelings, some of which may surprise you and which I don't think the principal expected to hear when he asked me to speak. Right now I am feeling more secure. I feel more comfortable at this school. I feel safer about being here and being gay."

There was a stunned silence, though no jaws dropped (except the headmaster's). The audience listened quietly to the rest of Mark's brief speech. He said that being part of the championship was the highlight of his life; it reinforced his feeling that Dwight-Englewood was a great place but that the school needed to move forward in its treatment of gay and lesbian students. He spoke confidently and proudly, without embarrassment or apology. He concluded by saying, "Over the past year you've honored me by sharing so many confidences. I'd like to repay that honesty." There was applause at the end, but some remained quiet; many students had no idea how to react. Mark walked out of the room wringing wet.

He headed to his first class of the day — and his students were not there. He found them behind a divider, talking in an adjacent room. When they returned to their regular classroom, they gave their teacher an ovation. "I guess they just needed a little bit of time to think it over and talk things through," he says.

The rest of the year went fine. Players — none of whom had had any inkling that their coach was gay — continued to respect him; in fact, some sought him out more frequently to discuss personal issues they had kept hidden from everyone else. A few players joined a gay-straight alliance Mark helped form. No students came out to him, but several sought support for friends. Late that spring — a year after coming out to Chris — Mark opened the yearbook and was shocked to find it dedicated to him. Those fall and spring semesters remain the highlight of his professional career.

There are several reasons, Mark thinks, that his coming-out process was relatively easy and pain-free. Many, though not all, relate to soccer.

Winning a championship helps, of course. If Mark had been associated with a losing team, he would have had neither the confidence nor the opportunity to speak as candidly as he did. Whatever he said would have had lesser impact; people listen to winners more carefully than losers.

At the same time certain things set soccer apart from other sports. To begin with, Mark says, soccer seems to attract more "sophisticated, individualistic people" than other sports. Some of that may be attributable to the fact that it is a game played all over the world; even at a relatively homogeneous school like

Dwight-Englewood, the soccer team was "like the U.N." Athletes exposed to teammates and foes from many countries may be more tolerant of other differences, such as sexual orientation, than those who hail from like backgrounds. Soccer is a game in which "people feel free to be who they are."

In addition, Mark notes, while soccer is "the consummate team sport," it is one in which players spend a great deal of time working on individual talents, developing individual styles. In football and baseball there are rigorously prescribed ways to perform skills or run patterns. Even in a relatively free-flowing game like basketball, much of the action is planned; players must arrive at certain places at exact times, or the play will fail. Soccer players are constantly analyzing, improvising, and adapting; they are not afraid to take opponents on one-on-one if the situation warrants it and to succeed or fail on their own.

"Players literally teach themselves," Mark says. "And people who think on their own tend to be able to see things objectively." In soccer more than any other team sport, a player is *expected* to make his own decisions on the field without input or instructions from the coach. Football action stops every several seconds, and onto the field runs a new man bringing news of the next play, which everyone else must adhere to perfectly. The final two minutes of a basketball game can take twenty minutes to finish; coaches call constant time-outs, gathering their teams around while they diagram plays on their ever-present clipboards. Even in baseball the coaches' role is paramount. Players cannot decide to bunt, hit away, perform a suicide squeeze, even advance to the next base without signals from older men dressed in uniforms crouching near the sideline.

But soccer is different. A soccer coach performs his primary job during practice. Once the opening whistle blows, players are on their own. They and they alone decide where to move, whom to pass to, when to shoot. Soccer places a premium on creativity, independence, and freedom; athletes who possess those qualities on the field usually view the entire world that way too. It is

a problem-solving sport — and soccer players are adept at solv-
ing problems both on and off the field.

Mark is aware of American soccer's "image problems" and feels that in an almost perverse way, it makes soccer players feel special, apart from the crowd — much as gay people do. "Anyone who plays soccer knows it is one of the most demanding sports there is," he says. "The conditioning and games are so much harder than basketball or baseball. Soccer players know that if they can play soccer, they can do any sport. *We* know it's a ball buster, not a wimp sport, but we also don't have to make excuses or prove it to anybody who doesn't feel that way. Soccer players have a self-confidence that spills over into other areas of life."

Mark mentions the bizarre experience of players who, while cooling down from a ten-mile run, watch their football counterparts struggle to complete one lap — all the while enduring their taunts about playing a "wussy sport." The soccer players he coached always felt secure about themselves and seldom responded to teasing.

Such athletes also do not feel the need to demean others who are different. "I've never heard the womanizing, woman-hating, 'pussy'-type comments in soccer that I heard in basketball and baseball," says Mark, who played all three sports in high school. "I guess if you feel secure about yourself, you don't feel the need to constantly put down other people."

Confidence was never a problem with Mark, even when he was grappling with what it means to be gay. He grew up "a big fish in a small pond": Northampton, Massachusetts. In those days it was still an old mill town; Barbara Walters had not yet dubbed it "Lesbianville, USA" on television's *20/20*. In addition to playing sports, he served as student council president. He did not lack fellow athletes to fool around with but was not official-ly out to them — "there was no vehicle for that" in the mid '80s, he says. He wondered a bit about what being gay meant in the grand scheme of things but had little hesitancy about coming out to one of his high school coaches as a senior. The man helped Mark realize that being gay was normal and assured him that everything would take care of itself in college. (Mark later learned, to his surprise, that the coach was gay. "He was good-looking, well-dressed, and preppy," Mark says. "All the girls had crushes on him. There were no signs.")

Mark describes his family as traditional Irish-Catholic. "We weren't close," he says. "We had dinner together, that was it. It was not very nurturing." He did not come out to his parents until after high school.

By sophomore year at Amherst College, he was out to friends. Two were soccer teammates. One was just like Mark — happy, easygoing, secure. His reaction to Mark's announcement was simply, "Yeah, me too." The other player was "neurotic, all wigged-out about being gay." But having a pair of gay teammates made things easier. Mark saw that males could be masculine, succeed athletically, and be no different from other people. In time the rest of the team learned about Mark and his teammates and had no problem with them.

College sports proved to be a great confidence booster for Mark. Though the training and competition levels at Amherst were high, he felt secure enough in both his athletic ability and his sexuality that he did not suffer the crippling fears or anxieties that derail some athletes. In fact, he found a close connection between soccer and sexuality. "To see that I could perform with these great players and still be accepted as a gay man was great," Mark says. Being a good athlete helped, of course. "It might have been a different story if I'd gotten cut," he muses. "Then I might have wondered, *Gee, maybe I spent too much time in bars. Maybe I should've been out juggling a ball. Then maybe my life would be better.*"

Since Mark was a three-sport athlete, the only peers he knew before college were jocks. He always found the sports world more comfortable than the gay community because he spent more time in it. "Male bonding occurs a lot more with athletes

than nonathletes," he says. "The chance to form male friendships in sports is pretty unique. I knew more about what athletes
liked to do than what gay guys liked to do. I always felt comfortable going out after a game for beer and pizza. I didn't feel
the need to duck out to a gay bar." And he was confident enough
with his jock buddies not to get drawn into the macho game,
trolling for chicks as if they were fish.

But by his second year at Amherst, Mark recognized that
there was a price to pay for hanging out with jocks. He was
not meeting gay men or attending gay dances. With his two
gay teammates he had what he thought was the best of both
worlds — but gradually he realized that the world is wider
than he thought.

As a sophomore he understood that "the jock mentality is a
bit limiting." The conservatism of many athletes rankled; he was
anxious to test the waters, politically and sexually, elsewhere. For
his junior year he transferred to the University of Massachusetts.

The next year he switched his major from political science to
business. "I was in a more 'practical' school, so I thought I
should do the practical thing," he says. After graduation he
worked for the United States General Accounting Office but
soon realized that finance was not for him. What he really wanted was to teach and coach; it represented a return to his values
and roots. He spent a year at a public high school in a situation
he called "every teacher's nightmare: lots of discipline, not much
education" before reluctantly taking a consultant's advice and
ending up at Dwight-Englewood. He realized after visiting the
private school that accepting the job would mean going back in
the closet — there were no support groups on campus, no out
faculty members — but he also recognized that it would not be
forever. In fact, it took just nine months for Mark to come out
to Chris Schmid and six more to tell the entire school. Now it is
hard for him to imagine ever hiding his homosexuality again.

Mark is no longer at Dwight-Englewood. Despite having
the best year of his professional career, he found his social life

still lacking. His support network remained in Massachusetts. He had no interest in the New York scene just across the Hudson River; at any rate, he had little chance to get there. He was stuck on a prep school campus with "straight faculty and seventeen-year-olds." His next step was Northeastern University Law School in Boston; after graduation in 1996 he took another big step. For a while he had planned on criminal law but instead took a lower-paying job as Boston mayor Tom Menino's liaison to the gay and lesbian community. "I think this is something more useful," Mark says.

Yet wherever the legal profession eventually takes Mark McGrath, his fond memories of that championship season — and of coming out to Chris Schmid, his team, and the entire school — will remain. So too will the image of his first National Soccer Coaches Association of America convention, in 1992 in Pittsburgh. The annual winter meeting draws over 3,000 coaches, from youth and high school to college and professional levels. One night he ventured out to Pegasus, a gay bar. "It's a place you obviously don't go to by accident," he notes. There, he saw a number of young athletic men — men he recognized as fellow coaches. Like him, they moved confidently in both the gay and jock worlds.

The yearly soccer coaches' convention was important for another coach too. In fact, it was so monumental, he called it a life-changing event. The quiet, self-described "nonactivist" used the 1995 meeting in Washington, D.C., to come out to nearly a hundred fellow coaches and administrators. It was the most nerve-racking thing he'd ever done, but it created sensations of freedom, strength, even exhilaration he had never dreamed possible.

John Natale's road out of the closet began in the summer of 1994, when the NSCAA was planning its forty-eighth annual convention. A workshop proposal called "Homophobia and Soccer: Issues for Coaches, Administrators, and Players" was accepted — it had been rejected the previous year — and organizers searched for speakers. Several sources recommended John, the president of the International Gay and Lesbian Football Association (throughout the world soccer is known, rather logically, as "football"; American football is called "gridiron.") Despite his prominence in that group, he was not out at the Division III university where he served as assistant coach. Nor was he out to colleagues in the youth association he had helped found as an eighteen-year-old over a decade earlier. In fact, he was not even out to his family.

John consulted with friends and coaches in his city and with IGLFA members around the world. They urged him to speak; a college coach, they said, can give the issue of homophobia in soccer far greater visibility than someone working at a lower level. He checked his school's antidiscrimination policy; it covered sexual orientation, so he knew he could not be fired. Furthermore, soccer is not his full-time job; he owns a small general contracting company. Yet it was with enormous trepidation that he agreed to tell his story in Washington.

Though the homophobia seminar was scheduled at the same time as a clinic conducted by the popular U.S. national team coach, it drew a large crowd. Some were curious onlookers; others, committed activists. Many entered the room hesitantly, peering over their shoulders while seeking out-of-the-way seats. A majority were women or male coaches of women.

When it came time to speak, John told his story nervously but directly. He described how hard it was to stand there but added that it would have been harder still to stay away. He discussed why he was in the closet to his head coach, athletic director, and players and why even that day he refused to name his school. He talked about the pressures on gay athletes and gay coaches and offered ideas for those in attendance — gay or straight — to support their gay players and colleagues.

As NSCAA members congratulated him after his speech, he was shaking. He wondered if word would get back to the head coach, also in attendance at the large convention, or to family and friends back home. When a reporter from a soccer publication said he planned to write about the workshop, John worried even more; his fears eased when the reporter promised not to use his name.

A couple of weeks later, however, John felt double-crossed. The story included his name, school, and IGLFA affiliation. Though the article — which John admitted was balanced and well-written — did not actually say that John was gay, the implication was clear. He called the reporter and blasted him. The man could not explain why he used John's name.

But there was no going back. The head coach read the news while eating breakfast. "He said he spit his food all over the paper," John recounts. When the head coach called his other assistant, the man reacted well. "He and his wife have lots of gay friends," John says. "But I think I was the first gay person the head coach knew or, I should say, knew of. It freaked him out for a week or two."

Yet eventually the man came to terms with his assistant's homosexuality. During long discussions the head coach asked how long John had known, why he had hidden it, why people become gay, and whether he took precautions against AIDS. Eventually, when John and his two colleagues went for beers after practice, the straight coaches would ask which bartenders he found cute.

His homosexuality is not an issue with his colleagues, John says. His belief that sexuality is a private issue helped persuade them not to tell the players; if any asked, they agreed to answer honestly but did not plan to bring it up in a team context. They also decided not to tell the college athletic director. He is a very religious man, and they believe it makes better sense not to open that can of worms.

Soon after the newspaper article appeared, John realized he had to come out to his family. His father was deeply involved in soccer too, and John did not want him to hear from someone else. He sat his parents down, told them — and was amazed to learn that they had already assumed he was gay. It was anticlimactic; his father's biggest concern was that John not lose his coaching job. His parents also wanted to know why he had decided to speak in Washington. He said it was a growth experience, the next step he needed to take for himself. He told them, "It was a chance to say, 'This is who I am. If you don't like me, too bad.' I'm not an activist; I don't hold placards and bitch and complain. I did it because it involved the game I love." He described how liberated he suddenly felt. He thinks they understood.

John also found that everyone else in his family also knew he was gay. "It was like I was the last to know!" he laughs. His youngest brother told him he had wondered ever since he saw the men on John's (gay) soccer club. After John came out his brother joined the team; that brings to four the number of straight siblings who play.

John's gay club plays in a competitive city league against foes sponsored by banks and businesses. He is often asked why people feel a need to field a gay team. He responds, "For a man like myself who played most of his life on straight teams, it's more about what happens off the field than on it. It's a chance to bond with a group of men who understand who I am and accept me without question, in an atmosphere of complete openness."

Besides competing in league play, the team socializes often, at brunches, dinners, parties, and beach weekends, and travels to gay tournaments. In 1995 the IGLFA championships were held in Berlin; the next year it was Dallas, then Washington, D.C. John and his teammates meet gay players from as far away as England, Germany, Japan, and Ghana; over the years friendships bloom. "The bond of being athletes in the gay community is important," he says. "We give each other self-esteem and hope."

Like Mark McGrath, John notes that, more than most others, soccer is an accepting sport. "It's so multicultural," he says. "We meet people from Europe, South America, Africa, Asia, so it's natural to accept differences in language and culture. That carries over into straight players accepting gay ones. It may be different, but it's not abnormal."

Like Mark too, John is passionate about his favorite sport. "I eat, breathe, and sleep soccer," he says. "I get so much energy from it. Every time I play, I challenge myself. I'm almost thirty-four, but I play better and am in better shape than when I was twenty-one. Every day I learn something about the game and myself."

John's devotion to soccer includes a younger squad as well. In addition to founding the town program and overseeing its rise from thirty players to 800, he coaches youth teams. Several years ago his sixteen-year-old boys reached the state finals.

He is not out to the youth coaches or players — implicitly, that is. His father advised not pressing that particular issue, and he agreed. "People have enough in their lives to deal with already," John philosophizes. However, he is sure the word is out. In 1996 the youth program leaders organized a celebration for its founders. John was not invited.

"My family and others thought it had to do with the article in the paper," he says. "That was very upsetting. It left a fire burning in my belly. It really bothers me. The next time I see those people, I've got a thing or two to say."

In fact, ever since the coaches' convention in Washington, John Natale has been talking. His voice may be quiet, but his words — and deeds — are strong and clear.

The Semi-out Ivy League Runner

To high school athletes, college sports seem exciting, glamorous, almost mythic. They imagine a healthy environment filled with dedicated coaches, high-level competition, interesting travel, and lots of publicity and adulation. From an early age many youngsters aim to become college athletes; that dream motivates them, propels them through middle and high school, focuses their lives. Some actually reach their goal.

When they get there, however, they often find they have stepped not into Eden but rather Alice's Wonderland or the Wizard's Oz. The pressures of college — academic and social as well as athletic — weigh heavily. New coaches and teammates may not share the values so familiar and comfortable in high school. For many, the adjustment is quite difficult.

It's even tougher for athletes wrestling with their sexuality. For them, the promise of college — a new life away from home; a more open, accepting, "cooler" atmosphere than before; the growth and maturity so eagerly anticipated — may prove as elusive as a national championship. The letdown can be devastating — especially when it comes at a place reputed to be one of the gayest colleges in the country.

IN THE SUMMER OF 1993, Nick Boggs had high expectations for Yale University. The nineteen-year-old was well aware that the school's English program — his main academic interest — was top-notch; more important, he knew that the track coach had recruited a crop of good runners, and Nick was one of them. A highly rated scholastic runner in Washington, D.C., with personal bests of one minute, fifty-seven seconds in the 800-meter run and four minutes, nine seconds in the 1,500, he counted the days to New Haven. Previous coaches had always marveled at his runner's build and natural stride; with a few months of college training, he expected his high school times to be just memories.

They were, but not in the way anyone anticipated. In his first two years at Yale, Nick never approached his personal records; he was one of the few runners who actually slowed down. As his times plummeted, so did his grades; he slept through classes or simply skipped them. He ate poorly and drank frequently. He was in a difficult, codependent relationship. He was a mess.

Much — though not all — of his difficulties can be traced back to Nick's anguish over being gay. Though Yale has a well-deserved reputation as a gay-friendly school — a dozen or so gay and lesbian organizations serve the far-higher-than-10 percent of undergraduates who identify that way, and queer theory works its way into scores of courses — such heightened aware-ness does not permeate every corner of the campus. Behind Yale's fabled ivy walls lie dark closets filled with athletes. Cowering deep in one was Nick Boggs.

He knew he was gay, of course. Soon after arriving on cam-pus, he fell in love with a senior and moved in with him. But the upperclassman worried about the effect coming out publicly could have on his goal of being a movie star. He remained quasi-closeted, and that reinforced Nick's still-strong internalized homophobia.

He carried his fears and anxieties into the track program. There were several reasons he did not come out to his teammates and coaches. One was that he was still not sure he couldn't change; after all, he'd had a girlfriend for a year and a half in high school, and because he was such an excellent athlete, no one ever suspected.

In addition, he heard the locker-room talk, and he did not like it. "People always say runners seem liberal and laid back, but a lot of guys on the team were Republicans or from places like Texas or the suburbs, and they said so many homophobic, racist, or misogynistic things." Nick had heard such comments before, at Washington's exclusive St. Albans School, but he chalked those up to the preppy, affluent, all-boys environment. Yale, he thought, would be different.

Though Nick had been raised in both theory and practice to value individuality and multiculturalism — his father, Roderick, directed the Washington Lawyers Committee for Civil Rights and Urban Affairs, and until Nick transferred to St. Albans (for the track program) as a junior, he had been the only white runner on the Woodrow Wilson High School team — he still worried about being labeled "different."

After all, he was. Besides being gay, he was one of the few English majors on the Yale squad. He did not share his teammates' penchant for "rah-rah sports viewing" and betting at nearby Milford Jai-Alai. So even though the runners invited him out socially, he seldom went. "I was scared of rejection, so I stayed away," Nick says. "They were nice and didn't understand. I'm a really gregarious person, but with them I was completely silent. I never laughed or interacted with the team. When they made homophobic comments, I didn't know how to respond, so I didn't say anything. I thought if they found out, I'd have to quit, and I loved running. I didn't know what to do. At that point I hadn't even told my family, so coming out to them never entered my mind."

He had plenty of other things to think about. During his first month at school, his father drove up to Connecticut and announced that he and Nick's mother, Dianne, a music teacher, were splitting up. That bolt from the blue sent Nick into a tailspin.

The worse he felt — about the divorce and about his relationships with his teammates and closeted boyfriend — the worse he ran. The worse he ran, the more pressure he put on himself. That made him run even more poorly, and he spiraled ever further downhill.

Nick's world was collapsing. He and his boyfriend fought constantly. Nick could not fall asleep; to catch up he napped during the day, then either slept through practice or woke up too tired to train effectively. Academics suffered too: He missed classes as well as practices, and the high school A student suddenly found himself getting C's in college.

He cried often. "I was a complete wreck," Nick recalls. "My family and track were both falling apart. I was gay, in a new place, with no time to cultivate new friends. I was drinking every night. I don't know if I was an alcoholic, but I was definitely dependent on it. I was not ready to deal with everything, and I couldn't." He wanted to quit, but track was too important to give up.

He considered seeing a therapist but did not. The only people he knew well were his boyfriends' friends, and they were not on his side. Yale's gay community is very vocal, but Nick was not hooked into it. "My attitude at the time was, I'm gay, but I'm not like all those other people," he says. "I considered myself an athlete, not into fads or the mainstream gay culture. Besides, the person I was dating told me not to trust anyone in the gay community, so I didn't."

He had good reason to distrust other gay people: In the middle of his trauma, he was outed to his dormitory by another gay man. "The hardest part for me freshman year was the silence," Nick says. "I had no one to talk to. I was incredibly lonely. I was never quite suicidal, but almost."

Even road trips — respites from the Yale campus and all its distractions — proved disastrous. "Being around the team was so stressful," Nick explains. "My biggest fear was that they'd think I was attracted to them, which I wasn't, so I was always looking over my shoulder or monitoring what I did and said. On the road there was no escape; we were always together. And having to worry about sharing a bed with a guy in that homophobic environment was horrible. Sometimes I didn't sleep all night."

His times got slower and slower, but his coaches were mystified as to the cause. Their concern embarrassed him — "My self-esteem was completely wrapped up in my running, my times," he says — but he could not bring himself to disclose the problem. He suffered in silence.

He did come out to his twin sister, Amanda, a basketball player at Amherst College, late freshman year. She was fine with the news, but it was a difficult discussion for Nick. He remained uncomfortable coming out to people.

He still did not tell his parents. "I was furious at them for their incredibly messy divorce, and they were so wrapped up in their own problems that they didn't seem to care about mine," he says. "With my grades and my running, it was clear I was struggling, but they didn't even really ask why."

That summer Nick prepared poorly for the upcoming season. His spirits lifted in the fall when he was tapped for St. Anthony Hall, a prestigious literary society with a strong gay presence. It provided a safe haven. He made good friends and found an element of stability. His grades rose slightly, though his study habits were lackadaisical (and he chose courses based on the opportunity they afforded for sleeping in). He continued to drink.

The middle of sophomore year was the first time he thought of quitting track. He had never liked running indoors — his tall frame is ill-suited for small tracks, with their tight turns — but now he saw the endless laps as a bad metaphor for his life: "I was just going around in circles."

The track — for so long a comforting presence in his life — became a place to fear. When he lined up for races, he was plagued by anxiety attacks. Heavy thoughts filled his brain: *I'm gay. What am I doing here? I can't do this. I can't win.* He felt "like a ghost going through the motions."

Finally an assistant coach invited him to dinner. The man mentioned Nick's high school times, his great stride and wonderful talent, then asked point-blank what was wrong.

Nick was seized with a desire to come out to him, but the words stuck in his throat. He mumbled something about problems; the coach said he'd heard. Nick wondered if that meant his secret was out, but it turned out the coach was talking about Nick's family situation. He advised Nick to take time off if necessary but not to quit.

"I was so tempted to come out, but I just couldn't," he recalls. "I fell back on the divorce; the huge academic load I was taking because I'd done so poorly earlier; my job, which took so much time; my apartment without any heat. That was a critical moment. I always wonder what would have happened if I had told him then. Things might have been a lot different."

Although Nick did not come out, that dinner conversation proved crucial to his life. The assistant coach's words kept running through his head — and kept him running.

Yet running every day without the support and friendship of teammates while at the same time feeling marginalized and isolated took its toll. "Running is so dependent on emotion," Nick explains. "Even though I felt like I'd come out of something horrible and through the other end, I still was miserable." His times improved from freshman year — but still lagged behind his high school bests.

That sophomore spring Nick finally broke up with his boyfriend. The man, by then a graduate, had never supported Nick's running. He bothered him before meets, talking to Nick despite knowing that Nick was trying to concentrate. Though still running poorly, Nick gradually found a new network of friends. He was fed up with himself and determined to make a change. He decided to stop drinking and take control of his life.

With his times so poor, he was not selected for a major spring-break road trip. That proved fortuitous. Nick went home to Washington and came out to his parents. It was not a total shock — they had already met his former boyfriend — but still caught up in their divorce, they could not provide full attention to their son. "They gave me the token line about AIDS and how my life would be hard," Nick remembers. "I told them my life *had* been hard and that now I was going to be okay so long as people wouldn't make it hard." When he came out to his elder sister, Erin, a Georgetown University law school student, she had a similar reaction.

Happy to finally get the crushing weight off his chest but still feeling a hole in his stomach, Nick returned to Yale. He met a special person, ran one decent race, and wondered whether sticking with track was worth the aggravation.

During the summer he joined Frontrunners, a gay running group. Though one of the youngest members, he made many good friends. He luxuriated in Washington's active gay scene. At night he discovered gay bars, drank a lot, and loved it; by day he worked at a law firm, made a lot of money, and hated it.

Fall semester of junior year, when Nick studied in London, was a great time. He realized he could be happy even without running and Yale. He was intellectually stimulated, got good grades, developed strong friendships with professors, and dated a wonderful man. The lone negative experience came when he met an openly gay track coach. The man showed a more-than-athletic interest in Nick, which knocked him off his newfound stride. "I was looking for a role model and instead — well, he wasn't sleazy, but close," Nick says. "All the stereotypes came flooding back. I felt really sad."

In mid December, Nick began running again. Suddenly he was hit with another great revelation: Even though he was not a great college athlete, that was okay. He was still a good human being. He stopped drinking.

When he returned to Yale for spring semester, Nick's rebirth continued. He was stimulated by intelligent, supportive teachers, including a gay writing professor. In a seminar Nick discovered James Baldwin. He made great friends. He thrived both academically and socially.

His running got much better too. For the first time at Yale, Nick equaled his high school times despite training less rigorously. Though still not out to his teammates, he felt more relaxed. Again his assistant coach helped, assuring him he had the talent to be great.

During the summer he sent Nick lists of suggested workouts. Every day after his job as a researcher, Nick ran. "I love the sensation of running smoothly, the movement," he exults. "There's a real joy in it." He does not, however, rhapsodize as others do about the solitude of running. For him, the camaraderie of a team adds to the sport's enjoyment. That was a major reason he felt so bad about not being out to his teammates.

Nor did he expect that would ever happen. "I don't want to give myself up to their scrutiny," he explains. "I just want to train in peace. I don't want to be looked at differently. I just want to run."

Coming out, he felt, would create a huge divisive issue. Nick, a sensitive man, did not want to put himself in a position where he would be made to feel uncomfortable. His running, which he had worked so hard to resuscitate, would suffer again. There was no doubt in his mind; that would happen, he was sure, because for so long he had heard so many homophobic comments. They came from teammates, captains, and coaches.

"In a way I wish I'd gotten closer to people on the team," he admits. "But since I haven't, they have no investment in me. They don't know me; they don't know who I am. If someone asked, I wouldn't deny being gay, but I won't volunteer it either."

Nick knows he is not alone, listening in bitter, confused silence as teammates spout homophobia. Several athletes have left other Yale teams for exactly that reason, he says; he is the only one who has not. After graduation he hoped to let the athletic director know how many gay athletes have quit Yale sports.

Nick does not think his team's attitude is different from that of most athletic teams — and he recognizes that, despite Yale's liberal, gay-friendly reputation, its teams are no different from any other school's. "In this country sports is seen as a protected bastion of masculinity," he says. "People say things in a locker room they could never say anywhere else on campus. There are no watchdogs. They don't know I'm gay, so they talk about faggots. They don't know I have three sisters, so they talk about women in unbelievably crude terms. I feel awful not saying anything, but there's a tacit agreement that the locker room is an okay place to voice anything you can't say anywhere else."

Certainly Nick would like to talk about homosexuality to his teammates. He is, finally, proud of who he is. "Being gay has helped me in huge, wonderful ways," he explains. "Intellectually it's been incredible. It's allowed me to see the world in so many different ways I couldn't have if I'd been caught up in the masculine world. I understand people and how they suffer better because I'm gay. Being gay is not all I am. But it does allow me to see life in ways so many people — especially athletes, with their sheltered view — never do."

Nick's high school track coach always treated running as a metaphor for life. "I think I took that too literally," Nick says. "I made running a barometer of my worthiness." Overall, however, he credits the sport for much of the good that has come into his world. "As horrible as it was, it provided a structure for my life," he says. "It brought me so much pain but so much pleasure too. I have a healthy body; I'm happy. Without running, I might have become a total drug addict or alcoholic. It's been an overwhelming, positive force."

In one way his high school coach's metaphor is apt. Running taught him to forget today's race; there will always be another one tomorrow.

Right now Nick Boggs is training to run in the next Gay Games.

The Nonparticipant

Though drawn to sports by their size, strength, innate athletic ability, or perhaps a subconscious psychological element such as a desire to prove themselves in a "masculine"-appearing activity, some gay youths nevertheless shy away from participation in school or community teams. Though they love the physical sensations and emotional releases of athletics — the joy of running, jumping, knocking heads, and kicking butts; the endorphin highs, the exhaustion that leads to a good night's sleep followed by a fresh morning sensation; the quiet satisfaction that comes from setting a goal and finally reaching it — they are uncomfortable joining teammates and coaches in order to achieve those feelings.

Their reasons vary, from fear of discovery and negative early experiences to poor self-image, worries about fitting in, and locker-room terror. Yet whatever the cause, the result is the same: Young men with already too much on their minds rob themselves — or are robbed — of the right to take part in one activity from which they might gain some desperately needed self-esteem.

DON KEIZER'S FATHER stands six and a half feet tall. A former college basketball player who now teaches physical education in the Bronx, he intimidated his young son emotionally as well as physically. "Even when we were just playing catch, if I dropped the ball, he'd call me a faggot," Don recalls. "I tried not to be around him."

School was no better. His classmates in the New York City suburb of Nanuet called him a dork, a nerd, and a loser. "They always thought I was weird," he says.

In sixth grade, en route to a friend's birthday celebration at Yankee Stadium, he shared the backseat of a car with a twelve-year-old he did not know. The boy edged closer and closer. To protect himself Don yelled, "Get away, you faggot!" Secretly he was thrilled.

His frustration worsened in junior high and high school. **129** In tenth grade, battling depression fueled by dreary winter weather, he and his parents had a big fight. He fled to a friend's house. Instead of giving solace, the other boy prattled on about girlfriend problems. "I told him, 'You don't know what problems are!' " Don says — and came out to him. Looking back, he realizes that treating homosexuality as a problem is not the most positive way to come out. Luckily his friend was accepting.

For the next four months, he did not confide in anyone else. Eventually Don told a girl. She broke his confidence; other friends found out and deserted him. "They weren't afraid of me personally," Don says vehemently. "They were just pussies. They were scared of themselves."

One summer morning he fought with his mother. His father had already left for his job at a day camp — the same place Don worked. Suddenly Don spit out to his mother that he had "a problem." The news that he was gay surprised her; she told him he did not fit the stereotype. He asked what she would do about his father; she said she planned to tell him when he got home.

"I was so nervous all day, I couldn't stop shaking," Don says. "Every time I'd see my dad, I couldn't look at him. He got home before me. When I saw him he said, 'Don…' I said, 'Leave me alone. I don't want to talk about it.' He said, 'Don, you're my son. I know you didn't choose this.' "

That unexpectedly enlightened reaction stunned Don. Over the following months his father read articles and books, watched movies and television shows, asked questions, and listened to answers. In time he began recommending resources to Don. Today their relationship is so relaxed, his father can joke about fruits and bending over for bars of soap — "in a good way," Don notes — and together they laugh.

"He's so aware now," Don says proudly. "He's such a much better human being. I give him so much thanks. His support and my mother's and sister's have been great."

But Don's years in the closet took a toll on his athletic spirit. After a bit of Little League baseball — he once struck out eleven batters in a six-inning game — Don veered away from team sports.

"I had such low self-esteem," he explains. "I thought because I was different that I had to be better than everyone else. If I wasn't good enough people might call me the *f* word, and that would destroy all the team spirit. No one would be able to function together, and — I thought — it would all be my fault."

The eagerness he had felt in sixth grade to be part of a high school team faded. Within two years, feeling like a freak, he lost all desire to play sports. He even stopped following his beloved Yankees.

But with his acceptance of himself has come a discovery: He can channel his athleticism into a new arena. Don's work as a summer-camp counselor, where he is proud of his reputation as a talented athlete, has become one of his most important activities. And he is out at camp to anyone who cares to ask.

"All the other counselors know," he says. "The director knows, and he put his own son in my group. He has more trust in me than in anyone else." Even some of his campers know: Half of the current eleven-year-olds, he estimates, and all of the previous ones. He does not initiate conversations about homosexuality, but occasionally it pops up. For example, Don quickly disciplines campers who use derogatory language and is not afraid to say why. "I believe in coming out to children," he says. "You can influence them ten times more than you can a twenty- or thirty-year-old. By the time people get older, their minds are made up."

Don, an extremely popular counselor, has encountered no horrible reactions or insurmountable problems. Once in a while campers ask questions. Some are appropriate ("Do you have a boyfriend?"); others are not ("Are you the pitcher or the catcher?"). He does not always guess correctly about who will feel comfortable with the news and who will not. One day, while playing home run derby, he struck out a boy from New York City whose uncle is gay. Don figured him to be a streetwise kid not bothered by having a gay counselor. Instead the boy taunted, "Come on you queer, give me a break."

But another player, this one a suburban boy whom Don believed to be quite narrow-minded, retorted, "Shut up! Just because my counselor's gay doesn't make him any different!"

Don is known around camp as "Bob Backlund." That's the name of a World Wrestling Federation champion, and Don does impressions of him. In fact, Don is so taken by him, his ambition is to be a professional wrestler.

In place of team sports and in pursuit of that goal, Don has devoted tremendous time and energy to working out. In three years he has added thirty pounds to his five-foot ten-inch frame — that makes him 180 pounds — and sees an added benefit, beyond wrestling strength, to his good physical condition. "People respect you more if you're in shape, and you respect yourself more too. I used to be so skinny. Now I've got confidence and self-esteem, whether it's asking a guy out or getting kids at camp to listen to me."

He is most passionate when discussing pro wrestling, a "sport" that boasts millions of fans but earns little respect in the athletic world. "It combines athleticism, acting, entertainment, theater, choreography, fitness, performance, and a loud mouth," Don explains patiently. "I've loved it since I was four. I know it's fake, but it's fun. I'm not a masochist, but I like getting body-slammed."

Wrestling's reputation is especially low in the gay community, in part because of Golddust. As part of his "character" role, the WWF performer hurled homophobic epithets at his opponents — and the wrestling federation made excuses for it.

"Golddust pissed me off," Don admits, "but I've also heard that a lot of people in the WWF are gay. It's insulting to me that so much of the audience buys into what Golddust says, but a lot of the audience is white trash skinheads." Though he is both gay and Jewish, Don does not believe that self-described "double whammy" precludes a professional wrestling career.

He does not consider himself a jock. That is a social term, he says, designating someone who cares for little else beyond sports. To Don, all jocks are straight. He declared himself to be "jockish." That means, he says, that he plays and follows sports but does not excel in any one. His best activity is tetherball, which, while requiring excellent hand-eye coordination, is considered a game, not a sport. His experiences during junior high and high school have left him leery of participating in team sports such as baseball or football.

However, he notes, the gay community labels him a jock. His short hair, athletic skill, muscular build, and — yes — love for the Yankees cause people to see him as a "total straight-boy jock." That leaves him feeling conflicted. When he is with gay friends, he sometimes feels part of the gay community; however, at other times — when their interests diverge — he thinks of himself as an outsider. He felt that way sometimes even at the University of Massachusetts, where he lived on an all-gay floor but did not always feel comfortable with everyone there.

He wants to be seen simply as Don Keizer: not as gay Don, jock Don, or even "jockish" Don. Like all of us, he is unique; like most, he wishes others would see him that way without feeling the need to apply a label. After all, he wonders, how many gay psychology and elementary education majors dream of becoming pro wrestlers?

Time-out: The Author's Story

Every coach, athlete, trainer, sports information director, and significant other jock-type male interviewed for this book has a unique story to tell. Some have spent years grappling with what it means to be a gay man in sports; they balance — and keep separate — what seem to be two opposing elements of their lives. Others have managed to integrate the two fairly easily. But whatever camp they fall into, all recognize their status as something special. Face it: Being an athletically minded gay man is still an anomaly. Our achievements are seldom heralded; our role models, few.

Because we have not read much about ourselves, we've spent a lot of time thinking about our situations. When I began my interviews for this book, I thought I would have a difficult time getting people to open up and talk. That was not the case. Virtually everyone I approached, it seemed, had already reflected on his own life and was just waiting for someone to talk to. The stories I heard were intriguing and instructive.

I am no different. I too have a tale to tell.

IF YOU BELIEVE THE RESEARCH STATISTICS, in my career I have coached two to three dozen gay soccer players. After all, I've been a soccer coach for over twenty years. I am no mathematician, but I can figure out what 10 percent of the total is.

In all that time not one boy has even hinted he may be gay. In subsequent years I have learned that several former players indeed are. Some I've suspected; others I never would have imagined. I know there are many others I do not know about.

During much of that time, I never revealed my sexual orientation to my players. They might have guessed — I am unmarried, I live alone, I don't date women — and the older I got, the more the rumor mill probably churned. But I never brought it up, and no one ever did in my presence either. On my soccer teams "don't ask, don't tell" was alive and well.

A few years ago I finally came out of the closet — the locker-room closet as well as the many others I cowered in. My vehicle was my weekly column in the *Westport* [Connecticut] *News*. A driving force behind that coming-out decision was my work on the athletic field. Though I make my living as a writer, part of what I live for is soccer.

I was never a particularly good player — and I needed to have been great to break into the Staples High School starting lineup in the early '70s. The Westport school's soccer program was among the most successful in the nation; for example, during my senior season our team allowed just two goals, winning the second of what became a national record five consecutive state championships. I watched the goals and glory from the bench, happy to hide rapidly growing anxieties about my sexuality in the welcoming blanket of teammates and friends who were well-respected, hardworking, high-achieving, intelligent, creative jocks. They dated girls, I reasoned; I did not, but I hung out with them, and I, like them, was a jock — so obviously I could not be gay. No way. Right?

I had even less of a chance of playing soccer at Brown University, a perennial national contender, so I settled for second best: I covered the team for the school newspaper. To further embed my jock bona fides, I joined a fraternity. It was not exactly the most popular thing to do in the '70s, especially for a self-styled liberal on one of the most freethinking campuses in the country, but more important to me than independence was being viewed by others as a straight man. In fact, being myself — especially *discovering* myself — was the last thing I wanted. When I graduated I breathed a sigh of relief that no one had ever asked why I was the only frat man at Brown who never dated.

A job offer brought me back to my hometown of Westport. Social life in suburbia is limited even for straight people, but I found an activity that provided plenty of human contact and enormous satisfaction — and that I was particularly good at to boot: soccer coaching.

I organized youth teams, which my new friends and I soon formed into the Westport Soccer Association. Over the years we won numerous state championships. I also joined the coaching staff at my alma mater, Staples High (still one of the best high school programs in the country). I organized a dozen overseas soccer trips to Europe and Australia. I was selected State Youth Coach of the Year in 1980 and National Youth Coach of the Year a decade later. All the while I continued my soccer writing, winning awards for my coverage of youth sports. I traveled to World Cups and Olympics and met Pelé. Soccer was very, very good to me.

My coaching career taught me a great deal about adolescents: how they think, what they dream, who they are. Spending time at Staples gave me insight into high school education, so during the 1993 gay and lesbian march on Washington, I attended a reception hosted by the National Education Association. There I met Sasha Alyson, founder of Alyson Books. We discussed marketable ideas. The result was my first book on gay topics. *School's Out: The Impact of Gay and Lesbian Issues on America's Schools* was published in 1995.

My research included interviews with nearly 300 teachers, administrators, students, guidance counselors, nurses, librarians — and coaches. An openly gay football coach and a lesbian volleyball and lacrosse coach spoke eloquently of the coming-out process, highlighting its effect not only on them but also on their athletes and, ultimately, their entire schools.

The more I spoke with these courageous men and women, the more I recognized that by not being out, I was doing all my soccer players — straight and gay — a disservice. Every afternoon at practice I preached honesty, yet every time I changed pronouns when mentioning something as mundane as with whom I had dinner or saw a movie, I lied. Every day I preached tolerance, never hesitating to halt practice to address racial, ethnic, or religious slurs, yet my rabbit ears turned deaf whenever I heard the words "gay" or "fag." Every season I stressed respect for others — teammates, opponents, referees, parents — but my actions clearly showed I did not respect myself. Every player looked up to me as a role model for sportsmanship and fair play, for compassion as well as competition, for someone who stressed the importance of education and the arts along with athletics. Yet in the area in which I might be the most important role model of all — by proving that a man could be both macho and gay — I was frozen with fear.

Ever so slowly I inched out the closet door.

Midway through writing my book, I gave a talk in our school library about the project. Over 300 students attended, the most ever for such a program. (I have no illusions why: Homosexuality is far more enticing to teenagers than chemistry or the situation in Sarajevo.) I discussed the process of research, writing, and publishing as much as the content, yet of course every question centered around gayness. I had promised myself before that, if asked, I would say I was gay. Several students came close — in particular a football player, who challenged, "I got something personal to ask you," but then backed off with "I'll talk to you later" (he never did) — but no one dared pop the "Are you...?" question. Suburban boys and girls are too polite.

During that session I mentioned the pioneering gay-straight alliances popping up in high schools throughout Massachusetts. Immediately after, several girls asked me to help start a gay-straight alliance in our school. A straight teacher, Ann Friedman, agreed to work with me; our principal, Gloria Rakovic, recognized that the idea fit into her yearlong theme of "diversity." Within a few weeks our group had twenty regular members.

I grew more and more confident about coming out. I wrote a column for the local paper; it was set to run in late May. The day before, at our weekly gay-straight alliance meeting, we chatted about what we had accomplished in just a few months of existence. Someone commented, "I feel bad no one's been comfortable enough to come out here yet."

There was a brief pause, then I jumped in. "Pick up the paper tomorrow morning," I said simply. "Read my column." Instantly they got it. One boy, sitting in the front row, stared at me in awe. I knew then that, regardless of the fallout, I had made the right decision.

The next morning I was nervous yet excited. My column is usually well-read; this one, I knew, would be particularly so. I walked into the cafeteria — the student hangout — and felt a buzz in the air. Everyone had seen the article, yet no one had a clue what to say or how to act. I looked around; fifty or so Stapleites either stared right through me or glanced away.

Suddenly Tim Caffrey, the popular and respected soccer captain, walked over and stuck out his hand. "Great column, Dan," he said. "I'm proud of you."

That broke the ice. For the rest of the day, students approached me. Some complimented the piece; others patted my arm as they walked by. A few just smiled — friendly smiles, not mocking. I made contact with people I'd never spoken to before. I learned about gay and lesbian relatives, so many that I felt like saying, "Okay, if you want to talk about an aunt or uncle, line up here; a cousin, over there. If it's a parent or sibling, I'll see you right now."

The good feeling continued for days, with the soccer athletes among the most enthusiastic. Congratulations poured in; current players spoke to me in person, while former athletes called and wrote letters (and, this being the '90s, sent E-mail). "It's cool" was the gist of what most conveyed. "You're a good coach, we like you, and now we know a little bit more about you." The head coach of the varsity team told me how glad he was that I could finally be myself. I got a similar message from my former high school coach, now eighty years old and a man I revere so much, I still cannot call him by his first name.

Only two parents phoned; both were complimentary. One man said my column had allowed him to have the kind of honest discussion with his boy that every father always wishes to have; another said that that night they'd had the best dinner-table conversation ever. Both men ended their calls the same way: "Thanks for coaching my son."

The father of a former player called. His four sons kept telling him he was homophobic, he said; his gut reaction to my column convinced him he might be. But he wanted to talk with me and learn about homosexuality. I brought him books and answered his questions. Months later he told me he was a changed man.

I expected soccer people to be, if not accepting, at least not intolerant; after all, the game attracts a certain type of creative, intelligent, worldly person. I was less sure about the reaction of athletes and coaches in other sports, who at the time I believed to be less — well, creative, intelligent, and worldly. Yet they too went out of their way to let me know that, even if they did not delight in the news or want it for themselves or family members, it did not change our relationship one bit. Football, basketball, baseball, and lacrosse players complimented me on my "guts" (how's that for an athletic metaphor!), while coaches of those sports said it gave them a bit more insight into the person I am. The closest thing to a negative response came from a football coach, who happened to be reading my piece the same time I walked past his office. "Hey," he said immediately. "If that's what you are and that's what you want, it's fine with me." I could not have asked for more from him.

The fall season began. I did not stand on a soapbox, preaching about homosexuality and homophobia when I should have been teaching passing and shooting — but neither did I shy away from the subject. If someone asked why there was no practice Friday, I told him: I was attending the National Lesbian and Gay Journalists Association convention. If the T-shirt that made its way to the top of my drawer and then into my gym bag happened to be from a gay pride parade, I wore it. And if a player wandered, inadvertently or not, onto the rocky terrain of gay issues, I met him there.

One day a boy tried to explain why a certain teammate was disliked. "It's always been that way," he said. "Even when we were in elementary school, we had a TIAF club."

"What's that?" I asked innocently.

Suddenly the player looked stricken. He opened his mouth but was literally unable to speak.

"Come on," I prodded. "It can't be that bad. What is it?"

Finally, staring down at the ground, he mumbled, "Tom Is a Fag."

"Well," I said, "I appreciate your telling me. Kind of makes you think about the power of words, doesn't it?" At last, grateful to be let off the hook he'd hung himself on, he looked at me and nodded.

Another time the varsity soccer players shook hands with their opponents after an important victory. A boy on the other team who had had a particularly difficult afternoon muttered "faggot" at one of our players. He had been outplayed, and in his frustration that was all he could say.

I reacted immediately. "No, I don't think he is," I told the opponent. "I am. He's not." The stunned boy just stared; he had no idea how to respond. The players on our team roared and high-fived me.

The following summer I took fifteen players to the Netherlands, Denmark, and Sweden. They played hard and well and improved immensely; five straight times we beat or tied excellent European teams. But perhaps my most memorable moment took place off the field.

During the Gothia Cup, a large tournament in Göteborg, Sweden, players are housed in schools: Each team sleeps on cots in its own classroom. As can be expected when a group of sixteen-year-olds spends a week in such close quarters, the air gets ripe. Nonetheless, it is a rare opportunity for team bonding — and unexpected encounters.

The team in the next room, from North Carolina, was sponsored by a religious organization. In between practices and matches, they held prayer meetings. Once or twice zealous team members handed religious tracts to our players.

At breakfast one morning a boy on my team asked a bit mischievously, "Dan, are you going to say anything to those guys?"

"What do you mean?" I replied.

"You know, all the stuff they're saying about gays — aren't you going to do anything about it?"

"Well, I'll tell you what I'm *not* going to do," I said. "I'm not going to get into a big brawl just so you can watch!" That was the end of that — I thought.

Two days later the same boy approached me privately. "Dan," he said, "I finally went up to those guys from North Carolina."

"And...?"

"Well," he continued, nervously but proudly, "I told them they had, you know, every right to think what they want about stuff. But I told them they shouldn't say shit about gay people, because they probably didn't know much about them, and besides, they don't know who they're offending."

"That's great!" I said. "But why'd you do it?"

"Well," he concluded, "I told them I had a friend who was gay."

In January 1995, in what is believed to be the first event of its kind anywhere, I presented a workshop on "Homophobia and Soccer: Issues for Coaches, Administrators, and Players" at the National Soccer Coaches Association of America's forty-eighth annual convention, in Washington, D.C. Seventy-five college and high school coaches came to the session, out of a total convention attendance of 3,500.

The number did not disappoint me. I am sure many coaches did not make my workshop because they were worried about being seen, while a concurrent session featuring the national team coach drew many others. But the ones who came proved what I strongly believe: This is an important topic that must be discussed. Seventy-five people, after all, had never gathered before to discuss homophobia in soccer.

The Moonie-owned *Washington Times* had predicted that my presentation would be the most controversial of the entire convention and quoted one person as wondering why the topic needed addressing at all. "It's a bit like a talk on the Bosnian conflict at a shoe salesman's conference," the please-don't-quote-me-by-name coach said, managing to give short shrift to soccer, homophobia, Bosnia, and shoe salesmen all at once.

Earlier, when he had asked my reaction, I told the reporter I disagreed with that quote: "If we coaches are truly the people we say we are — teachers and educators concerned about the physical and emotional growth of every child we work with, straight and gay — then this is a topic we cannot ignore." But he chose not to print that.

In fact, the entire piece was decidedly negative, but I used that to my advantage in the introduction. "I could say, 'What do you expect from a paper owned by the Moonies?' — but I won't," I began. "That would stereotype every Moonie based on what I've heard, not what I know. There might even be Moonies in the audience — I don't know who you are or what you look like. That might embarrass you, if you don't want your Moonie-ality made public. After all, most people in America don't like Moonies. They don't want their kids coached by them. And they certainly don't want them to grow up to *be* Moonies!"

I had hoped to create a panel involving several openly gay coaches and athletes, nicely balanced among gender, age, and geography. What I found was that those people willing to talk were unable to go to Washington, while those able to be there were unwilling to speak publicly. So I gathered four "life stories" and presented them myself. Then I introduced a college coach active in both the Gay Games and the International Gay and Lesbian Football Organization. He spoke honestly — and with trepidation — about why he was not out on his campus.

Audience members asked many questions after our presentation. One man said, "I coach at the high school level. Doesn't a girl going on to college have the right not to play for a lesbian coach and not to play with lesbian teammates?"

"Let's turn the question around," I replied. "Would you get up in a public meeting and ask, 'Doesn't a girl have the right not to play for a black coach or with Hispanic teammates?' You'd *never* do that! Furthermore, what happens if she chooses a college because, she thinks, the coach is not a lesbian and there are no lesbian players? After she graduates and gets a job, chances are that she'll have lesbian coworkers — maybe even a lesbian boss. How is she going to get along with them if she hasn't learned those lessons earlier? The issue is not whether she has the right to play with lesbian teammates or for a lesbian coach but why that's a problem for her."

The next query came from an athletic director. "I understand everything you're saying, but why do you have to talk about it?" he asked. "Why can't you just let it be?"

I answered that the issue exists whether it is talked about or not, so it is far better to bring it into the open than bury it. "If a player on your team shuts himself off from his teammates because he's scared they'll find out his secret, you're not going to have the best team possible," I explained. "And if there's something tearing your team apart, like rumors flying around about a player and you don't even know it's an issue, you're not going to be a very effective coach."

The final questioner wondered about pedophilia. "I'm glad you brought that up," I replied. "I'm worried too. I'm worried about the 5 percent of pedophilia acts that are performed by gay men and the 95 percent performed by straight men — most of whom are married. I think we all have to be concerned about every person who is coaching every boy and girl."

It was a good ending to a remarkable day. Several dozen coaches had their eyes opened, their horizons broadened. There was plenty of information presented, lots of honest give-and-take. My only surprise was that no one approached me afterward and came out — either as gay or a Moonie.

Which brings us to the present. The Staples High School gay-straight alliance continues to meet weekly. The longer we exist, the deeper we integrate into the fabric of the school and the less often we find our posters defaced. Coming out has freed me as a writer to become both bolder and more honest. That is not merely a guess; several students have told me, "Dan, your columns are getting really good!"

As an openly gay soccer coach, I am happier, healthier, even more successful than ever before. I have the respect of my athletes and colleagues and, more important, of myself. At long last the themes I have for so long tried to convey in my twin careers of writing and coaching — honesty, integrity, being true to oneself — are part of my own life too.

To me, that is the biggest victory of all.

The Ex–Football-Playing Workshop Leader

With adulthood comes the ability to see things one might have missed at a younger age. Decisions once seen as logical, natural, even preordained — which sport to play, whom to hang out with, how to act — may be viewed through the lens of maturity in a very different perspective.

For some of us, the chance to revisit our high school years is gratifying, a pleasant stroll down memory lane. For others, that path is strewn with horrors. How, we ask ourselves, could we ever have thought that, done this, said such a thing? For a fortunate few, adulthood brings the opportunity to rewrite some chapters of an earlier life of which we may not be particularly proud.

Michael Kozuch is one of those lucky people.

MICHAEL KOZUCH WORKS as an educational consultant. A "safe schools specialist," he gets paid to conduct workshops on the best ways to create buildings in which everyone — students and staff, gay and straight — feels comfortable and secure.

It was not always that way. In fact, just over a decade ago, Michael was in a distinctly unsafe place: a high school locker room. It was somewhere he longed to be, yet at the same time it scared the hell out of him.

The ninth grader had never before spent time in a football locker room with a bunch of naked boys. For the first time he could compare himself physically: Was he growing at the right rate? Did he have enough pubic hair? For the first time too, however, he ran the risk of becoming publicly aroused. He compromised by stealing quick, furtive glances at his teammates, then staring conspicuously at the floor. To this day he laughs when he hears straight people express their fear of gay men in gang showers. He knows gays are the most terrified people there; they want to flee the fastest.

Yet something stronger than the chance to sneak peeks at bare bodies drew Michael to football. He had never played the game in his southern New Jersey hometown — baseball and soccer were his sports — but as he began high school, the lure of football was great. It offered friendship and camaraderie. It conveyed status. Best of all, football promised a way to affirm himself as a heterosexual male. For a fourteen-year-old boy just discovering sex (his favorite partner that summer was a friend who also planned to go out for the team), nothing was more important than the chance to be seen as straight.

Junior high school had been a time of intense conflict for Michael. A self-described "Stonewall baby" (he was born in 1970, one year after the uprising that gave birth to the modern gay rights movement) who grew up the fourth of six children in a Philadelphia suburb, Michael followed his fundamentalist Christian parents' lead, to the point of standing on street corners trying to save sinners. He felt alienated from everyone: not only his peers but also the clique of nice Christian people who loved Jesus Christ and hated homosexuals. "I was having a hard time reconciling who I felt I was with who I thought God wanted me to be," he recalls.

By eighth grade he thought he knew who he was: a straight boy. At least that was how he tried to present himself. He dated girls, laughed at faggots, and couldn't wait for fall to arrive so he could try out for football.

When he made the freshman team, Michael was pleased. When he found he was actually good — his speed, agility, and tenacity made him an ideal cornerback — he was elated. And when he found that his talent and leadership skills made him an important, respected member of the squad, he was ecstatic.

He was inspired by a coach who, though even smaller than Michael, taught him how to burst off the line, pursue an opponent, and tackle him. Michael learned to use his size as an advantage, mixing leg strength with impeccable technique and innate intelligence into a formidable defensive package.

Michael loved nearly everything about football. The team-work appealed to his desire to bond in a cooperative, gung ho way with other males. It was a tough sport; the action was grit-ty, hand-to-hand, down in the trenches, unlike baseball, in which players seem to spend hours just waiting for the ball to come to them. Football was even a way to connect with his father, a blue-collar worker who spent long hours at his job at an Army base. He had little free time but was always in the stands for football.

And of course Michael basked in the glory that reflected off even the lowly freshman squad. "I definitely liked the status," he says. "No one questioned my orientation, and I felt like I'd arrived in the heterosexual world. I even told myself I might be straight."

He was not, of course. And as fall wore on, the shine slowly wore off the football team. First came a split between two fac-tions: the "hard-assed, typical go-for-it jocks" who believed win-ning was not everything, it was the only thing; and Michael's group, which valued teamwork, coming together, doing the best they could while enjoying the effort. His best friend landed in the other camp. The problem persisted, and as a sophomore Michael decided not to play anymore.

However, the rift on the team was not the sole reason he quit. He had begun to be bothered by "the hypermasculine side" of football. "Hearing 'faggot' all the time — not only from players but from coaches too — really alienated me," Michael remem-bers. "I was uncomfortable not just with the homophobia but with the whole masculine aura. I saw the older kids having to prove their masculinity by beating up people in school. The juniors in particular were picking on one supposed 'art fag,' pushing and teasing him all the time." Michael participated in the verbal bashing — an attempt to cover up his own insecurities and fears — but drew the line at physical harassment. He thought to himself, *I can't be that violent.* He saw where the older players were leading his young teammates and did not want to follow.

At the same time he lived in constant terror of slipping up and somehow revealing his gay thoughts. His fear of being killed — literally — had, he believed, a concrete basis in fact: the football players' constantly threatening mantra, "If anybody's a fuckin' fag on this team, we'll kill him." He recalls that ninth-grade season as a time of both great joy and excruciating hell.

Michael's decision to drop football in tenth grade was not hard, he says. Yet he wishes in retrospect that he could have done more with the game. "I have no illusions that I could have gone pro, but it was something I really enjoyed," he says. "I still love football. Every Sunday I'm there, watching all day long."

For the next three years, Michael stayed away from school sports. He grew more and more alienated from his former jock buddies. Though he found a good new group of friends, it was not the same as before. Yet he also realized to his surprise that the football crowd's status — once viewed from outside — was not what it seemed to be while he was on the team. "When you're in that group, it's glorifying, but when you're out of it, you see that plenty of people don't like football players," he explains. As the team took the course he had expected — they were very successful on the field, less than sporting off it — he felt glad he was not part of it and congratulated himself on making the decision to leave. Looking back, he is amazed that as a sophomore he had the level of knowledge and foresight to do what he did.

"Football is *the* masculine sport in high school, *the* status symbol," he says. "It's the focus of homecoming; it brings a school together. It's played in the fall, when everything is fresh and people are full of enthusiasm. There's nothing like football in high school. But at the same time football players are — I'm speaking generally, but I think much of the time it's true — the most homophobic group on a high school campus. Football players are the only ones who use the term 'soccer fags.' It's all part of that hypermasculine atmosphere. I wish it wasn't so —

football players have status, so if they want to, they can be positive leaders — but it is."

Coaches feed that frenzy. While making exceptions for those like the freshman team coach who inspired him and his quiet head coach who unfortunately surrounded himself with loud, bullying assistants, Michael says too many football coaches' sense of superiority manifests itself by putting down anyone they deem to be weaker or less masculine than they are. "I guess it's part of the culture they grew up with, part of how they see the game and society," he theorizes. "As players move on up and become coaches, they carry that attitude along with them."

Yet dropping out of football did not end his dilemma. After an altercation with a team star, Michael carried a knife for protection. The boys shared a health class, and anytime the discussion veered toward homosexuality, Michael was petrified. His face would redden, and he was sure everyone was looking at him, discerning his secret.

When Michael entered Stockton State College in Pomona, New Jersey, he again wanted to fit in. Again he tried to do so through sports, this time rowing. Again he simultaneously loved and hated it.

"It was an incredible experience!" he says. "I thought football was tough, but this went so far beyond that. You got up at 5 A.M., did this amazingly intense training, had a special diet...it just consumed me."

Unlike football, however, the crew team had zero status on campus. No one even knew Stockton had a squad. Yet from the start Michael felt comfortable. There was a true camaraderie he never sensed on the football team; perhaps, he says, the presence of women added an important dimension.

One teammate was gay — everyone knew it, but no one spoke about it. While they appreciated him and his work ethic, they also made fun of him. Michael describes him as "comic relief, the way gay people on TV shows often are today." Still

struggling with his own sexuality, Michael tried to connect, but 149
the man rebuffed his attempts. "Neither of us was ever able to
say the word," Michael says. "There was a barrier neither of us
could get over."

Michael's crew career ended when he transferred to
Northeastern University, a large Boston school with a world-
class team. "I wasn't good enough to row in the Henley
Regatta," he laughs, "so that was it." He majored in business.
"After all, it was the '80s," he says. "I was still closeted, still a
conservative Republican. I was going to make a lot of money on
Wall Street. I couldn't wait to get my BMW."

Fast-forward to the '90s. Michael now lives in
Massachusetts, not New York. He has worked for Senator Ted
Kennedy. He drives a Honda.

Coming out took a long time, but it focused him on his life's
work. The process began during freshman year in college, but
his first steps were tentative. He scampered back in the closet
and spent two more years dating women. Finally, however, in
Boston — far from home and his fundamentalist upbringing —
Michael looked in the mirror, opened his eyes, and admitted
that he liked what he saw.

He moved to Oregon, joined Queer Nation, and became a
political activist fighting that state's antigay ballot initiative. In
Washington, D.C., he helped Senator Kennedy during the gays-
in-the-military fight. Today, back in Boston, he is an educational consultant and a national expert on safe schools.

Safe schools is a big topic throughout Massachusetts. In
1993 Governor William Weld signed the historic Gay and
Lesbian Student Rights Law, prohibiting discrimination in public schools on the basis of sexual orientation. Gay students are
guaranteed redress any time they suffer name-calling, threats of
violence, or unfair treatment. Administrators and school boards
are mandated to intervene and protect gay students.
Massachusetts students have the right to form gay-straight

alliances; in fact, schools now have the legal obligation to provide the same materials, space, financial support, publicity, and other services to those groups that they give to all other student clubs and organizations.

To help schools comply with the law and raise awareness of the special issues facing gay youth, Michael and other educational consultants run workshops and training sessions for teachers, administrators, school boards, parents, and students. From his travels around the state, he has gained intriguing insights into the differences between gay athletes and coaches and their straight counterparts.

There are even differences between gay male coaches and lesbians. The latter, Michael says, are among the easiest people to reach. Whether closeted or not, as females they are used to struggling for equal access to the facilities, programs, and respect males enjoy, so they can relate homophobia to other examples of oppression.

However, Michael rarely meets male coaches at workshops. When they do appear it is often because they were forced to. They sit sullenly, arms folded and faces frowning, sending the not-very-subtle message that this is one issue they have no interest in discussing.

No matter where in Massachusetts his safe-schools sessions are held, Michael says, the topic of football always arises. The football team — and jocks in general — are seen as major stumbling blocks to schools' abilities to become comfortable, affirming places for *all* students.

"Football players are leaders of homophobia in many schools," Michael admits. "But they also get bad raps. They *can* be reached. In fact, if you can get to just a few coaches or kids, they can make an incredible difference in a school environment. Because they are leaders, and students — even teachers — look up to them, they hold a very important key."

The way to get to them, he continues, is to show them that gay people exist in sports, as they do in all other areas of life.

The message must be, "We're on your teams. We're next to you. And we're hurting. We need places to be homophobia-free so we can keep playing, so we don't drop out, so we don't kill ourselves."

The nearly complete lack of positive role models hurts, Michael says. More women athletes have come out than men. While Greg Louganis's announcement was important, he says, "it's diving. He's not in the NBA or NFL. To get kids to see that gays are everywhere, they need to see it in 'macho' team sports."

Some people are making differences on the local level. A football coach in Salem serves as adviser to his school's gay-straight alliance. The environment there, Michael says, has "changed incredibly."

Another positive change took place at a school in southeastern Massachusetts at which the assistant principal is also the baseball coach. When he learned one spring that several players were making derogatory comments and writing graffiti about a classmate they believed to be gay, the coach hauled the boys into his office and told them that if he ever heard of such behavior again, he would call the colleges they had been accepted at and ask that their sports scholarships be revoked.

"You wouldn't do that," one dared.

The coach picked up the phone. "Try me," he challenged.

"It's incredible the influence a coach can have, either positively or negatively," Michael says. "If you set the right tone, all kinds of things can flow from that. If you say nothing, of course, it continues. Or else it gets worse."

In his workshops Michael stresses that gay athletes' issues differ even from other gay students'. "Athletes spend so much time in environments where homophobia is rampant," he says. "That's not true in a place like the drama club, where support is easier to find. I'm not saying it's easy being a gay actor — you can get harassed by other people for being in the drama club — but the homophobia on a team comes from within, from the people who supposedly are your friends. Jocks — and I was one — are the initiators of homophobia, not the receivers of it. Being an agent of homophobia, which can happen when you're closeted, causes enormous pressures on a teenager."

That's why Michael Kozuch believes so strongly in the importance of young gay athletes having out role models. Seeing a gay coach in his school would have made growing up immeasurably easier, he said. He needed to see stereotypes shattered, but there was no one around to do it.

However, his late-'90s perspective as an educational consultant makes him far more optimistic than when he stood, titillated yet terrified, in his mid-'80s football locker room. "I see more athletes and coaches coming out in the years ahead," he says. "The single most important thing any gay person can do, bar none, is to live life openly and honestly. Once that happens we'll see a change. Coming out is happening in so many areas today; it's just a matter of time before it comes around to sports. People might not think it will happen, but look out. The wave is coming, and pretty soon it's going to hit."

The Phys Ed Teacher

The popular image of the physical education teacher is not pleasant. Large clipboard-clutching men with bellies spilling over their gray shorts bark commands: for calisthenics, dividing into teams, taking showers. Their drill-sergeant personae — "You're all weak, lily-livered pansies; the only difference is that some of you are weaker and more lily-livered than others" — instill fear in all but the most supremely confident athletes, making gym the least-looked-forward-to, most-skipped class this side of math.

Like most stereotypes, it bears a kernel of truth — and much falsity. There have always been compassionate, empathic gym teachers, men who understand that not every boy can throw or catch a ball and that towel-snapping torture is not a proper rite of passage. Especially now, in the '90s, as Korean War veterans retire from teaching and children of baby boomers take their place, phys ed class is undergoing a transformation. Team sports are fading; in-line skating and step aerobics are taking their place. Coed classes have eliminated much of the misogyny that for decades passed as motivation and humor.

And some of the male physical education teachers are no longer repressing their homosexuality.

WHEN PETE DIBENEDETTO REPORTED for his first teaching assignment seven years ago, he was twenty-three years old. His desk was squeezed between those of two veteran teachers, both well past fifty; each had several children, their faces beaming from desktop photographs. The morning conversation ran to topics like "those fuckin' faggots on *In Living Color* last night." It was a rude awakening for the young teacher.

Phys ed was almost a calling for Pete (who asked that his real name not be used). Growing up in the Washington, D.C., suburbs to which he now returned, Pete had never experienced the terror of jock-oriented gym classes run by Neanderthal men. Quite the opposite, in fact: Though not the best athlete around, he had always felt accepted and appreciated by his gym teachers. They took time to teach him skills and motivated him to improve. And while he knew he was gay — a self-realization that for many males turns each PE period into an obstacle course of fear — Pete never felt threatened. Gym was always fun, so when he grew up it was natural to want to pass that pleasure on to others.

Pete's path to sports had been neither straight nor smooth. When he was young his parents signed him up for a youth football league; everyone in his family participated, and in his small town it was the thing to do. Pete was good at both offense and defense, was elected captain, and continued to play all through middle school — but he never enjoyed it. The contact, violence, and macho posturing were not for him.

"I played well, I was respected, and I was part of the football gang," he says. "No one doubted that I was one of the toughest guys around. But the social piece — the growling, the grunting, the wanting to inflict bodily harm on someone else — never felt right. It was a gross motor sport, and I liked fine motor activities. I guess I had the skill but not the mentality to be a real football player."

In eighth grade he finally weaned himself from the game. It was not easy. Soon after he stopped playing, his father remarked to another parent, "He's just chicken." The comment has stayed with Pete for nearly two decades; he still remembers exactly where he was when he heard it and with whom his father was talking. Later his father began lying to others about Pete's decision, claiming his son had back problems that prevented him from continuing. "My dad just couldn't deal with the fact that I didn't like football," Pete explains. "It would have been much easier for him if I wasn't good at it. But because I was, he had a hard time rationalizing why I wasn't playing. And, of course, at that age I was unable to communicate to him why it just wasn't for me."

Basketball had always been his favorite sport; however, he realized with frustration, he was not proficient at it. He ran track in junior high and joined a recreational volleyball league in tenth grade. But the sport that wound up giving him the most satisfaction was gymnastics. "It demanded precise technical skills," he explains. "And it was more of a loner activity."

That was about the time Pete was recognizing that in some ways he was not "normal." He made out obligatorily with girls but preferred being around boys. "I didn't necessarily want to roughhouse with them, I just wanted to spend time with them," he says. "I wanted guys as companions, friends, people I could rely on."

Privately he was praying to God for guidance or deliverance from this evil that had been visited upon him, but publicly he was sailing right along. "I was the classic overachiever," Pete says. "President of my eighth- and ninth-grade class. Student government president in eleventh grade. In the upper clique. I masked it pretty well for a while."

Because he had looked up to his gym teachers, Pete decided to major in physical education at college, a branch of the University of North Carolina. His gymnastics background led him to cheerleading, an activity he loved from the start. He enjoyed the physical aspect of it, leaping around and partnering with a smaller girl, and the social atmosphere also seemed comfortable.

"It was a gay-friendly environment," Pete says. "Most people on the team were aware that college cheerleading is stereotyped as a gay sport, but it didn't bother them at all. There were openly gay people on the team, and everyone accepted that as fine."

Pete was not one of those out cheerleaders. In fact, he did not even self-identify as gay until his senior year. He thought all gay males were effeminate — "women trapped in men's bodies" — so he told himself that his feelings meant he was bisexual. He dated and slept with women. Finally, just before graduation, he saw a gay man he knew with a date so masculine that Pete just said, "Uh-oh." That handsome man became the first male Pete ever kissed.

His other college activity, volleyball, proved just as satisfying as cheerleading. Because he is not tall — five foot nine — Pete primarily played back-row defense. "It's like being a soccer goalkeeper," he explains. "You're agile, you have to dive and sprawl. You get the ball up to the front guys, who are six foot four and really appreciate the work you do for them." His rapport with his volleyball teammates was good. They knew he was a cheerleader and were fully aware of that sport's stereotype, but no one ever made a flip comment or caused him discomfort.

Despite having experienced tremendous inner turmoil, Pete considers his college days his best times ever. He felt he was constantly growing, always doing and learning something new. He had many good friends. If he had those years to do over, he says, the only thing he would change is coming out sooner. The first person he told was a female friend during senior year. The night he came out to her as gay, she came out to him as a lesbian. It took a bit longer before Pete found the courage to tell his roommate, a fellow cheerleader who tried to deny the sport's stereotype by adopting a supermacho attitude. Ironically, that man now lives in Greenwich Village and participates in AIDS walks and similar activities. "He's not gay, but he's grown a lot," Pete says.

"I've been lucky," he adds, "or maybe it's the activities I've chosen. But whatever it is, I always seem to be surrounded by gay-friendly people. I know that wouldn't have been the case if I'd stayed in football."

Pete's first job out of college was with one of the largest school districts in the country, just outside Washington, D.C. He was hired as the only physical education instructor for a 450-student elementary school; in addition, he coached both boys' and girls' varsity volleyball at a nearby high school and was county coordinator for all cheerleaders. He felt thrown into a vortex — and he loved it.

He also made a conscious decision not to come out of the closet at work.

His reasons are complex. Though he is protected by a strong union and his county's antidiscrimination clause includes sexual orientation, Pete decided that being an openly gay physical education teacher — at the elementary school where he began, the middle school where he now works, or in any of his other positions, including coordinator of health and family life curricula — was a battle he did not want to fight.

"Too many people connect homosexuality with pedophilia," he says. "If I came out, there would be this focus on the fact that I'm in the locker room with their sons every day. Parents can be completely unobjective when it comes to their kids. They already make seventeen excuses why their child didn't do his homework, so just think what they would say about a gay phys ed teacher in the locker room with their kid. I do too many good things every day. I don't want to jeopardize that."

Two of those good things take place in the locker room itself. One is supervision: He makes sure no one is ever teased, taunted, or otherwise terrorized for having any type of difference. The other is saying something every day before students leave for their next class. His words can be as simple as "Be nice" or as strong as "Today praise two classmates for good things they do — and don't criticize anyone for anything." Whatever the message, he makes sure he imparts it to each class.

Pete's greatest fear is that coming out would cause him to be moved out of the classroom to an administrative position. "They'd call it a promotion, saying that because I'm Teacher of the Year, I'd make a great assistant principal at school X," he says. "But I love teaching. It's clearly what I was meant to do."

That does not mean he will never come out. He envisions a day when he does become an administrator and then reveals his homosexuality — being "postjudged" rather than prejudged, to use his term. It intrigues him that at that point students and their families might look back and say, "Mr. DiBenedetto? Gay? I never knew!" That, he believes, would help demolish stereotypes more than coming out now would; today, he says, the probable result would be a major controversy he does not wish to become involved in. He knows he may be exaggerating his fears — "There might be only a handful of people who have a problem with it," he admits — but he feels he has not been around long enough to take the chance.

His decision not to come out publicly hardly means that no one knows. He is certain some colleagues have figured things out, though no one has yet raised the subject explicitly. Of the four principals he has worked with, three — all women — have tacitly broached gay issues with Pete and let him know that they are supportive. (He has seen a son of one of those women at a Washington gay bar.) The only principal who has been "a jerk" is a male.

Administrators and coworkers may know that Pete is gay because he never hides his participation in activities like AIDS walks. He posts fund-raising notices in faculty rooms and defends gay issues whenever they arise in staff meetings. In conferences with parents about curriculum items, he says, "Like it or not, some of your kids will grow up to be gay or lesbian. I will not tolerate a negative atmosphere in our classrooms about these things."

Pete describes his attitude this way: "I'm not hiding anything, but I'm not screaming about anything either. I assume that by this time people know." Colleagues have long since stopped trying to fix him up with females, and when he is invited out socially, he is usually told to bring his "roommate" along. He does.

"I don't know what it would mean for me to 'come out' publicly," Pete protests. "Would I send a memo? Make an announcement over the intercom? As it is right now, I don't hide. If somebody, whether it's a parent or kid, asks flat out if I'm married or seeing someone, I tell him or her, 'I don't discuss my personal life with you, and I won't ask you to either.' I've reached a point in my personal life where the questions are asked less and less, so I think it's ceased to matter. I'm not out per se, but I'm also not pretending to be someone I'm not."

Nonetheless, as a volleyball coach, physical education teacher, and administrator dealing with health and family life, Pete knows that gay and lesbian issues are on students' minds. On his volleyball team "faggot" or "gay" is the worst put-down his players know. (Interestingly, he has never heard a female athlete call another girl "dyke.")

He has learned to turn a deaf ear to most banter. "When a boy calls another guy 'fag' and the second one says, 'I don't think so' with an exaggerated lisp, that's playful," Pete maintains. "I don't consider it harmful or hurtful. I've become desensitized to it. Kids are kids; they're not yet the people they will be later in life."

However, when he senses the barbs are aimed at a youngster who may in fact be dealing with sexuality issues, he intervenes. He addresses everyone within earshot, telling them it is not right to purposely harm someone else. That happens more often in elementary and middle school phys ed locker rooms than on high school sports teams; it is a function of age and maturity. In addition, he notes, he knows his interscholastic athletes better than his PE students, so it is easier to determine when the line between lighthearted joshing and deliberate cruelty has been crossed.

He believes he has a good sense of which youngsters will turn out to be (or already are) gay. "I see the MO," he says confidently. "I know who I'll be meeting in a bar soon." He treats those boys differently from the straight ones: He is both easier and tougher on them. He protects them from some abuse but at the same time gives them opportunities to fend for themselves. "This is a straight world," Pete explains. "I want them to be able to hold their own place in it." He feels a special responsibility to help those who are his phys ed students succeed in the real world. "I make sure they have the physical skills to compete with other guys," the instructor says. "I think every kid should know how to shoot a basketball and hit a baseball. I take extra care to see that those kids can do that."

Pete knows that many gay men have had horrible experiences in locker rooms and during phys ed classes. He himself did not, but he feels a special mission to make certain no student from his school will one day look back in anger at gym class or gym teachers. "Every child will learn, and every child will have a good time here," he says determinedly. "We want all kids to be turned on to sports, not turned off." To make that a reality, he instructs all teachers to assign teams personally (the best athletes cannot pick them) and to patrol the locker room carefully.

His concern encompasses all potential outcasts, not only gay youth — for example, overweight children. Pete's grading policy differs from most phys ed teachers': Instead of giving A's for top accomplishments and lower marks for lesser achievements, he asks each child to set individual goals, then grades accordingly. When a good athlete once protested that obese boys and girls could earn high grades in phys ed, using the analogy "Smart kids get A's in math, and dumb ones get F's," Pete responded, "That's true, but it doesn't make it right. I grade the right way." He notes that he does give poor grades to heavy children — but only if they do not try.

It has taken Pete several years to reach the point he is at today, where he can run his locker room and classes the way he wants. For the first few years of his career, he worked for people he did not respect: the tobacco-chewing, sedentary, cursing-and-mocking stereotypes of his profession.

Gradually he became confident enough to voice proposals for change. One winter he suggested that instead of separating classes by sex — the boys going off to wrestle, the girls doing aerobics — they split the time instead. First all would wrestle — together — then all would do aerobics. A male colleague asked, "But who will the girls wrestle?"

"Other girls," Pete replied logically. His fellow teacher stared at him as if he had three heads but ultimately acquiesced. "I think he recognized that I as a young person had new ideas, and he at least had the intelligence to consider them," Pete explains.

Now at the point where he can hire the people he wants and institute his own reforms, Pete has become a public advocate for a new style of physical education. (Pete never utters the word "gym," calling it "a building, not a class.") PE, he says, is an equal-opportunity educational event. "We teach every child: white, black, Hispanic, male, female, straight, gay," he says. "I see every boy, every day, coming through that locker room. That's a powerful thing. We can abuse kids in that situation, or we can make their day a little better. My hope is that no matter what any particular kid looks like or thinks, we help that kid think better of himself or herself."

Growing up gay has had a major influence on his career, Pete admits. "It's made me not a competent teacher or a good teacher but a *great* teacher," he says. "I do things with kids very few other people can do. I think you have to suffer yourself before you can sympathize with others. I suffered — not a lot, but I played a sport I didn't like, and I spent time worrying because I couldn't stop looking at the guy next to me on the bench. I watched guys get picked on for being gay when I knew I was exactly like them and wasn't getting picked on. The only difference was that I was on a team.

"I didn't stand up for those kids then, but I can stand up for them now," Pete continues. "I know what being a member of a minority is. I want all minorities in my classes to have a significant physical education experience. A straight teacher doesn't know what it's like to be a minority. Yet at the same time I have the luxury as a white man to live in the majority. That's why I can deliver the program that I do and why it's so important to me to keep doing that. I *can* do it, so I will."

The Quiet High School Athletes

Many readers will no doubt be drawn first to the big stories in this book: those filled with drama, controversy, the occasional fistfight or firing. Playing sports, after all, is about conflict.

But playing sports is also about learning to compete quietly and win gracefully, and it is in those realms that one finds many more tales — less remarkable than the headline stories, perhaps, but just as important. They are worth including too, because by their very unremarkableness they show how far the issue of gays in athletics has come.

Here, then, are a few brief tales of gay high school student-athletes doing ordinary things every day. Some are out to all or some of their teammates and coaches; others are not. But whatever their degree of openness, being gay scarcely affects their contributions to their teams or prevents them from enjoying sports.

Come to think of it, that's pretty remarkable in itself.

EVERY FALL GREG MORISSE GOT DEPRESSED. With no sport to play and plenty of time on his hands, the Bloomfield, Connecticut, high school student was forced to examine the Big Questions of Life. The answer to one — "Who am I?" — was particularly disconcerting. Greg was gay and figured that meant he was destined to spend the rest of his life alone.

Winter was always better. The tall ponytailed boy played volleyball, surrounding himself with teammates who liked him for who he was. He enjoyed the comradeship, the sense of working together for a common goal. He gained confidence that he was a good person.

Over the years, as the Bloomfield volleyball team grew closer, got better, and neared its goals, Greg's confidence soared. By his senior year he was able to face the realization that he was gay with hope, not fear. He understood that being gay did not mean he was a bad person. On the contrary — he felt great.

For years, until high school, Greg considered himself a nerd. **163**
He was picked on by others for being smart or wearing braces;
he picked on himself for feeling attracted to males. But as a
Bloomfield freshman he lucked out: Eight volleyball-playing
seniors had graduated the previous spring, and Greg and his
ninth-grade teammates were seen as the talented replacements.

Meanwhile, Greg's struggle with his sexuality was particularly intense. He made up his mind to switch and be straight. For
three months he dated a girl. They were soul mates; he felt fulfilled. At the same time he realized he could not live a lie.
Without telling her why, Greg broke up with her. The realization that he had caused another person pain was especially hard
for him and intensified his belief that he would live the rest of
his life without loving anyone.

For the next two years, he focused on schoolwork and volleyball. But as a senior he became infatuated with a male student
and realized that it was time to face up to his sexual reality. He
came out to several friends and one English teacher; all were
supportive. He then told his former girlfriend, who was "extra-
ordinarily accepting and helpful." When Greg came out to his
parents in a letter, they too were very affirming. "Everyone was
totally wonderful right from the start," he says. "It's like a dream
come true to have such a great situation."

A fellow student, an out lesbian, took Greg to Hartford's
Your Turf support group, where he met other gay youths. For
the first time he understood that he would not have to be alone
forever. He attended his first gay pride parades, in Hartford and
New York, and was overwhelmed with excitement.

During his whirlwind senior year, however, he did not come
out to his volleyball teammates. Part of him wanted to — he
knew they would accept him easily — but another part held
back. The team was focused on winning the state championship,
and Greg did not want to do anything that might cause a dis-
traction. So he said nothing outright, though he learned later
that some players heard about him from friends. (As he expect-

ed, they had no problem with the news.) The team fell short of its goal, dropping a hard-fought match in the state quarterfinals, but Greg felt good about his own and the team's performance as well as his handling of the entire situation all season long.

In fact, he did come out to his coaches, both of them math teachers he had had in class. Greg told them one day before heading off to a Your Turf meeting; they pledged their unqualified support.

Greg offers a few reasons for the solid reactions of his teammates and coaches. One is that they appreciated him on the volleyball court before learning he was gay. "They could see I wasn't an effeminate, flippy, hairdresser-type person," he says. "They knew me well and liked me, so when they found out I was gay, it wasn't like I was someone different than before."

In addition, he explains, volleyball is a true team sport. "In soccer, theoretically one person can run down the whole field and score," he says. "In basketball, the same. But no matter how well I set the ball, I still have to get it to a hitter. Everyone relies on everyone else and knows you need teammates to get the job done. It doesn't matter what your teammates are like so long as they can play volleyball."

And, he adds, volleyball players are often more intelligent than athletes in other sports. "My coaches always say you need brains to play volleyball," Greg says. "You have to have court awareness and anticipation and be able to figure out all sorts of problems very quickly."

Though his sexual orientation did not influence his choice of volleyball as a favorite pastime — "When I was younger I didn't even want to think about being gay," he says — Greg realizes his good fortune in picking a game played by intelligent people and coached by open-minded men. "I see other coaches in our school who are like, 'Do as I say or run fifty laps,' " he says. "In volleyball the coaches chew my face off if I make a mistake, but they do it in an intelligent, supportive way. They're not so right-wing that they don't see individuals for who they are."

Volleyball has brought Greg much success. As a sophomore he was named his team's most improved player; for three years he made the All-State squad and for two years was involved in both the Junior Olympics and Connecticut Nutmeg State Games. He plays whenever he can, luxuriating in the good feeling of jumping, hitting, and working in tandem with teammates who like him.

But the most important thing he has gotten out of volleyball is more intangible than any trophy or plaque, more long-lasting than memories. Volleyball gave Greg Morisse friends who care, the confidence to be himself, and the realization that no one should live life alone.

Growing up gay in suburban Connecticut is one thing. Doing it in heavily Mormon southeastern Idaho is another indeed.

"Keith" (who asked that his real name not be used) did just that. He was a football player for a brief time, a high school skier for longer. Though sports and school were fine, his home life was not.

The town Keith lived in from age five to eighteen had just 1,000 people. Everyone attended church every Sunday, everyone made sure every picket on every fence was painted white, and everyone knew everyone else's business. Or tried to.

Keith started experimenting with sex the summer before seventh grade; that was the first time he realized he was gay. But he kept the news to himself, despite fooling around with ski teammates. To this day he does not know how many were gay and how many simply liked "experimenting." But he does know he enjoyed the opportunities he had during those ski trips. "I didn't feel guilty then," he says. "It felt so right and perfect."

However, the next day his Mormon upbringing, with its clear condemnation of homosexuality and strong promise of hell, kicked in. He never raced well after having sex.

That bothered Keith, because the ski team was his favorite high school activity. "I love winter sports," he explains. "Skiing is a team competition, but you're on your own." Slalom and giant slalom races offered a chance to get away from school and have fun. Winning was less important than simply being on the mountain.

In that respect skiing was a lot different from football, which he played in junior high. He loved games but hated practice, especially in the heat, and quit in high school. He expected that would make his father upset, and it did.

The first place Keith saw an openly gay person was not Idaho. It was San Francisco, where in the winter of 1996 he participated in a high school journalism convention. Keith went by himself — not even his adviser could go — so as soon as the required meetings were over, he took off exploring. He had read *The Culture of Desire* a short while before — a sociological work about contemporary gay life — and was eager to find the gay community that author Frank Browning so evocatively described. Those adventurous few days in San Francisco convinced him it was time to come out.

The first person Keith told was his best friend. He chose a peculiar venue — church — but her reaction stunned him: "I always knew you were, but that's cool. You're my friend." He gradually told others; after he gave a speech in government class explaining exactly why he favored the legalization of gay marriage, everyone in school knew. Though he expected to be shunned, no one cared — not even the "cowboys." He had spent most of his life in his small town; everyone knew him and liked him (besides ski team and journalism, he was president of the speech team, vice president of the debate team, and editor of both the newspaper and broadcast program). This latest information was not enough to change their feelings about him, even if the Mormon church branded him a sinner.

Keith's father was a Mormon leader, which meant that despite the church's focus on family, he was often away from his own. That particularly upset Keith's mother, who had converted to Mormonism when she married his father, and was one of the primary reasons his parents did what few Mormon couples do: They divorced.

Keith came out to his father and stepmother somewhat involuntarily in April 1996. Someone searched his large walk-in closet and discovered gay books — lying on their sides on the top shelf. His parents confronted him about what they called his "gender-identity problem" (they could not say the word "gay") and sent him to a church counselor.

The Mormon belief in "moral cleanliness" prohibits homosexuality, sex before marriage, even masturbation. The only exception, Keith learned, is masturbating to female pornography in an attempt to cure male homosexuality. "It's a secretive program," he explains. "There are a lot of secrets in the Mormon Church."

In that same spring of 1996, gay issues flooded the Mormon news. Salt Lake City student Kelli Peterson had tried to form a gay-straight alliance at East High School; legislators attempted to stop it by banning all extracurricular clubs. On his trips to Salt Lake, four hours south of his Idaho home, Keith met Kelli. They became good friends.

Through her, Keith met several sports-minded guys. Many were gay. One 23-year-old came from the same small town as Keith; in fact, he had once dated the same girl as Keith. The two young men held hands in a car until the older one said, "Don't act like you're gay." That appalled Keith.

"I can't date people like that," he explains. "He's a big jock — a football player and bodybuilder. His father works for a Mormon college, and his parents don't know about him. I don't have time for people who worry about things like that."

Keith has met many gay jocks who, fearful of losing friends and respect, try to stay in the closet. Slowly, however, some have begun to come out.

"People are becoming more accepting, even in Idaho and Utah," he says. "This really is the gay '90s. That's why I came out. I figure if they can't accept me, too bad. It took me only two weeks to go from 'No, I'm not' to 'Yes, I am. Do you have a problem with it?' I guess I finally snapped. I just decided I wanted to live life and be who I wanted to be. More and more of the gay jocks I know have the same attitude: 'Don't be a flamer, just be yourself.' You can be a jock, be masculine, and still be gay. Flaunting just isn't the way I am, and it's not the way most jocks are."

At six foot seven and 260 pounds, Durwin Leonard looks like the basketball player he is. But his extreme soft-spokenness — you must strain to hear him — belies the stereotype of the big, hard-driving hoops center. Durwin is also a gymnast. And he is gay.

Durwin (who asked that his real name not be used) was born in the Midwest and was adopted by two doctors when he was just two weeks old. His adoptive parents moved to Washington, D.C., where he attended an elite private school. When he was in second grade, his parents enrolled him in Little League baseball (which he never liked) and youth basketball (which he eventually did).

His third-grade coach was hard on him because Durwin was the biggest boy on the team. When Durwin sprained his ankle, the man made him do endless push-ups in lieu of jumping rope. That caused him to rip muscles in his arm; the skin split at the elbows. Further complications led to a kidney disorder, and Durwin was hospitalized.

After he finished fifth grade, his parents moved to Chicago, where he became more serious about sports. However, athletics occupied a less prestigious niche at his new school. He was glad to return to Washington in 1993, before ninth grade, because interscholastic sports was again a big deal. Though already six foot five, he was placed on the freshman team to refine his skills. In the spring he tried throwing the shot put and discus for the track team and liked it; his coach liked it too, especially when Durwin hurled the discus a substantial 119 feet.

That summer Durwin was invited to join a Junior Amateur Athletic Union basketball team. The squad traveled to Florida and Washington State. Durwin's interest in the sport bloomed.

When he was a sophomore, school became more hectic, but his involvement with athletics grew. He played varsity basketball. The demanding winter turned even more stressful, because that was the year he came out. His parents believe homosexuality is bad — "Not out of malice or hatred but because that's how they grew up," Durwin says. Fearing he was destined for hell, he attempted suicide.

His mother and father took him to a psychiatrist. All the while he continued playing on his school team. "Don't ask me how, but my game got better, and my grades went up," Durwin says. He was practicing three to four hours a day, six days a week. Each night after basketball he spent several hours on homework.

However, those athletic and academic improvements did not last. Durwin had fantasized that coming out would solve all his problems; he would feel more comfortable with himself, and the people close to him would change too. That did not happen, and his basketball game soon declined.

Rumors about Durwin swept the small school. Though there was a gay-straight alliance on campus, he did not feel comfortable attending meetings. There were no fellow athletes he could talk to either. That made him feel especially bad. "I thought a team was supposed to be unified," he says. "I always heard there is no *I* in *team*."

Before one game, while the trainer taped his ankle, Durwin overheard his teammates talking about him. Their comments were not kind. That upset him greatly. For the first time he realized his teammates were not his friends.

However, Durwin finally confided in his coach and found him to be supportive. He took the tormented player aside from time to time for long, confidence-boosting talks. "I give that man a lot of credit," Durwin says with emotion. "He told me I was more than a gay person, that sexuality is only one part of a human being. He's a very caring, sensitive person." But despite his new ally, Durwin did not feel better. Everyone else in school — including his basketball teammates — was making him feel worse.

In the midst of all this turmoil, Durwin's parents were divorcing. He moved in with his father, but that did not work out well. With so much on his mind that spring, Durwin did not go out for track, opting instead to serve as assistant manager of the girls' lacrosse team.

Feeling betrayed by his teammates, Durwin figured he was through with basketball forever. To put his past behind him, he applied to boarding schools. One of the very best in the nation accepted him.

That summer he worked two jobs, at a drugstore and teaching English as a second language to elementary school students. In the fall he left for his new school filled with enthusiasm. From everything he had heard, it was an open and accepting place.

His first week there the basketball coach sought him out and convinced him to play. He luxuriated in not having to tell his fellow students he was gay; there were plenty of others like him around. He made many friends and for the first time in his life felt part of a school community. He was the starting center for the basketball team (which finished a strong third in the league), and his sexuality was never an issue. However, a few members of the dorm staff made life hard for Durwin. Torn between a desire to stay in school and an overwhelming feeling that his safety could not be assured, he decided to move back home — this time with his mother.

It was not a good decision. At his new school he signed up for modern and African dance. His mother did not feel the arts were an appropriate course of study, especially for a young man of his size. As their relationship deteriorated Durwin began taking drugs. Finally he left home and moved in with a female dancer.

Eventually Durwin discovered acrobatic gymnastics. For as long as he can remember, he has been fascinated by movement; however, it took a decade for him to find a sport that emphasized it. He joined a good club team with a Russian coach. He lost weight and gained muscles. Within a few months he entered a qualifying meet for a national tournament. He missed by just a

few points, but that did not matter. Durwin was finally content. **171**
His grades soared. He scored 1320 on his SATs and considered
graduating early.

On looking back, Durwin says, he probably should have
focused on an individual sport from the start. "I didn't fit in with
the rest of the people," he explains. "I'm a pretty passive person.
If I want to, I can kick everyone's ass, but I don't think that's the
right way to live. I'm stereotyped as a jock because I'm so big, but
my life is so much more than that. I like computers and going to
clubs. People don't always see that when they look at me. I think
stereotyping someone for any reason — the sports they like or
the people they find attractive — is bad. Everyone should be free
just to do what they want. What's so hard about that?"

An articulate, earnest young man, Ben Claydon has no problem being gay. But his acceptance has come at a heavy price:
Twice he was kicked out of his house, the last time permanent-
ly. To support himself while living on the streets, he sold drugs.
But through it all he has maintained his dignity, held on to his
pride, and played sports.

Ben attended Southern California public schools until ninth
grade; then his parents sent him to a tiny (ninety students) private school. His early years had been filled with confusion. "I
grew up watching cartoons in which the princes always get the
princesses," he recalls. "The guys in my school always got the
girls. But my parents were pretty conservative, and at home we
never talked about anything. I couldn't tell them what was going
on in my mind."

In junior high he was constantly angry for reasons he could
not fathom. He bottled up his feelings for weeks at a time; then
he would lash out and fight. When he reached high school and
attempted to sort out why he felt the way he did, he blamed his
father and mother. He tried to alter the way he acted. But because
he did not acknowledge the real cause of his confusion — his sexuality concerns — not much changed.

"I was a leader in school; I was on the soccer, lacrosse, and volleyball teams; but still I didn't fit in," Ben says. "I dressed differently, and I acted differently. Guys on teams always seem to know how to talk to each other, tease each other, get on the other team's case. I didn't know how to do any of that." Unsure of himself in adolescent-athlete situations, he had two distinct personalities. At times he remained quiet and shy; at other times he exploded in anger. "That was the wrong way to deal with my confusion," he explains, "but it was the only way I knew."

Upon reflection, Ben realizes that the reason he did not know how to act among peers was that during the long period they were learning about social relationships, he was too busy dealing with his own sexuality issues. Finally, in his last two years of high school, he figured out the root of his problems. At that point he started becoming "socially acceptable," a process that did not entail changing his behavior but simply being himself. Once he grew comfortable with who he was, others saw him as "more normal." The fights stopped; the friends flocked to him.

Though out at school, Ben never flaunted his homosexuality. For one thing, that is not his style. For another, he does not think sexuality is something to shove in people's faces. "It's not right to show off your wealth, is it?" he asks. "Well, sexuality is the same thing."

The first sport Ben was attracted to, back in elementary school, was soccer. His classmates, predominantly children of Mexican migrant workers, played the game all the time, and he enjoyed it too. But he did not consider himself an athlete until private school. Every student was required to play sports. He decided reluctantly to make the best of things, but the more he played, the more he enjoyed himself.

He found soccer to be more gay-friendly than "very jock-o" lacrosse. But no matter which team he was on, Ben never felt out of place because he was gay. One reason, he says, is that his habits and mannerisms are "stereotypically straight." He walks, talks, and dresses exactly like his teammates; no one would pick him out of a crowd. "Some people act one way when they're in a gay coffeehouse and another way in other situations," he says. "I can't do that. I act the same way all the time — the way I was brought up to act by growing up in a straight society. Most gay people grow up the same way I do, but then, when they come out, they jump headfirst into the gay community. I pretty much stayed in straight society."

That does not always sit well with his gay friends. "Sometimes they say I'm not one of them because I'm interested in sports, or they say I'm hiding being gay because I don't act a certain way," he says. He often finds straight friends more accepting than gays: "Straight people see me as a normal person doing normal activities, which is fine with them, but if gay people see me not doing gay stuff, they make comments or get mad." That is one reason Ben spends most of his time hanging out with straight friends. At times he "feels" gay only when he has sex.

"I like to hang out with gay guys for a change of pace and because that's who I'm attracted to sexually," he says. "But I also like girls and straight guys. I like people. I like soccer. I like lacrosse and volleyball and biking. There's lots of parts to me. I don't pigeonhole people, and I don't want them to pigeonhole me."

The Organizer

Many boys who grow up to be gay know from an early age that they are "different"; in fact, that knowledge predates any identification with sexuality. Feeling different in any manner is excruciating for most youngsters; for gay youths, sometimes the only way to exist is by developing subconscious coping mechanisms.

Some gay youngsters cope by being overachievers: The boy who is simultaneously class president, honor student, all-state musician, and king of extracurricular clubs earns kudos for his otherworldly accomplishments, all of which naturally leave no time for dating. Other children cope by underachieving: If all the adults in his life become focused on his low grades and poor attendance, no one will ever probe into the true cause of his unhappiness. Some gay youths cope by becoming sexually promiscuous (what better way to deflect attention from one's gayness than to have multiple opposite-sex partners?); others abuse alcohol or drugs (what better way to numb the pain?). Too many adapt the ultimate coping mechanism: suicide.

Athletics offers yet another means of coping. A boy who plays sports automatically rises a notch or two above his peers on the social pecking ladder. Athletics is widely seen as a healthy way to express youthful energy — and no one has a greater need to run around and act aggressive than a tormented, secretive gay child. Besides, since most people think gay boys don't like sports, the finger of suspicion seldom wags at those on the playing field.

Of course gay males play sports. But not every one is attracted to athletics from an early age. Making the leap from "differentness" — expressed, perhaps, as solitariness or engaging in gender-atypical activities — to that ultimate bastion of maleness, sports, is not easy. Once the gap is bridged, however, an entirely new world opens up.

ON THE FACE OF THINGS, Jeff Pike should always have been an athlete. He grew up on the University of Connecticut campus —

specifically, on its playing fields. His father served twenty-six 175 years as head athletic trainer there; the soccer and football stadiums, basketball court, and hockey rink were Jeff's second homes. He understood the rhythms of the sports seasons; he knew how locker rooms smelled, athletes bantered, and coaches yelled; he heard the roars of crowds and saw the adulation athletes received.

Yet it took Jeff many years before he considered himself one. As a child, he says, he was "the fruity, fairy type." All through elementary school he did "traditional female things": He sang, performed in plays, drew in the art room — and hung around with girls. He had no male friends.

He did have mad crushes on university athletes in a variety of sports, including football, soccer, and basketball. He loved seeing them train and play; he also enjoyed watching the cheerleaders. He would mimic their routines in his living room, always stopping when someone came in.

Despite his parents' athletic interests, they were not concerned about his disinterest in sports. They supported him as he did his own thing; he never sensed disappointment in him or his behavior.

However, as Jeff grew older, he felt it from another, more important source: his male classmates. "While everyone else was out protesting the war in T-shirts and blue jeans," he says with some exaggeration, "I was wearing these bright, wild Bobby Sherman clothes. I was this happy kid, until they all started making fun of me." That was during seventh grade, in the early '70s.

Jeff reacted by censoring himself. He became acutely aware of every action: how he walked and talked, whom he spent time with, what he did with them. He abandoned his dream of becoming a performer or artist. But he did it all without anger. "Instead of getting mad at people who were turning on me, I decided to beat them at their own game," he says. That game, of course, was sports. Jeff realized that, with the exception of throwing, he could perform any athletic endeavor better than other boys. He found a new niche and became a different person.

For as long as he could remember, Jeff had suffered from low self-esteem. Suddenly, as his involvement in sports bloomed, so did his confidence. "I never knew I could have such physical strength," he says. "I got this great feeling of power from what my body looked like." That power was fueled, he admits, by a sense of revenge. He was winning at the other boys' own games.

As he played soccer and ice hockey, as he ran track and swam, he surprised himself by actually enjoying the physical activity. It was a welcome release from frustration, a socially approved way of letting off steam. If the coach said, "Run as fast as you can," he ran faster. Chasing down, controlling, then passing a soccer ball provided overwhelming feelings of physical power, technical accomplishment, even emotional achievement. Because he was playing with talented athletes, his skills improved dramatically; that too added to his growing self-confidence.

Jeff now knows that another factor helped explain his new-found sense of enjoyment. "Games have rules," he notes. "I knew how to play within the rules. That wasn't true of the rest of my life, where I had no clue how to 'play.' I'd spent all my time up to that point saying to myself, *If I'm such a good person, why am I being treated so poorly?* With sports I knew exactly what I could do and what I couldn't do, and those were on the exact same terms as everyone else."

E. O. Smith High School, with its highly regarded faculty and a student body made up in part of many sons and daughters of University of Connecticut professors, was a great experience for Jeff. A self-described "big fish in a small pond," he played for excellent coaches, enjoyed the respect of fellow athletes, and tasted a fair amount of success. "I was doing something very healthy and getting positive feedback for it," he says. "I wasn't a great athlete, but I felt like I was an important part of the teams I was on. My confidence grew, and so did my physical abilities and strength." The soccer team was particularly successful; paced by Joey and Billy Morrone, Tom Nevers, and Jim Lyman, all of whom went on to star at the University of Connecticut, the E. O. Smith Panthers gained statewide notice.

But sports was not all Jeff did. He had the lead role in several school plays, he sang in the chorus, his artwork hung on the walls, and he earned straight A's. He also worked a paper route starting at 5:30 A.M. After practices, games, and homework, it is no wonder he fell into bed most evenings by 9. He never dated, though he managed to find dates for the few big high school events he attended.

While his teammates respected his athletic skills and work ethic and he felt comfortable with them on bus rides and in locker rooms, Jeff did not spend what little free time he had with them. He ate lunch with a small group of friends; they were dateless together and always had a good time. Today, he says, "eight or nine" have come out as gay or lesbian.

But in the mid '70s not one of them knew about anyone else. The only person in town who suspected Jeff's secret was the first boy with whom he fooled around — in fifth grade. Later that same year, the day after their sex ed class discussed homosexuality, the boy suddenly and viciously taunted him on the school bus. Jeff was devastated. But throughout junior high and high school, he remained above suspicion. Even the boys who derided him as "fairy" and "fruitcake" never called him "faggot," an important distinction to him. He might be gayish, he consoled himself, but he definitely was not gay.

The E. O. Smith swim team used the university's pool for practices and meets. One night during Jeff's senior year, he noticed an attractive man in the locker room. The two men looked each other up and down; without even knowing the term, Jeff was cruising him.

As electricity leaped between them, they talked. The man, a university student, offered to drive Jeff home. Completely forgetting that his sister was waiting to give him a ride, Jeff agreed. The only reason he did not leave with his new friend was that she came running up to him outside.

Two days later, in an empty school hallway, Jeff's track coach motioned him over. "So I hear you met my roommate," the coach said. He then told Jeff that his roommate was gay. Jeff's face turned red with embarrassment, but his coach's words were kind. To this day, two decades later, Jeff remembers them. The man told Jeff that if he wanted to hang out with the roommate, he probably should talk with his father to figure out what it all meant. Uncertain even of the source of his confusion, Jeff never broached the subject with his father. To his relief the coach never raised the subject again, but Jeff always sensed he could talk with him about it. "I have great affection for track because of him!" Jeff laughs.

After graduation Jeff headed to Boston University. He graduated in 1980, but it took thirteen more years before he finally admitted to himself why he selected a school in that city. It was because the man he met at the University of Connecticut pool had gone there after college to become a nurse.

Minutes after his parents dropped him off freshman year, Jeff began searching for the man. In four years at BU he never found him. Recently, however, they reconnected and discovered to their amazement that they had lived near each other during Jeff's first year.

Jeff ran track as a freshman, but the team featured several world-class athletes, and though he sliced several seconds off his personal bests, he came nowhere close to winning. Jeff's coaches were knowledgeable, but he realized he was not cut out to be a BU athlete. He played a bit of soccer, then turned his attention to intramurals.

During this time he began coming out on campus. Deciding "since I'm gay, I might as well do gay things," he returned to his earlier dream of becoming a dancer. But sports still held a strong allure, and in the summer of his junior year he discovered Boston's booming gay softball and volleyball leagues. Though he never mastered the mechanics of throwing, he was an excellent hitter and fielder; in addition to his athletic skills, he was recognized as a superb problem solver and quickly became a leader in the city's gay sports scene. He wrote the Beantown Softball League constitution and organized fund-raisers for his team and AIDS organizations.

Gay sports were the vehicle by which Jeff entered the gay community. Once he felt confident there, he threw himself into the Gay Games. He served as president of the entire Team Boston contingent for both the 1986 event, held in San Francisco, and the 1990 games in Vancouver, Canada. He was a medal-winning swimmer, a volleyball athlete, and a dance performer. But after the 1990 games he burned out as an organizer and focused his energy on playing for Boston's gay soccer team. He remains active with the games, however, as a board member of the Gay Games Federation and chairman of its cultural committee.

The Gay Games had an important effect on Jeff. "They uplifted and inspired me and so many other people," he says. "They would be a tremendous success even if they were held in a cornfield in Iowa. People have the experience of a lifetime, competing and achieving athletically as gay men and women. That's true in many respects of all gay sports. In athletics people are able to find new confidence that they then use in facing other parts of their lives."

Sports — an activity Jeff came to embrace only after other parts of his life were not working — has shaped the way he lives today. Athletics showed him his power to accept challenges and overcome obstacles on and off the field. "The rules were always the same, which I appreciated, but each new situation required me to be spontaneous," he explains. "The more games I play, the more situations I realize I can control and ultimately win at. That's the lesson I try to share with other gay athletes: Go in, play, make mistakes, recover, use what you learn, and keep going."

Was the closeted Jeff Pike, a youngster who grew up in a sports family and discovered his athleticism relatively late, different from a similar youth who might today live near a college campus, questioning or doubting his own sexuality? "Yes and no," he replies. "No, because the anxieties and fears of being a teenager will always be there. Those feelings will always keep a child from being who he wants to be until he decides on his own that he wants to try something else."

But the similarities pale when compared with the differences between yesterday and today. "The world in general is so much more aware now of gay people," Jeff concludes. "Everyone knows we exist, that we play sports, and that we're good athletes. There are so many more opportunities for gay athletes to participate in sports today, and so many more athletes are taking those opportunities, no questions asked. I see a lot of hope."

The Catholic School Girls' Coach

One of the enduring myths about homosexuality is that gay men hate women. In fact, many gay men feel more comfortable socializing with females than they do with males. They form strong, deep friendships with members of the opposite sex in ways straight men and women seldom do.

Another myth is that gay male coaches use their position of authority and power to indoctrinate or otherwise influence young boys. In fact, plenty of gay men do not even coach males; they work in women's athletics. Men — gay and straight — coach females for a variety of reasons. They like the fact that because women's sports were ignored or marginalized for so long, the opportunities for growth are great. They appreciate working with females who, compared with male athletes, are far more willing to listen and take instruction, far less apt to cop an attitude. And, quite simply, they enjoy being around the opposite sex.

That, in a nutshell, is the story of Mike Bryant. That he is a gay man coaching women is intriguing. However, that does not make him unique.

FOR AS LONG AS HE CAN REMEMBER, most of Mike Bryant's friends were girls. They still are.

Growing up in suburban Seattle, he played junior high and high school basketball — of course, as a six-foot-tall twelve-year-old, that would have been hard to avoid — and while he liked his teammates, they did not hang out together off the court. Mike preferred the company of his elder sister Karen ("KB") and her friends. KB, three and a half years older, was a noted basketball player, first at Woodway High School in Edmonds, then at the University of Washington. She and her friends were funny, friendly, and not intimidating. They liked him and treated him well. And they were exceptionally good basketball players, always ready for a good pickup game.

Growing up in KB's shadow was both good and bad. It provided Mike with a social life and nice group of friends; on the other hand, KB was an excellent athlete, while he labeled himself "mediocre," and that was a burden.

Yet Mike stuck with basketball long after abandoning other sports like soccer and baseball. Besides his sister he was influenced by his high school coach, a man Mike calls "a fascinating guy, an intense man, and a great teacher. He turned me on to basketball like never before. My team had always played together and done well, but he was the first person to make me realize that I could really accomplish something in the game, like my sister had."

Yet he was not Pacific Ten caliber, and when he followed KB to the University of Washington, his playing career ended. At the same time his real life began.

Though he felt his first same-sex stirrings as far back as age eleven, Mike did not allow himself to think about them. Even in high school he never connected his thoughts with the word *gay*. Not until two years into college did he first begin dealing with his feelings. It was not easy.

The catalyst was volleyball. Though he never played it in high school — there was no boys' team at Woodway — Mike had always enjoyed the game and helped coach and manage the girls' high school squad. At UW he joined a club team. Things went well. But then he developed a crush on a teammate who happened to be a roommate, and trouble began.

"I was so scared, so freaked-out, and I had no idea how to deal with it," Mike recalls of his sophomore winter of 1991. "I was in an apartment of my own for the first time, and I couldn't really talk to anyone about it."

One night, on purpose, he overdrank and overdosed. "It was such a weak suicide plan," he says. "I strategically planned it so the guy I had a crush on would find me when he came home that morning from his girlfriend's house." That is exactly what happened. The teammate took him to the hospital, with absolutely no idea what had caused the incident.

"I didn't want to see or talk to anyone, including my family," Mike continues. "I told them I had done it because of the pressures of school. I found out later that they talked among themselves and questioned my sexuality, but no one said anything to me."

Two women he knew from the health club he worked at invited Mike to live in their basement apartment. Molly O'Neill and Margaret King are outspoken activists in Washington's lesbian and sports communities. Being around them and their friends was good for Mike. For the first time in his life, he saw happy openly gay people.

To get away and clear his head, Mike moved to San Francisco. He enrolled at Foothill College, a two-year community school, and played a season of volleyball. He met many gay people but, unsure of his teammates' attitudes, was not yet fully out of the closet.

His volleyball prowess caught the eye of the Pierce Junior College coach in Los Angeles. As soon as he enrolled there, Mike knew things would be different.

He lived with relatives. Through her work with AIDS patients, his aunt knew many people in the gay community and talked enthusiastically about them. To this day Mike does not know if she spoke so candidly because she knew about him, but her unquestioning acceptance of homosexuality smoothed his path.

He also learned that two volleyball players from the previous year were completely out with no repercussions at all. As his comfort level grew, his coming-out process accelerated. He wrote a long letter to his parents. They responded with complete support.

"The team sort of figured me out by asking about my social life," Mike says. "They started feeding me names of gay clubs in West Hollywood. Then one night we all went together to one, which to me was the greatest thing in the world."

Rejuvenated, Mike moved back to San Francisco and then, six months later, to Seattle to finish up his degree at the University of Washington. He graduated as a sociology major in 1996, eager to embark on a career as a coach.

He already had two years of experience. Mike's coaching career began when the girls' basketball coach at a large suburban Seattle high school asked him to help out as her assistant and junior varsity coach. He agreed — after all, the coach was his sister KB — but only after discussions with her about how to handle the *G* thing.

"We talked, and I decided I wouldn't lie if I was asked," Mike says. "But I also didn't want to create any unnecessary problems, so I wouldn't say anything on my own." (The year before, a coach was fired on suspicion of being a lesbian.) Yet homosexuality turned out to be a nonissue; the players did not suspect, and because some had crushes on him, Mike felt his secret was safe.

He learned a lot from his sister and from the coaching experience, so when a casual friend asked him to join her at a nearby Catholic school as assistant varsity and freshman volleyball coach, the UW student eagerly accepted. He had just settled in and was relearning the volleyball ropes when suddenly, three matches into the season, a fight erupted between the head coach and her players. She walked out, and Mike was asked to step in. Luckily, his afternoons were free.

Once again the season was a success. For the first time ever, the team qualified for the state tournament, finishing as one of the top sixteen teams in Washington. Just as important, he developed a solid rapport with his players and the administration. When the girls' basketball head coach position came open recently, Mike was the natural choice to fill it.

"I love everything about coaching: strategy, teaching, working with kids," he says enthusiastically. "All the stuff I learned from my own high school coach — applying new ideas, learning about commitment, coming together as a team, working for common goals, accepting failure, appreciating success, taking nothing for granted — I'm trying to pass on. It's so important to provide something they can look forward to every day and learn from."

He especially likes the fact that he's providing that "something" to females. "I've never really coached guys, except at camps and a few high school events, but it's clear that guys respond to screaming and yelling and that girls don't," he says. "I think I have a better rapport with girls."

Mike believes that the rapport he and his athletes have established is closely connected to his homosexuality. "The whole emotional side, the way women are, is very much a part of my life," he says matter-of-factly. "I'm a nurturing, emotional person, and that's part of my being gay."

Indeed, much of male athletics turns him off. "On straight basketball and volleyball teams, as well as other sports, there's so much of what I call a 'straight attitude,'" he says. "Everyone screams and yells and curses. I hate that about sports. I don't need that male-dominated attitude, and I don't want to be around it." For that reason Mike seeks out coed teams and leagues as well as pickup basketball games with and against women. "They appreciate playing basketball for its own sake, not just to prove who's better or tougher," he explains. "Besides, I like their company — and a lot of them are better than me!"

Gay volleyball and basketball leagues hold particular appeal. "They're very competitive, filled with great athletes," Mike said shortly after returning from a national gay volleyball tournament in Dallas. "Gay leagues allow you to use your skills but still feel comfortable being on the court with people who share your beliefs and your lifestyle."

Though Mike has never hidden his homosexuality at the school where he coaches, neither has he gone out of his way to advertise it. As a result of his easy relationships with women, administrators — to whom he is not out — assume he and certain female coaches are dating. His assistant coaches are under no such illusions; he is out to them, and their acceptance is complete. "I don't know if the topic of my homosexuality is ever going to come up in a school context, but if it does, I know I'll have support from my fellow coaches," he says. "Some of them have been outspoken, some just give quiet moral support, but they've all made me feel welcome. I've had nothing but good experiences here."

That may sound surprising coming from a coach at a Catholic school, but Mike says the issue of homosexuality seldom arises. Perhaps, he surmises, that is because the school's staff, parents, and students are fairly liberal or because the church in general (at least in Seattle) is changing. "I myself am not very Catholic, though my mom's side of the family is," he says. "But I've had lots of discussions with people trying to understand what the church says, and from what I hear it's becoming more accepting. Overall, though, gay stuff just doesn't come up much."

Nor does it come up in the context of his coaching. Mike Bryant's goal is simply to be the best coach possible; sexual orientation has nothing to do with it. His ultimate goal is to work with college women. For now, however, he is happy coaching high school girls.

"I'm making a difference," he concludes. "I've learned so much about volleyball and basketball and life that I can apply to my coaching and teaching. I can't imagine doing that in male sports, because of the attitudes there. Working with females is where I really fit in and feel comfortable. It's where I think I can contribute the most."

The Reflective Runner

At some point in their lives, many athletes switch sports. The foot-ball player may move over to lacrosse; the skier will take up crew. Often these athletes cannot express what motivated them to change beyond a vague feeling of burnout or a desire to seek a new challenge.

Occasionally, however, a young man recognizes his decision to try a new sport as a major life event. He understands that underlying the seemingly simple act of trading in, say, a bat for swim goggles lies a deeper, more fundamental exchange of one set of values for another.

It is extremely rare, however, for an athlete to express his reasons articulately and passionately; some things are too personal or perhaps better left unsaid. For an eighteen-year-old to be able to bring soccer, running, and homosexuality together and then cogently describe the subtle nexus between them is remarkable indeed.

"STRAIGHT PEOPLE LEAD UNEXAMINED LIVES. They never have to question themselves or their place in the world. They have no problem fitting in on a team; if they're a left wing, they know they have an obligation to cross a ball to a certain place, and they do it without thinking. If their teammate fucks up, they see nothing wrong with calling him weak or saying, 'Do better, pussy.' "

That's David Zucker's shoot-from-the-hip view on straight people and their place in team sports. He is anything but straight and anything but a team player. At eighteen years old, he knows himself as a proud gay man, he loves to run, and he is quite clear about the relationship between the two.

"Gay people are not free to do everything straight people are," he says. "We can't hold hands in a lot of places, we can't express affection openly, we can't even talk candidly anywhere we want. So we become self-reliant. We reflect on our place in the world. Since we can't be open about our dreams and desires, we keep them to ourselves and wonder about our lives and ourselves when we're on our own. Eventually we reach a point where we say to ourselves, *I'm unique; this is me*, and then we're eager to get in touch with other unique aspects of ourselves. That's why I gravitated to running. It's a place I can be by myself, be alone, and just think."

Though it seems David has spent a lifetime honing those thoughts, in truth they are only a year old. The realization that he is gay came relatively late; his switch from team sports to running followed that epiphany.

David spent the first years of his life in Southern California. When he was eight his mother, who had severe emotional problems, committed suicide. His father, always a workaholic, dived even deeper into his business. David and his two siblings spent most of their time at school or day care; when his father wanted to date, he dumped the children at the mall. "We were always on our own," David recalls.

When David was ten his father remarried, and the Zuckers moved to suburban Chicago. David could not stand his stepmother; she was terribly dogmatic, he says, and besides, she wanted to raise him as a Christian, while he felt strong ties to his Jewish faith. After he tried to run away, his parents sent him to an Episcopal military school, Howe Academy in Indiana.

It was there, as an eighth grader, that David learned about masturbation and had his first sexual experience. It was with another boy. "I had always been kept away from anything sexual. I didn't know what gay was," he says. "But this kid two doors down took a liking to me and started doing things. I was diggin' it. I didn't know it was bad. I'd never even heard of 'gay.' " The first time he ejaculated was with his friend. "I said, 'Whoa, what's going on?' " he recalls. "I'd heard the word 'coming' before, but I didn't even know it involved a penis."

He and the boy continued their activities all year long, though in public his partner was a virulent homophobe. "He kept saying, 'Suck my dick' and 'There's the faggot shower,' "

David says. "That's when I figured out what 'gay' was, that it had to do with sex. But I didn't understand why he didn't like gay people. It was my first taste of homophobia."

David did not label himself gay, however. He moved back West and spent ninth through twelfth grade at Midland, a rustic, summer camp–looking school in Los Olivos, California, with just eighty students. Teachers and pupils handled all maintenance chores. One of the major lessons was self-reliance.

Midland also taught David how to use his mind and body and how to interact with all kinds of people. "In public school if you don't get along with someone, you just go home at the end of the day," he explains. "There you had to figure out how to accept that person and do well with him or her. I got a terrific education in life. I wouldn't trade it for twenty million bucks."

David also learned about sex and drugs. He was no angel child; he had problems with authority. But he adapted.

On breaks — the school calendar was six weeks of class, one week off — there were always parties. During one bash David, by then a senior, enjoyed a "fabulous" five-hour fling with another male. At that point he realized he was not, in fact, bisexual. "I resolved it then and there," he says forthrightly. "Before that I had stared at guys' haircuts and bodies but put it in the context of how it helped them get girls. But when I walked out of that party, I knew for sure I was gay. It was wonderful." In retrospect, he recognizes that the signs had always been there — he looked at men's underwear in Sears catalogs and got erect while wrestling with friends — but it took that blissful night to understand the signals.

David was a popular student who had served two terms as student body president. He also participated in many sports: soccer, lacrosse, baseball, even polocrosse (a game similar to polo, played on horseback but with lacrosse-like sticks rather than mallets). With the realization that he was gay, however, came a new understanding: Team sports were not for him.

"People on teams are so focused on winning that they forget about teamwork," he says. "It's pretty clear that in a team context the whole team wins, but everyone forgets that. When someone makes a mistake, everyone is derogatory and jumps all over him. Well, everyone makes mistakes at some point. I started to see that games just weren't that big a deal."

But if winning faded in importance, other elements of athletics — exercise, fitness, health — did not. In fact, those benefits replaced competition as the reason David ran. "When I run I feel great," he says. "The oxygen flows, the endorphins kick in. I get in a rhythm, a state of flow. I lose all sense of time and forget everything else that's going on. It's like dreaming while being awake."

And when he runs, he thinks. "For me, running is a chance to get in touch with everything in my subconscious," he says. "When I think, I can miraculously come up with answers to so many questions, whether it's relationships, the place of beauty in our society, or an essay I'm writing — my aim is to be a reporter for National Public Radio. In a team sport you can't do that; you have too many goals, objectives, external pressures from teammates and coaches and referees."

There is no pressure in running. David runs anywhere: hills, valleys, city streets, and parks. He does not run for distance or time. When he wants to stop, he stops. He can run races — half marathons, ten-kilometers, even marathons — but that is not his style. He prefers running as a means of thinking and getting fit, mentally as well as physically.

David believes it is a "gay thing" to enjoy individual sports over team sports. "We can't feel comfortable on teams," he says. "There's too much emphasis on competition and winning and putting people down in order to feel you're a winner and they're a loser. A team is just a microcosm of society. Everyone fulfills individual roles en route to a bigger 'team' role."

Gay people, he continues, are more independent than that. "We can't trust society to allow us to be ourselves," he says. "If society can't provide comfort for gays, then we have to feel comfortable in other ways. One of the ways we do that is by recognizing that we're unique. Then it becomes more natural to want

to express our uniqueness in other unique ways, by doing individual things like running rather than by succumbing to being
part of a big, faceless team."

Running has not only given David Zucker feelings of health
and serenity; it has allowed him to reflect on and solve one of the
major problems of his young life. Early in his senior year, he
thought his postgraduation plans were firm: He had been
recruited for an elite U.S. Navy nuclear power program and
wanted to participate. He even signed a form saying he had no
propensity to engage in homosexual acts. But then came his
awakening as a gay man. As he ran and pondered who he was
and where his life was going, he realized he did not want to join
an organization that would not let him be himself. Thanks to
some "cool guys" at the recruiting office, he got out of his military obligation.

That situation caused David to miss deadlines for some of
the major colleges he might have applied to. So off he went,
thoughtfully yet gaily, to Cerritos College, a two-year school
near Long Beach, with plans to write, figure out how to attend
a four-year university — and, of course, to run.

The Impostor

When is an athlete not an athlete?

When he has no interest in sports — when, in fact, he actively dislikes them. When he joins teams for reasons having nothing to do with the thrill of competing, the excitement of learning new skills, or the pleasures of running, jumping, throwing, and shooting.

The vast majority of gay youngsters become athletes despite their sexual orientation. They make difficult, tortured journeys through the swamps of self-hatred before arriving tremblingly — in some cases terror-stricken — at the locker rooms and playing fields that are truly their birthrights.

But a small number of gay youth become athletes because of their sexuality. For them, thrills, excitement, and pleasure come not from participating in games themselves but from proximity to the boys who play them. They join teams not to compete but to get close to teammates.

Yet these "pseudo-jocks" have no easier time accepting their homosexuality than their athletically minded counterparts who suppress or deny same-sex attractions. In fact, in many ways these unathletic athletes' knowledge of what they are doing may make their lives even harder.

GREGG JOSEPH PULLS NO PUNCHES when discussing sports. "I hated track," he admits. "I despised swimming. I had no interest in basketball, and because I wore glasses I couldn't even see a baseball." Yet in junior high this self-admitted sportsphobe played on four teams: track, swimming, basketball, and baseball.

He is equally candid when explaining why: "The sport thing was an absolute excuse. I idolized guys with perfect, muscular bodies. Playing sports was the best opportunity to be around flesh."

Little in his '70s childhood suggests that Gregg would turn into any kind of athlete, pseudo or real. He and his two brothers enjoyed a typical suburban Long Island, New York, upbringing, right down to their seemingly happily married parents, who later divorced.

Gregg (a pen name he uses when writing erotic fiction) always liked boys. And long before junior high sports, he found a way to surround himself with them. "I would ask my mom to ask certain boys' mothers if they could come over and play," he says. "I choreographed my own fun. I was certainly conscious of my desire to be with certain boys and not others." One day he challenged a young boy to a fight over a girl. However, he knew that reason was just a pretext; what he really wanted was the chance to wrestle around with a guy.

In junior high school in the late '70s, Gregg realized that his attraction to males was sexual. He can recall the exact moment: Sitting on a beach one late summer afternoon, watching older teenagers bodysurf naked, he spontaneously ejaculated for the first time. "I didn't even know what coming was," he says. "But I knew there was a connection between what I was seeing and what just happened." It took him a long time to accept what he was, but he knew he could not deny it — or change it.

An intelligent boy with a logical mind, Gregg set about making the most of his predicament. The school swim team seemed to offer the best opportunity to see exposed flesh, so he joined up. The fact that he was heavy — and had never swum competitively — did not deter him. In fact, in a strange way it even helped. Without the pressure to win, he appointed himself masseur for the better athletes, helping them "relax" after workouts or "recover" from injuries. It was a supporting role not out of character for an overweight youngster. Gregg loved it.

The locker-room scenes fed his every fantasy, providing hours of masturbatory material. Even better were late-night bus rides home from away meets. "Guys would fall asleep on each other," Gregg remembers. "It was a wonderful way to touch without being seen. I pretended I was with a lover."

The most difficult part of being on the swim team was hiding his erections. Being fat and unnoticed helped. Having his brother on the team did not.

Not until many years later did Gregg learn from a former teammate that many swimmers on that squad were either gay or fooling around. "I didn't even know!" Gregg laments. "Or maybe it was because I was this invisible heavy kid and nobody wanted to include me."

Body image presented a major issue for Gregg. He conflated fitness with masculinity with acceptance with popularity — feelings common in many junior high boys, whatever their sexual orientation. Like many young males in the throes of puberty, he emulated older boys; like many with low self-esteem and confidence, he envied them too. In eighth grade Gregg decided he would have a body like his heroes — or if he could not, then at least he would get as close as possible to those who did.

The easiest means of accomplishing that, he determined in his logical way, was to go out for track and field. An added benefit was that track shared a locker room with the lacrosse and baseball teams, and Gregg had major crushes on many ninth graders who played those sports. To shower and change with them would be a dream come true.

His locker-room behavior was brazen. He constantly invented excuses to walk up and down the rows. One day he mentioned that he had forgotten something; the next time he said he was "on an errand." Almost daily he found reasons to brush against naked bodies.

"I groped for a whole semester," Gregg recalls, almost in wonderment. "I was possessed. After touching someone, I would be sure not to wash my hands." To this day he remains thrilled by "accidental" contact. In all that time he remembers only two comments from athletes. A boy once joked about his frequent forays; another said, "Hey, man, it's not *that* crowded in here!" Both remarks haunted him. Still, he did not stop.

Yet each time he prowled the locker room, Gregg felt guilty. If he had not, he notes, he would have approached one of the boys and acted to make his fantasies real. Instead he gazed, schemed, and touched, clandestinely (he hoped). "I kept thinking 'it' was horrible — even though I had no idea what 'it' really meant," Gregg says. Today he understands "it" to be an unhealthy reaction to frustration, fright, and ignorance.

His obsessions kept him from participating in other activities one part of him wanted to try, including singing and theater. But at the same time he did not relate to the people involved in those endeavors — at least, he thought he did not. "I had enough problems dealing with being 'a brain,'" he says. "I couldn't be artsy-fartsy too. That would have been too much to handle."

His parents were pleased with his transformation into an athlete, especially the year he made the prestigious basketball team. They attended every game. His mother was delighted that Gregg lost weight; she bought him new clothes and told him he could be a model.

Of course, Gregg never mentioned his motivation to anyone, in part because he was so confused himself. "When I finally became 'one of them' — a good-looking jock on varsity teams — I realized that it didn't solve anything," he says. "My fantasies were continuing the same as before. Girls were coming after me, but it was boys I wanted. I wanted their respect and adoration, and I wanted it to also be tactile, romantic, and sexual."

He accepted those feelings on one level; on another Gregg fantasized that his athlete friends would find out he was gay and then abuse and humiliate him. That was a frequent masturbatory fantasy.

"So at the peak of my athletic performance — when I achieved athletically what I had always dreamed of achieving — I still felt like an impostor," Gregg says. He was exactly where he wanted to be — roaming locker rooms, showering with naked boys, glorying in the adulation awarded to athletes, even in junior high — yet he remained unfulfilled.

So even though he had finally become good at sports, he had no desire to continue as an athlete past junior high. "I had it, and yet I couldn't do anything with it," he says. When he entered high school, he dropped team sports completely.

196   With nothing to do now after school, he cruised the mall. One day he met a boy who liked him. The feeling was not reciprocal, but Gregg allowed the boy to perform oral sex on him several times. Because he did not care for the boy, those were not enjoyable same-sex experiences. But they were his first.

Suddenly rebellious, Gregg began cutting class. It was a way for him to feel in charge, not defensive. His innate intelligence kept his grades high, so no one seemed particularly bothered by his declining attendance.

One reason he avoided school was that the dating scene was becoming intense. Dutifully he tried to go out with girls, but there was nothing there. He did not even feel like experimenting sexually with them.

In college Gregg continued to be uninterested in organized sports activities unless they were completely social like volleyball. He labels this "repressed guilt" for having abused the trust of his teammates for so long when he was young. Though older, he could not view sports in any context other than as a frustrating, unfulfilling outlet for his still adolescent sexual desires.

But every repressed emotion must eventually find a means of expression, and Gregg's has emerged in writing. A professional journalist specializing in European affairs, he has a sideline gig: writing erotic sports fiction. He focuses not on the mechanics of sex but on the dynamics of situations, the sensual discoveries of participants, and on fantasies and taboos, such as the transposition of roles between coaches and athletes. "I think a lot of people have an interest in gay jocks — not just the act but the foreplay," he says. "I write about the stuff you don't see in videos: 'What can I get away with?' 'Is he or isn't he?' "

He admits that his interest in the genre springs from never having come to terms with his athletic self. His teenage locker-room fantasies remain unrealized today. "If I can't experience it, at least I can write about it," he says with a touch of self-deprecation. "It's part of my coming-out process. I'm not completely out yet, and I don't know when I will be."

Gregg thinks that process was stunted for him by his junior high behavior — not by his furtive gazing and groping but by his fear of doing anything more. "I'm incredibly disappointed that that was all I did," he says. "I sold myself short. I had so many hang-ups about my body, about my sexuality. The only thing I was confident in was my ability to do well in school, and I just dismissed that out of hand. What I wanted was to be beautiful and have a good body. If I'd been totally honest about that, I would have had much earlier and better sexual experiences. It would have been so interesting, so wonderful if I had just approached the right guy. It would have liberated me."

However, he admits, perhaps that wistfulness is just another fantasy. It would have taken massive amounts of counseling and self-acceptance — neither of which was terribly in vogue nearly two decades ago — for Gregg to have taken the huge step from feeling attracted to boys to feeling secure enough to approach one honestly and positively.

Today, he continues to try to reach that state. At thirty-two he is not particularly confident about himself, still does not feel fully comfortable inside his own skin. Every morning he repeats the same mantra: "Today I will be true to myself."

Most days he fails.

The Media Relations Director

College athletic programs are known for their athletes and coaches; those are the ones who get ink and airtime, reap fame and glory. But behind every college team lurk support staff: the countless trainers, managers, and administrators who make sure every athlete is healthy enough to compete, each coach has enough equipment to run a program, and the buses roll on time.

Standing behind those support people is an even less visible group: the sports information or, as it is called in the communications-conscious '90s, the media relations department. These men and women, known only to athletes, coaches, and journalists, have one mission: to spread the word, as often and as positively as possible, about a school's teams and players. To do that they produce media guides and write press releases, arrange interviews and shepherd their charges through them, suggest story ideas, plug stars' accomplishments, and smooth ruffled journalistic feathers, all the while serving as intermediaries between young athletes and the often demanding adults who run athletic departments.

Sports information directors and their assistants often arrive from the fringes of athletics. As youngsters many felt more comfortable with the printed word than the pitched or passed ball; while their friends were playing games, these boys and girls chronicled them. Because of their interest in statistics and stories, they might not have fit in well with the rest of the playground crowd. But as they grew older and discovered their niche in a media relations office, they learned something else: Their status as noncompetitors in a competitive world enabled them to fill a role in athletics no one else could.

Their daily contact with athletes and coaches gives sports information people special entrée into an often inaccessible environment. Their facility with words, their ability to listen, and their position as nonathletes enable them to hear and see things — and not repeat them — like no one else in a locker room. They become athletes' and coaches' confidants, advisers, mentors, and friends.

The best sports information people deal honestly and directly with all kinds of issues, on and off the field. Dave Lohse is one of the best.

LITTLE IN DAVE LOHSE'S BACKGROUND suggests a life outside the mainstream. From age four until college, he lived in Griffith, Indiana, southeast of Chicago. When he was eight his parents took him to his first baseball game at Wrigley Field; it marked the start of a lifelong love affair with the Chicago Cubs. The same year he discovered the football Bears; they won the NFL championship that winter of 1963 and, unlike with the Cubs, he learned the joy of cheering on a champion. Passion for the hockey Blackhawks and basketball Bulls followed. "I've been a Bulls fan since 1967, their first year," Dave says with a trace of defensiveness. "I didn't just jump on the Michael Jordan bandwagon."

In 1964 he was transfixed by the Olympics. "Looking back, I realize my fascination with Don Schollander was not just that he was a tremendous swimmer," Dave recalls. "He was this beautiful blond boy from Yale. Of course, at the time I didn't know I was thrilled with more than his athletic ability."

Dave was not a gifted athlete. His career in organized sports was limited to Little League baseball, though he enjoyed shooting hoops in the driveway and throwing a ball against the house. His interests were not confined to athletics: He loved music (his first album was the sound track to *Oklahoma!*) and politics. He thought of himself as a "Renaissance kid," hardly the norm in his working-class environment. Until his senior year in high school, he had few friends.

"I was always the odd duck," Dave says. "My parents were not big sports fans. My dad worked in a steel mill and never finished high school. He liked working in the wood shop and on cars, and I loathed that." Yet his parents took full advantage of their proximity to Chicago, introducing Dave and his elder sister to museums, art exhibits, and sports events, and he appreciated that. "Lots of kids in my neighborhood never even went into the city," he says. "So my parents did right by me."

Under the tutelage of gifted journalism teacher Pat Clark, he saw his high school writing career flourish. The yearbook he worked on earned national awards. High school was also where he wrote sports stories and columns for the local paper, then branched out as a stringer for dailies in Gary and Hammond. Between those activities and managing the baseball and cross-country teams, he did not have much time to make close friends — or date. In fact, not until twelfth grade did he go out with a girl. He was, however, valedictorian of the class of 1973.

Dave made Phi Beta Kappa at Purdue University; he majored in political science and for a while thought of becoming a lawyer. He worked for three years as a student assistant in the sports information office but considered that an avocation, not a vocation. His college years were also marked by a long bout with ulcerative colitis. His weight seesawed between 140 and 220 pounds.

He applied to seven graduate schools for political science. All seven accepted him, and six offered money. But the one that did not — the University of North Carolina at Chapel Hill — was the only one he really wanted to attend, and in the fall of 1977, the lifelong Hoosier headed south. He soon procured a teaching assistantship and supplemented that with work in the sports information office, so once again he was immersed in satisfying work. But the political science department's emphasis on methodology rankled him, and the next year he moved over to the graduate school of journalism. In August 1979 the assistant sports information director left. Dave, the logical successor, has been at Chapel Hill ever since.

Dave Lohse's first inkling that he might be gay came when he was thirteen, but in the blue-collar culture he grew up in, he did not even know what the word meant. He was nearly twenty before he first acknowledged his feelings to himself, though in

retrospect he realizes many signs were there long before that.
For two decades he endured a torturous struggle to accept his
homosexuality. "I went through so many different phases," he
says. "It was a very unhappy existence. I was working in an environment I perceived to be less than tolerant, one that emphasized youth, beauty, and athleticism. I was constantly bombard-
ed by those messages. I was in total conflict about who I was, but
of course there was nothing in my makeup to make me come
out. Those who knew me probably suspected — I never tried to
be anything other than who I was — but I was just not ready to
come out."

His perception that the UNC athletic department was a "less
than tolerant" place came mainly from his own internalized
homophobia, Dave emphasizes. He believed that if people knew
he was gay, he would immediately lose his job, his friends, and
his colleagues' and athletes' respect. He had never heard homosexuality referred to in a positive way, so he had no reason to
believe anyone in the sports world would support him.

His internalized homophobia is so deeply rooted that Dave
battles it even today. "It's horrible to admit, but I'm still terribly
intolerant of effeminate men," he says. "It's just a major turnoff
to me. I guess that's part of my upbringing and the environment
I work in. I consider myself very much a 'mainstream gay guy.'
In fact, I'm so 'normal,' I sometimes feel like a misfit in the gay
community. My interest in sports and my intellectual interests
seem to intimidate people."

On the other hand, he has had no trouble fitting into the
straight world. His heterosexual friends and coworkers, along
with the Tar Heel athletes, have accepted him completely. "I
owe them a lot," Dave says. "I've never been hassled. I know
that's not always the case, and I feel incredibly lucky."

Dave dates his coming-out process to June 1992. For many
years he had spent one week every summer working at the
American Legion Boys and Girls State Camp in Indiana. He had

gone there while in high school, then served as a staff member for seventeen years. At age thirty he was named the youngest assistant dean ever.

Dave cherished the trusting relationships he had formed with many youths at the camp. He knew several were gay, but he had never come out to any of them. That summer of 1992 one of the attendees was a high school soccer player. From their first meeting Dave sensed the boy was gay. The final night the boy knocked on Dave's door and said he was upset about going home. Dave knew what was coming next.

After hemming and hawing, the youngster asked, "Do you ever have thoughts...?"

"You can tell me anything," Dave replied. "I'm gay. Nothing you say can shock me."

The boy responded, "You're so brave and courageous!"

Dave was stunned. "I'm thirty-seven," he told the teenager. "If you only knew!" It was a gut-wrenching experience because he recognized that a seventeen-year-old boy was psychologically and emotionally far ahead of where he was.

Several weeks later Dave came out to his first straight friend, in Indiana. The friend laughed, said he'd always known, and added that the news made no difference; he liked Dave just as he was.

Emboldened, he returned to UNC. "I'd been so distraught, I was thinking about leaving my job," Dave recalls. "I was grossly overweight — 220 pounds does not look great on a five-foot seven-inch frame — and extremely unhappy." He sought psychological counseling, which helped immensely. The process of coming out at work and to friends began, then evolved quickly and with little drama. Someone looking for an incredible coming-out story will not find it at the Carolina sports information office.

Though relatively hassle-free, Dave's coming-out process is far from over. He still retains vestiges of the internalized homophobia he picked up during two decades in athletics. He is hardly ready to hoist a rainbow flag and lead a parade. "I dislike the phrase, 'I'm proud to be gay,' " Dave says. "I hate that gay pride shit. What I say is that I'm *comfortable* being gay. It's not a feeling of pride but of uniqueness — particularly in the field I'm in."

As athletes and coaches learned Dave Lohse was gay, he asked himself why it had caused him so much stress for so long. "It was like a fairy tale," he says. "People greeted the news with such a sense of maturity, I was flabbergasted. I have no idea if anything has been said behind my back, but to my face I've had no problem at all."

Athletes feel at ease talking with Dave about homosexuality. "On road trips, in buses, kids are not afraid of asking questions," he reports. "They want to know about my life, my world."

Players and coaches have no problem touching him. When Carolina wins a big game, Dave gets the same hugs and pats on the butt as everyone else.

Athletes do not censor themselves around him, and that's fine. "Kids are kids," he says. "In this day and age, they call each other 'faggot.' It's inevitable, and I'd feel terrible if they felt so constrained around me that they had to watch every word. I know it's not intended personally. It's not the word, it's the context. In athletics you have to get used to 'faggot,' just like you get used to antiwoman stuff. It's not particularly becoming, but it *is* part of the athletic culture."

Dave got a taste of that culture the day he called a freshman swimmer at his dorm room with a question about the media guide. The athlete and his roommate had left a "somewhat homophobic" message on their answering machine. Though not offended, Dave mentioned it to the swim coach, who gave his athlete a tongue-lashing. The young man apologized profusely, saying, "I had no idea! You're not a flamer!"

"I could have stayed in the closet successfully at work for the rest of my life," Dave says. "But I came out for myself. I was tired of living a lie, of having to cover all my tracks. I wanted to be who I really am and not have to worry about making up stories or censoring everything I said."

Dave admits he might not have felt as comfortable coming out in a sports information department somewhere else. His longevity at UNC, his fifty-four writing awards from the College Sports Information Directors of America, and the recognition he received for his six tours of duty for the U.S. Olympic Committee helped; so did the overall atmosphere at Chapel Hill. "UNC is a great school with top-notch academic and athletic traditions," he says, sliding into his booster mode. "There are very few colleges like this, and it's also a quintessential college town. Chapel Hill is extremely liberal, the size of our gay male population is probably higher than average, and Carrboro, our sister city, has an openly gay mayor. So environmental factors certainly helped."

However, he adds, he also spent nearly two decades underestimating the athletes and coaches he worked with every day. "Until we test the waters, we'll never know how people will react," he says. "Because the closet seems the norm in college athletics, we assume people will react negatively when we come out. And then, since most people in athletics don't come out, the closet continues to be pervasive. I think gay people would be surprised to find how little people care one way or the other."

Since he came out several Tar Heel athletes have spoken to him about their own sexuality. Dave tells them he'll be supportive if they decide to come out; if they choose to remain in the closet, he assures them of his complete understanding. But he emphasizes to all that whatever they do, they should know that the UNC athletic department is a far more tolerant place than they ever dreamed.

Not long after coming out, David Lohse received a major promotion, to "director of media relations and publications for Olympic sports." He also shed over fifty pounds.

The Partners

In their search for athletic success, gay athletes sometimes stumble upon personal fulfillment. Finding a gay man who enjoys sports is called serendipity; finding one who enjoys sports and reciprocates the physical and emotional attraction you feel for him is called love.

But as is often the case with love, things don't always happen the way we planned. Careers must be juggled, and compromises must be made in order to allow love to bloom and grow. That's the way of the world; love is love, gay or straight.

Yet being gay and in love in the predominantly straight world of athletics can be difficult. If you are a rowing coach looking for a job, do you come out in the interviewing process? If you are a high school swim coach, do you mention your lover's name to your team? Gay athletes spend months grappling with questions their straight counterparts never dreamed existed — and years wondering what the answers mean.

CHARLEY SULLIVAN'S COACHING CREDENTIALS seem impeccable. As a junior at Princeton, he helped the private Hun School resurrect its rowing program; after college he coached, in succession and quite successfully, boys' and girls' rowing and football at two prestigious private schools, Groton and South Kent, as well as a suburban Virginia public school. While a graduate student in history at the University of Michigan, he coached varsity men's and women's and novice men's rowing. In three years he helped Michigan crew rise from mediocrity to among the best club programs in the country.

Yet Charley Sullivan cannot get a collegiate coaching job. He is convinced it is because he is gay.

Tension began to build at Michigan when he and Rob Koplan, a swimmer and coach, announced their engagement. Relations with the men's rowing coach soured; that's when

Charley moved over to the novice boats and began his job search. But the *G* word was out, and in the small world of collegiate rowing, that made a difference.

Charley is sophisticated enough to know that homophobia pure and simple does not cause every rejection. Where searches have been conducted by athletic-department committees, he has received interviews and reached the final selection stage. His best experience occurred at the University of Iowa. He was flown in and treated royally, and when he spoke openly about his homosexuality, no one seemed to care. The job ultimately went to someone Charley calls "one of the best young women's rowing coaches in the country," so he did not feel bad. In fact, that experience convinced him he was indeed an excellent coach, worthy of serious consideration. Another school told him early on that they would be hiring a female; he had no problem with that — after all, it was a women's team — though he notes wryly, "It's illegal to say that ahead of time."

But he did not fare as well at other, less competitive schools, and that set him wondering. Sometimes he did not even receive the courtesy of a return letter or phone call.

He was one of four finalists at his own school, Michigan. However, they called only three candidates for interviews. All were women; all had far less experience than he. After talking with fellow coaches (including several lesbians), he is convinced the reason he has not gotten most jobs is because of his sexuality.

"With the résumé I have, if I wasn't out, I'd have a job," he says firmly. "And it's not just that I'm gay. I'm an activist too."

For example, while coaching in Virginia, he talked often to his high school athletes about staying healthy. In the course of those conversations, he did "very basic" AIDS education. "I didn't presume anyone was gay or straight; it was all inclusive," he recalls. "But the principal freaked out. He said I had no business doing it, that it was covered already in the health curriculum. I was told to be silent."

At South Kent, when several students broke into his apartment to try to settle their debate about whether he was gay (they

found male literature in a closet), he made certain they were rep-
rimanded, then came out to the entire school. (The boys did not
know he was already out to the entire faculty.) "I didn't want
people to think I was ashamed of being gay," he says.

Most of his athletes responded well to his openness. Before
South Kent raced against a "bigger, richer, more athletic,
smarter" school, the opposing coach informed his team that
Charley was gay. At the starting line the other rowers taunted
South Kent for being coached by a "faggot." The coxswain kept
up the abuse the entire race.

"My kids said 'Whatever' and blew them away," Charley
relates with satisfaction. "They said, 'We may be coached by a
faggot, but we kicked your ass!' "

Charley is sure he could get a high school coaching job
again, but he's done that. He wants to stay with a college team.
When it became clear that would not happen, he took a job
teaching French and history at a private school in Birmingham,
Michigan. He is not coaching at all now because they do not
have any sports he knows well. He is, however, the head of the
school's gay-straight alliance.

The reason he has not been offered a college job, he says, is
that intercollegiate athletics is ruled by a cult of masculinity. He
knows the environment well. He himself was not out while rowing at Princeton. It would have been too difficult, even though
he knew other men on his team who were gay.

At Michigan, where he was openly gay as a history-depart-
ment teaching assistant, he spoke with varsity football and hockey athletes who were gay. The homophobia they described — on
the part of coaches as well as teammates — was scary. "The only
men's coach here who did a good job fighting that was the gymnastics coach, and he's gone," Charley says. "He was a straight
guy, but he knew he had gay athletes, and he knew that if his
team was going to be a *team*, they had to be together. He actually brought in a counselor to work with everyone." There is not
one openly gay male coach at Michigan, Charley says. And he

does not see the one man he assumes to be gay coming out any-time soon: "That would mean the end of his career."

The coaching fraternity is not filled with nasty people, Charley emphasizes: "It's just the way they see the world. Gay men call into question what many people think athletics should be about and what people should get out of it. People get very uncomfortable with homosexuality. At Michigan and other places, the athletic department has been largely independent of the powers that control the rest of the school. Athletic departments have been run by older men who don't see the world through today's eyes. They worry about alumni and public support."

The result is that everyone — athletes as well as coaches — stays in the closet, even at a place as liberal as Michigan. "While students are forcing the rest of the university to move forward, it's not happening with athletes," Charley says. "It's a lot harder for an athlete than a regular student to insist on being treated well. Gay athletes don't come out because of all their fears: losing a scholarship, losing playing time, not getting a shot at a starting position, getting beat up in practice. Here we are, at a school with all the protections in the world, and there's still so much fear and worry among athletes."

That fear, of course, is felt not just by athletes and coaches. Administrators fear the truth too. That is why Charley Sullivan still does not have a rowing team to call his own.

Yet Charley is only one side of the Michigan story. The man he shares his life, home, and bed with tells a very different tale about Ann Arbor. It is there that Rob Koplan has finally been able to reconcile the two most important facets of his life: his homosexuality and his swimming. For the first time ever, he is open and honest about everything.

By the time he entered high school in San Antonio, Texas, Rob knew he was attracted to men. Thinking it to be an illness, he kept his feelings to himself. The result was extreme loneliness.

Several schoolmates were "obviously gay," but Rob told himself he could not be because he did not act like that. At sixteen his mother sent him to a summer camp to meet "nice Jewish girls." Instead he met a nice Jewish boy and realized he was indeed gay.

Rob had always been a good athlete. But because he was constantly teased and felt he did not fit in with his peers, he never went out for team sports. His passion was swimming; of particular appeal was the fact that it was an individual pursuit.

As a high school freshman, Rob was "gawky and uncoordinated." People perceived him to be effeminate — except in the water. But swimming, running, and working with weights produced a well-defined body. By the end of his senior year, the self-proclaimed "nerdy wimp" outraced his entire class in the 600-yard run and knocked off more sit-ups as well.

At Austin College, a small liberal arts school an hour from Dallas, Rob had a better self-image. Though not "an elite, Bruce Hayes–type swimmer," he was pretty good, earning district championships in the 1,000-yard freestyle and 200-yard backstroke.

He was exactly similar to Hayes in one crucial area, however: his homosexuality. Freed from the shackles of the people he'd known for twelve years, he felt more accepted than in high school. Still, he did not come out until the end of his senior year at college. Though at Austin it was cool to go to a gay bar, Rob did not; he was too afraid. "Basically, I wasted four years," he says.

He always wanted to teach, but his parents objected. "You can't do that — you're gay!" they said. Nevertheless, he got certified and in 1984 was hired by Newman Smith High School in Carrollton, a Dallas suburb, to teach English and history and to coach.

Heeding the advice of friends — "Be cautious" — he edged out of the closet to a few faculty members. His rule of thumb was not to come out indiscriminately but also never to lie. Whenever a question of the rights of gay people arose, Rob spoke firmly in their favor.

During his seven years of coaching, he grew close to the swimmers and their parents. Some parents knew he was gay, though the issue was never discussed. "The educated, astute ones and I made veiled comments, so we knew where we stood," he says.

His homosexuality never posed a problem for them, but in Rob's final year the principal made things uncomfortable. "He didn't want 'an issue,' " Rob says. "He told me that kids thought I was gay and that things might become difficult." Rob, who also taught health, knew he would be leaving soon, so in response he became bolder. One day he brought in a video on gay teenagers.

He knew he was leaving because that year, at a gay swim meet in Washington, D.C., he had met and fallen in love with Charley Sullivan. They dated long-distance, and after the semester ended Rob moved to Michigan, where Charley was a graduate student.

Rob did not have a job, but he was not worried. He was used to the teacher shortage in Texas and figured work would be easy to find. It was not; the Ann Arbor area suffered from a teacher glut. So Rob substitute-taught in the public schools and coached swimming and cross-country at a private school.

He was hired for the coaching job by an out lesbian. That in itself represented a big change for Rob. "When I moved I didn't want people to assume anymore that I was straight," he says. His very first day in the faculty lounge, someone asked what brought him north. A relationship, he said. "What does your wife do?" someone asked. "My wife is a man!" he replied.

The swim parents were fine with his homosexuality. Most cross-country parents were too, except for "a few homophobes" who would not admit the source of their concern. "This is a very politically correct town," he says. "They had to find another way to complain, so they criticized my coaching."

The differences between Texas and Michigan were immediately apparent. "I hate to use a cliché, but it was like a huge weight was lifted off my shoulders," Rob says. "It felt so nice to be totally honest. Now I don't have to worry about what I say or who I say it to."

His effect on athletes — gay and straight — is apparent too. Rob believes that every year of coaching marks another team of teenagers who will not become gay-bashers. One day a girl came out to him as the daughter of a lesbian. "Kids of gay people are in a whole other closet," he says.

He is completely open about his relationship with his lover. "It's nice when kids ask about Charley," Rob says. "In Texas I used to just say I was going on 'a date.' " Their commitment ceremony four years ago became the first same-sex announcement in *The Ann Arbor News.* Four swimmers and a number of Charley's rowers attended; several swim parents sent congratulatory cards. They have been invited as a couple to family events such as graduation parties.

In recent years Rob has noticed a subtle but positive change in his athletes' attitudes. He is not sure whether it is attributable to his move to Michigan, the passage of time, or other factors, but the reason is immaterial. "There's more information available to kids," he notes. "I didn't hear the word 'homosexual' before ninth grade. I never knew there was a gay world out there. Now they know. So whether kids today think it's sick or a choice or just know someone who's gay and that's fine, at least for them, homosexuality exists, and they're thinking about it."

Besides his relationship with Charley, swimming is the most important part of Rob's life. "When the endorphins kick in, that's an indescribable feeling," he says. "I feel so good when I swim and so awful when I don't. Even if I have to drag myself to the pool, I feel better afterward."

And gay swimming events are especially important. Thanks to meets, Rob and Charley have friends in Ann Arbor and across the country they would never have met. Swimming, Rob says, is a very gay-friendly sport.

"It must be something in the water," he laughs. "When *Swim Magazine* ran advertisements for the Gay Games in 1994, someone from Dallas — I think he's a closet case — wrote a horrible letter, from a Christian point of view. Well, the magazine was just deluged with responses against that letter. People came out of the woodwork. It gave me a really good feeling that I'm involved in this sport, swimming and coaching every day."

The Gymnast

With the possible exception of ice skating, gymnastics is probably the sport most Americans associate with gay men. Maybe it's the form-fitting tights gymnasts wear; perhaps it's all the running, jumping, leaping, and splitting they do. It could be the close physical contact — putting hands on arms, legs, and butts without benefit of football, hockey, or lacrosse pads — or the fact that gymnastics celebrates beautiful bodies and graceful movements more than any other sport. And don't forget: Girls are gymnasts too — a definite concern to any man worried about being thought of as "effeminate."

Whatever the reason, gay males who are attracted to gymnastics face stresses unique in the sports world. They start out being looked at with suspicion by friends, athletes in other sports, even parents and teachers. They then must confront their own complex feelings as they watch, spot, learn from, and teach other males. That the gymnastics environment is in many ways homoerotic cannot be denied; on the other hand, the line between homoeroticism and homophobia is thin indeed, and because male gymnasts know their sport is disdained by many men, they may go overboard trying to counter the stigma they feel.

"It's a schizophrenic sport," one participant says. That characterization applies to his own feelings as well. The life of a gay gymnast is filled with plenty of trips, stumbles, and falls — not all of which take place on the mat.

FOR TEENAGER JEFFERY NUNES, it was both the best and worst of times. Each day he spent hours surrounded by handsome young men with hot, buffed bodies. It was perfectly natural to look at them as they waited in line to practice or perform; once they took to the rings or floor, in fact, he was supposed to scrutinize their every move. Better yet, he could touch: pushing a shoulder down during warm-ups, placing a hand on a hip to spot.

However, that was as far as things could go. "It was wonderful and terrible all at the same time," Jeffery recalls. "It was like being a kid in a candy store without any money. There was so much conflict in my life. I was watching these guys' backs, chests, and muscles. I could smell them. But I couldn't do anything about it. It was so hard. I ended up leading an incredibly active fantasy life."

Even worse than not being able to go beyond touching to *touching*, the teenage Jeffery had to endure comments about "fags," jokes about "faggots," and dozens of daily actions small and large, subtle and overt, through which the guys Jeffery had crushes on sent a clear message to the world: *I may be a gymnast, but I'm not gay.*

Even if they were.

For Jeffery, the conflicted life of a gymnast began early. His first exposure to the sport came watching Olga Korbut compete in the 1972 Olympics. It seemed fun, and he soon learned of opportunities nearby. Los Angeles's Venice Beach was filled with men doing tumbling stunts. Jeffery befriended one, who taught him cartwheels and aerials. Adding to his excitement was the fact that, at the time, Venice was a clothing-optional beach. Jeffery was hooked.

His new friend told him about an open gymnastics event held every Labor Day since the '50s at Muscle Beach, just south of the Santa Monica pier. Bars were built in the sand; men performed on rings, while others tumbled. Jeffery was amazed and thrilled. He met a former national floor-exercise champion who taught him the basics. Jeffery preferred tumbling to rings or bars — it was something he could do on his own, without any equipment — and soon became a Santa Monica regular. Every Sunday he biked to the beach and spent the afternoon with his new friends.

Jeffery knew he was gay, of course. He attended military school, however, and kept his sexuality hidden from his classmates. Only years later did he learn that many of the boys he had crushes on were fooling around with each other. "I didn't understand sex and being gay then," he says. "One day I read *Everything You Always Wanted to Know About Sex but Were Afraid to Ask*, and under 'Homosexuality' it said gay men wanted to wear dresses and be women. I had no interest in that, so I kept telling myself I obviously wasn't gay."

However, shortly after coming out to himself at fifteen, he met his first lover: a man in his twenties. When his mother found out, she told Jeffery he had two choices: Change or become a prostitute on Hollywood Boulevard. He knew he could not change, but she sent him to a psychiatrist anyway.

She told him too that she knew there was something wrong with him because he spent so much time hanging around "all those muscle men." She said those kinds of people were notorious for seducing boys. "That put the brakes on my coming out," Jeffery says. "I knew gay people, but I couldn't talk about it with them."

Among the gay people he knew were several gymnasts. "I'd been out, I knew the language and how to do things, but most of the gymnasts I was playing around with weren't as comfortable," he recalls. "When I saw them later, they made a very strong effort not to let anyone else know." One man spent an entire post-encounter drive home discussing his many girlfriends.

Jeffery's mother was not alone in stereotyping gymnastics as a sport filled with gay predators. "Within gymnastics there's an effort — maybe not conscious, but it's there — not to associate it with anything or anyone gay," Jeffery explains. "Because it looks like dance — and my mother lumped the two together — there's a lot of fear about homosexuality. So as a result, people in gymnastics get overly macho in order to disprove it. They make horrible comments or show off all their women."

Yet the homoerotic elements are undeniable, Jeffery says. They begin with beautiful bodies and graceful movements — "Needless to say, the sport requires you to be young and in excellent shape" — and extend through to the physical aspects of stretching and spotting. "To practice center splits, you sit down opposite your partner," Jeffery says. "You both spread your legs straight out to the side as wide as you can, then take turns grabbing each other's arms and pulling toward you while locking your feet against his ankles." In another version one partner spreads his legs while attempting to touch his belly to the floor. The second man kneels behind him and pushes on his lower back to help him into the split.

However, the homoeroticism of gymnastics is not the sport's sole attraction. "Plenty of heterosexual men find enjoyment in expressing themselves through their bodies," Jeffery says. "Doing handsprings is like being on a roller-coaster ride without a seat. You literally fly through the air."

Indeed, Jeffery speaks as enthusiastically about tumbling's emotional and kinesthetic appeals as he does about its sexual stimulation: "The tumbling in streets and parks; the adagio, which is guys throwing people around; the men in their sixties out on the beach teaching things to kids on teeterboards; the unorganized, fun workouts we had at open facilities at high schools and colleges — those are what I remember most. One day eight guys and I spent ninety minutes doing continual back handsprings, twists, and layouts in rotation. There was so much camaraderie. We all felt a real connection with each other."

Though gymnastics may look like an individual sport, Jeffery appreciates the strong element of teamwork. "We challenged ourselves and each other," he says. "It was almost like a game. The best sessions were when people challenged each other to do things they wouldn't or couldn't have done on their own."

The sport gave form and focus to Jeffery's life at a time he needed it most. In eleventh grade his mother kicked him out of her house, forcing him to live with friends and other families. After graduating from Beverly Hills High School, he attended Santa Monica College and then the University of California, Los Angeles. He graduated with a degree in electrical engineering and works now at the Jet Propulsion Laboratory in Pasadena, doing circuit analysis.

Interestingly, Jeffery never competed on a gymnastics team. His high school did not have one, and at UCLA he worked thirty hours a week while carrying a heavy academic load. But there was another reason: He wanted the sport to stay fun. He worried that if he competed on a scholastic team, tumbling would turn into a chore.

At UCLA Jeffery also got involved with the gay and lesbian student union. "I was lucky," he recalls. "I had come out really young and learned to completely accept myself and not worry what other people thought about me. My big worry was that if people found out I was gay, they wouldn't let me in the gym. But still, it wasn't until UCLA that I really started to integrate my whole personality."

Now that tendinitis and a demanding work schedule have put an end to Jeffery's tumbling days, he looks back with regret on only one thing: his inability to connect with more gay gymnasts. It was not, however, due to a lack of effort. "Nobody talked about it," he explains. "There's a facade in the sport that no one's gay."

Today, when he watches a competition or sees boys experiencing the same thrill of the sport he discovered on the beaches of California, Jeffery Nunes thinks about one thing. "I wonder what it's like for a young kid today," he says. "Homosexuality is generally more accepted and talked about than it was when I was growing up, but I can't imagine it's any easier. There's all that contact, all those beautiful bodies..." He pauses, lost in reflection. "It's still a sport with a lot of conflicts."

The Hockey Player—Coach

It takes dedication to be an athlete. Along with hours of training and competition, special diets, tiring travel, painful injuries, and long rehabilitation regimens come serious mental pressures that rival the most extreme physical exertions.

No wonder athletes dedicated enough to reach high levels develop fierce loyalties to their particular sport. As they invest incalculable time and energy, their game grows into an integral part of their being. They define themselves by their sport, and separating themselves from it is difficult indeed.

But at some point in many gay athletes' lives, they must reconcile their love for their sport with their emerging sense of sexuality. It is difficult enough in individual endeavors like running and swimming; in a team sport like basketball or baseball, it is harder still. But in the rough-and-tumble world of hockey — a sport that, for complex reasons including history, geography, and demographics, may be the most macho of all — that realization and the reactions that follow can be truly harrowing.

YOUNG HOCKEY PLAYERS hang two types of posters in their bedrooms and lockers. As with any sport, there are the superstars they idolize and aspire to be just like: Wayne Gretzky, Mario Lemieux, Mark Messier. Just as frequently, however, one sees goons: Huge men with shirts pulled over their heads, blood dripping from their noses, battling with fists and sticks. In no other team sport is violence so tolerated, let alone admired.

That image, John Spear says wryly, is hardly the stereotype of gay men.

This is the same John Spear who for two years held the school record for penalty minutes at Williams College. And the same John Spear who spent a decade and a half listening — on the ice, in the locker room, at the training table — to the most obnoxiously homophobic taunts imaginable. The homophobic actions he witnessed were even more appalling. But he always listened and watched in silence. He never came out to his teammates or in later years to the players he coached because he knew that if they learned he was gay, they would hate him and reject him. Or worse.

Hockey players are not like other athletes, John explains. On the one hand, the game costs a great deal of money: hundreds of dollars a year for skates, pads, gloves, helmets, and assorted other equipment. Add the expense of ice time, travel, and visits to the emergency room, and it becomes a very self-selective (read *white, suburban*) sport. It is hardly a coincidence, John notes, that prep school hockey teams are better than their few public school counterparts.

On the other hand, hockey's roots lie deep in Canada's ponds. The National Hockey League — the only goal many young hockey players dream of — is filled with players who signed pro contracts while still teenagers and for whom college is as alien a destination as Africa.

But whether they are wealthy, sheltered prep school students or poor, poorly educated men from the provinces, hockey players share certain traits. They inhabit a physical world, one that extends far beyond the ice. The popular image of hockey players as hard-drinking, hard-fighting, hard-carousing he-men is, John says, not off the mark. He's been there; he's seen it with his own eyes. For a long time he also accepted it without thinking.

"The hockey culture starts young," John says. "And it's a lifetime culture. Hockey players don't have a lot of time for much else; they don't get the chance to do many other things." Hockey culture prizes toughness or at least a tough facade. It is a weakness to show weakness. There are only a few ways hockey players are expected to act, and different is not one of them.

"The ideal hockey player is big, strong, mean, aggressive, violent, and very skilled athletically, all at the same time," John explains. "That's not what a gay person is."

There was a time when hockey epitomized all those things to John. But as he grew older he appreciated other aspects, like the "intoxicating" feeling after a big win. At Williams he captured that sensation by making a collage of victory celebrations from various sports. He thrived on the feeling of "putting in so many hours, putting up with so much crap, then winning and enjoying it." It was no longer about being the one who scored the winning goal but simply about participating in winning.

That was certainly not the prevailing attitude, even at a prestigious institution like Williams. He recalls with sorrow an unrecruited freshman who tried out for the team. The young man was not big and strong; he may have been skillful, but during dry-land training, no one could see him skate or shoot. "Because he never spent a day in the weight room — and was a vegetarian — everyone rejected him as a 'fag,' " John says. Once during tryouts the freshman was first in line at the dining hall. He got his food and found a table, expecting other players to join him. No one did.

The locker room was the same; everyone stayed far away. The coach never had to decide whether to keep him, because he quit. John later found out the young man was not gay, but by then it hardly mattered. He had not fit the image of an ideal hockey player, so there was no place for him. "We handled things our own way," John says. "I still regret that."

For most of his four years at Williams, a small school nestled in Massachusetts's Berkshire Mountains with as solid a reputation in athletics as academics, John was not ready to come out. He had grappled for years with his homosexuality, often in the context of hockey, and nothing he had learned disproved his early feeling that the rink is an unsafe place for gay men.

His family had not sent particularly affirming messages either. As a child John lived in south Boston, which is to the rest of Boston what the Gay Games are to the official Olympics: night and day. An early '70s memory of John's is of relatives and neighbors screaming in protest as one or two school buses with police escorts carried black children from neighboring Roxbury into "Southie." A more recent and raw image comes from three years ago. Family members hoisted large signs with pink triangles overlaid by the international red-slash "not" symbol, symbolizing opposition to a gay group's marching in the annual St. Patrick's Day parade. John is out only to select relatives; his mother fears retaliation if others knew.

He moved to Lowell, an old mill town northwest of Boston, and started playing hockey in 1980, the year the U.S. Olympic team upset the Russians. Lacing up a pair of used ten-dollar skates, he could not get enough. Soon his life revolved around winter, spring, and fall leagues and summer camps. He saved all his money for new equipment. He joined as many teams as he could; sometimes there were four games a week plus practices. While his parents' memories are no doubt of 5 A.M. breakfasts at Dunkin' Donuts, John says, all he recalls is fun.

He became an avid fan of nearby University of Lowell, perennial NCAA Division II hockey champions. One night he actually turned down tickets to a Boston Bruins play-off game in favor of Lowell. He kept scrapbooks of his idols. When he actually met college players at a summer camp, he felt his life was complete.

When John was a ninth grader, his father, a food service distributor, was transferred to the Albany, New York, area. John played hockey and lacrosse at Shenendehowa High School in Clifton Park, captaining both sports senior year. Though his grades and SAT scores were high, a counselor told John — the first member of his family ever to apply to college — that he would not get into Babson or any other place he wanted and suggested local two-year schools. When he was accepted by all of them — and several state colleges as well — John realized that advice was off-base. He opted for a postgraduate year at prep school to prepare for the best college possible.

He chose Northwood School in Lake Placid, New York — coincidentally the site of the same 1980 Olympics that had first turned him on to hockey. In fact, the Olympic rink was his home arena. The thrill of skating on that ice for the first time remains indescribable, John says.

Northwood was a hockey power, a conduit to Division I colleges and, in a few instances, the NHL. It also helped him academically. Graduating second in his class and with even higher SAT scores than before, John found himself recruited by such schools as Brown, Dartmouth, and Amherst. His self-esteem soared; eventually he chose Williams, largely because the athletes welcomed him on campus visits and because he believed he could make an impact on the poor-but-improving hockey team.

He certainly did. A new coach his second year introduced a new system, a quicker style of play, and aggressive recruiting. By the next winter the Purple Cows were nationally ranked. When John was elected captain, he felt fulfilled.

But senior year brought personal anguish as well as satisfaction. That was when he first came to terms with being gay.

John dates his same-sex feelings to age fourteen, when he and a hockey teammate had a fling. At that age he had no problem being gay, but the boy he was "dating" — "Put that in quotes," John requests — eventually turned on him. He told John that he himself was not a "fag" but that John was. "That made me feel scared, small, and determined not to be gay," John says. "Athletically I had always had the belief that hard work could accomplish anything. If I spent enough time on the ice and in the weight room, I thought I would reach whatever goal I set." He applied the same philosophy to homosexuality: "I figured if I could work out three hours a day, date enough women, and think enough straight thoughts, then I wouldn't be gay."

But by senior year at Williams, reality caught up with John. The rationalizations he had clung to for so long — because no one around him looked or acted gay, that meant there were no gay athletes; since there were no gay athletes, *he* certainly could not be gay — crumbled under feelings he could no longer

222   repress. He began rejecting everything that for nearly four years had enamored him of Williams: sports teams, with their eat–live–train–party-together mentality; the us-against-them philosophy with which so many athletes view the outside world; and the comfortable, clear assumptions that allow jocks to pigeonhole anyone who is different.

As hockey season ended John formed friendships with people who harbored no athletic impulses at all. He quickly learned that there is more to life than sports — but that lesson carried a price. As he recognized that the one thing in which he had invested the most time, energy, and emotion was not going to be his way of living forever, he felt lost. He had had fun playing hockey and playing the role of hockey player, sure, but now he questioned how important all that really was. He regretted not spending more time on academics. He wished he had spent a semester abroad. He realized he was miserable.

His first job after Williams was at, of all places, Northwood School. He was hired to teach English and psychology and coach hockey and lacrosse. Despite his busy schedule John found time to think about what it means to be gay. The Adirondack Mountains offered spectacular opportunities for outdoor activities. During solo pursuits like hiking, rock climbing, and, particularly, running, John gained insights. As his miles increased, so did his comfort level. "Some people come out with a bang," he laughs. "I came out with a fifteen-mile jog."

But though his personal torment eased, his school situation remained tangled. The Northwood athletic culture, he began to see, was overwhelmingly homophobic, racist, and sexist. As he listened to his hockey players' comments and saw their actions, lacing up his skates became harder and harder.

He knew he was not ready to come out publicly. Just as he would not teach a novel until he understood it inside out, so he could not reveal his homosexuality until he understood his own reactions to hearing "You're all fags!" used as motivational

devices by coaches and players or seeing a once-respected colleague flap his arms and talk effeminately while telling a gay
joke. John did not feel comfortable confronting such people and
grew increasingly uneasy around teachers, coaches, players, and
students who thought nothing of acting that way.

One day the headmaster called him in. A man named Al
Chase had sent a letter to the admissions office. Saying he had
an openly gay son and was seeking a school that would affirm
him, Al posed specific questions about Northwood's support for
gay students and staff. John was called in, not, he says, "because
I was a flaming fag but because I was a flaming liberal" and was
asked how the school should respond. The headmaster believed
the letter was a setup by a gay organization. (It was a setup, but
not in that sense. Mr. Chase, a former private school teacher,
was acting on his own. He had no gay son but wanted to know
how 115 different private schools handled gay matters. The
responses impelled him to develop a newsletter devoted to gay
and lesbian issues at boarding schools.)

John told the headmaster to answer the letter naturally.
Thinking out loud, the headmaster said he would respond to the
question "Do you have any openly gay teachers?" with "We do
not but would hire one unless he preached or taught his own
personal agenda." For the query regarding Northwood's antidiscrimination policy, the headmaster said the school's inclusion of
the word *gender* was sufficient to cover *sexual orientation*.

"That was a good clue to me that the headmaster was not
quite 'with it,' " John says. "He wasn't homophobic, just clue-
less. It was scary, but I didn't want to be the one to educate him."

However, as an English teacher he had complete control
over his curriculum. He could teach any piece so long as it was
American literature. Because he noticed so many problems at
school surrounding race and gender issues, John introduced his
classes to books like *The Awakening* by Kate Chopin (which has
no overt lesbian scenes but leads naturally into excellent discussions about gender roles and expectations and, ultimately, sexu-

224   al orientation) and Alice Walker's *The Color Purple*, which does include lesbian romance. When he taught *One Flew Over the Cuckoo's Nest*, John was careful to mention something he says he missed the first six times he read it: that he thinks Randle Patrick McMurphy, the protagonist who is persecuted and institutionalized, is gay. As he walked across campus from his classroom to lunch to his apartment, he heard students discussing, of all things, homosexuality.

In his second year as a teacher, his students slowly opened up to him. One, a soccer and tennis player, sought John out after class and on the field. First he spoke indirectly about his feelings as a Northwood athlete; eventually he came out as gay. He said John was the first teacher who ever discussed gay people as "normal"; the boy added that he felt comfortable talking because John was a jock who did not look like the people at pride parades wearing purple hair or makeup. (That annoyed John, as it does today. "I get concerned when people say I don't look gay," he explains. "It's an unearned privilege I don't necessarily want. I don't feel like a jock or butch; I feel gay. It's supposed to be a compliment, but I don't take it that way.")

After a female colleague in English came out as bisexual, they collaborated on an essay for "Speaking Out," the newsletter on gay and lesbian issues at boarding schools published by Al Chase, the man who had sent the letter about his fictitious gay son to the Northwood headmaster. Like all good teachers, who know that administrators hate to be surprised, John and his coauthor told the headmaster about the piece before it appeared. He responded that it was great to have Northwood included. John gave him a copy when it was published, but he did not read it.

When he finally did, several months later, he was upset to learn that the female teacher was counseling a lesbian student and giving her gay-themed young-adult literature. Making matters more difficult in the headmaster's eyes was the fact that the girl's father was a board member and was having difficulty accepting her sexual orientation. Very late that year the headmaster refused to renew the bisexual educator's contract, accusing her of counseling students who needed psychological help and promoting a personal agenda. Upset, John told the headmaster that that decision was so poor, he did not know if he could continue to teach there. The headmaster asked him to reconsider, but John realized he could not continue working in such an uncomfortable environment.

The difficult decision was made even tougher because it occurred after students and many colleagues had left for the year. John could not say good-bye. Looking back, he says, "I have a lot of unfinished business there."

He is already taking care of some of it. After leaving Northwood, he entered graduate school in education at St. Lawrence University. Four former students were there; he came out to them. Word filtered back to the private school. Eventually he hopes to return and talk to students and faculty.

He is well-positioned to do that. Today, John serves as director of field services for the Gay, Lesbian, and Straight Education Network, a national service and advocacy organization with over 6,000 members and seventy chapters.

He still follows hockey avidly — though with a new twist: He is more aware of the gay side of the sport. One year after quitting Northwood, he took part in a GLSEN retreat in Rhode Island. After John told his story, a man asked, "Why is it that every gay person I know used to play hockey?"

"I don't know anyone else," John replied.

"They're there!" the man said.

John now realizes that gay men are everywhere — including the sport he grew up loving yet eventually left because he felt so isolated. He has discovered gay hockey leagues in New York City and is thrilled that it is an official Gay Games sport. He has also learned that there are gay players in the NHL.

None, however, is even close to being out, and that disturbs him. "It's devastating to a lot of kids," John says. "If I had known of a gay Bruin, it would have made my life a lot better." As a career closeted hockey player himself, however, he understands their reluctance. Hockey fans are tough; they have clear expectations of what a "real" player is, and — even more than in many other sports — could be merciless on one who broke that mold. In addition, hockey management — coaches, scouts, general managers — is filled with former players; they grew up in the same culture and share the same expectations of what it means to play hockey. They could make it extremely difficult for a gay athlete to stay in the league.

Even at the college level, at a school as relatively enlightened as Williams, John realizes that plenty of work remains to be done. Not long ago he returned to his alma mater to talk about discrimination and sports. He related four specific stories, about sexism, racism, anti-Semitism, and homophobia.

His former hockey coach was in the audience. After the speech, talking with John, he mentioned three of the stories specifically and said that on his team, with him as coach, those would not have happened. The one incident he did not bring up was the homophobic one.

"It was great to see my old coach and teammates," John says. "It was extremely important to see them. I don't know if what the coach said was inadvertent or intended. But I was profoundly, deeply disappointed." Thanks to GLSEN and his own visibility today, John Spear is in a position to make sure no hockey coach — or any other type of coach or teacher, for that matter — remains silent about homosexuality again.

The National Education Leader

Most people involved in athletics have a fairly parochial view: They know their sport, their league, perhaps their region of the country. That's to be expected; few of us have the time or the resources to develop a broader perspective.

But some folks do enjoy a national view. While the executive director of the Gay, Lesbian, and Straight Education Network is not normally involved in athletics issues, he does have contact with gay jocks; coaches are teachers too. And when he talks to them, he speaks their language. After all, Kevin Jennings was once a coach himself.

KEVIN JENNINGS'S RÉSUMÉ GLISTENS. A native of rural North Carolina, he was the first person in his family to go to college (and not just any school: Harvard). As a senior he was selected to give the commencement address. After a decade of teaching history at a pair of elite private schools — Moses Brown in Rhode Island and Concord Academy in Massachusetts — he helped found what was then called the Gay and Lesbian Independent School Teachers Network, for educators in New England. The organization, which was renamed in 1991 as the Gay, Lesbian, and Straight Teachers Network and again in 1997 as the Gay, Lesbian, and Straight Education Network, has mushroomed to seventy chapters across the country, with over 6,000 dues-paying members. Kevin has become a national spokesman in the fight to end homophobia in America's schools; his pithy, passionate quotes on subjects ranging from the importance of coming out to the need for gay representation in curricula have empowered millions of people while inflaming millions of others.

But of all the things Kevin has done, many of his fondest memories involve athletics.

He knows firsthand the power of sports to raise a boy's self-esteem — or shatter it. The youngest of four athletic brothers, he looked forward each school day in the mid '70s to phys ed. But his seventh-grade teacher — a man who "seemed to have a smoldering rage burning inside him" — made every gym class an ordeal. Kevin already feared that his eyes might linger too long in the locker room on the male bodies to which he was increasingly drawn, but that terror paled compared with what happened during a winter unit on wrestling.

As the phys ed teacher droned on about the scoring system, Kevin could not stop staring at a classmate. Suddenly the teacher halted, fixed his gaze on Kevin, and said slowly and clearly, "Stop looking at his legs."

After a few seconds of unbearable silence, the teacher returned to his lecture. Kevin, however, never went back to being the person he was before. He never again played on an organized school team. He never again felt as if he belonged at school. And he never forgot that moment.

Yet he eventually returned to sports, this time as an educator. At Moses Brown and at Concord, Kevin coached boys' squash and soccer and boys' and girls' volleyball. Of all the things he accomplished at those schools — including being one of the first openly gay teachers anywhere in the country — it is his volleyball teams he misses the most.

"As a coach you get close to kids in ways you don't or can't in other areas," he explains. "You ride in vans for hours, have dinner together at McDonald's. You talk and share things in a way not possible in any other school environment. A closeness develops through sports that just does not happen in the classroom."

He had no problems as an openly gay coach. Time and again his athletes came through for him. Kevin's girls once played a team whose coach, everyone knew, was a closeted lesbian. His players worked extra hard in that game. "They felt they had to uphold the honor of openly gay people everywhere," he says.

Another day a boy asked, as youngsters often do, "What kind of girls do you like?" The other players hustled the newcomer aside. "He's gay, stupid," they told him. "Don't be a dick."

In fact, Kevin says, though he received support from every quarter, the strongest of all came from his male athletes. "They knew me best as a person," he says. "They saw that being gay was a part of me; it wasn't all of me. They knew I was a good coach. I was enormously competitive — the athletic director nicknamed me 'Sarge' because of it — and the boys liked that." Today, the private school people he keeps in closest touch with are former players.

Still, Kevin knows that openly gay male coaches remain an infinitesimal minority in America's schools, and he understands the legitimate reasons why. Even he had conflicted feelings about using the only men's locker room at Concord. He showered at home rather than place himself in a situation where a disgruntled or disturbed person could accuse him of something.

Speaking generally, he says, "If administrators want to get rid of you, they will, no matter how many protections exist. They'll find a way." Thus, many coaches equate coming out with touching a third rail: It brings shock, perhaps death.

Yet, he continues, the perception of persecution is more dangerous than the reality. Most administrators do not want to get rid of most coaches, no matter what their sexual orientation; good coaches are simply too hard to find. Most understand that a coach's bedroom and weekend life has nothing to do with his behavior on the court or field. Most also do not want to risk controversy, and these days the fallout over the dismissal of a gay man might be more damaging than the revelation that a man is gay.

Kevin strongly advocates that coaches come out of the closet. "Gay male coaches break stereotypes," he says. "It is important for everyone to see that gay men can be good, successful teachers of athletics and athletic values. On a more personal basis, they have a unique opportunity to influence individuals." He recalls his fateful day in seventh-grade gym class and subse-

230   quent withdrawal from athletic activities. "Not until college did I realize I was deliberately avoiding something I loved and that was important to me," he says. "If someone had been there to say, 'This is your arena too,' I would have stayed. I look back on my own adolescence with tremendous sadness. An openly gay coach would have helped so much."

But Kevin does not place the burden of education on gay coaches alone, nor does he limit the lessons learned to gay athletes. Because coaches in general have more access to students than do classroom teachers, he believes it is imperative for all coaches, of any sexual orientation, to lead the fight against homophobia.

"The reasons are so clear," he says. "Coaches deal with a segment of the population that is stereotyped as homophobic. I'm not sure it's true, but what is true is that athletes are *told* to be homophobic. They hear messages about the need to 'crush weakness,' and homosexuality is seen as a weakness to be crushed. Homophobia has become a part of sports. So coaches can reach kids who need to be reached, where they can be reached, in a way they can be reached. If a coach fails to act when he hears a homophobic comment or sees a homophobic act, then he just reinforces the message that homophobia is okay. For gay kids — and straight ones — that's horrible."

From his national perch at GLSEN's New York headquarters and his ceaseless travel around the country, Kevin is aware that many coaches are indeed doing the right thing, speaking out against homophobia and disciplining homophobic athletes. But he also knows their numbers are low.

At virtually every school where he conducts antihomophobia training workshops, he hears the same refrain: "This is so great. If only we could get the athletic department here." Many educators see coaches and phys ed teachers as the most conservative, intolerant people in their schools; however, because they're off coaching in the afternoon or are not seen as "real" teachers during the school day, they often are absent from his sessions.

"It's stunningly shortsighted not to view coaches as equal to history or English teachers, as not part of the educational process," Kevin says. "That fundamental shift must take place before homophobia can be met and conquered." He cites his own career as an example. "I see my coaching as some of the best teaching I did, and I don't mean just how to serve the ball," he says. "I taught students to be focused and disciplined, to work with others, to overcome adversity. And I taught them about diversity."

He is both nervous and excited about current trends. The anxiety arises when he hears about places like Salt Lake City, where trouble erupted when East High School students petitioned for a gay-straight alliance. Some citizens were outraged; legislators responded by banning all extracurricular activities (except sports). At a basketball game fans from rival West High chanted derisively, "Gay club, gay club!" For the West High athletic director to take no disciplinary action, Kevin says, was devastating not just to gay students but to all students. "It sent a horrible message to everyone that certain differences are not to be tolerated," he says. "It said it is okay to hate."

Yet he is thrilled at what he discerns to be a growing desire on the part of gay youth to participate fully in all school activities on their own terms — including sports. "Gay kids don't necessarily want to separate themselves out in special schools like Harvey Milk in New York or EAGLES in Los Angeles," he says. "They want to do the same things every other kid does, and that means playing on teams. More and more we're seeing openly gay kids insisting on their rights and making waves if they don't get them."

However, unless homophobia is addressed whenever and wherever it occurs, the potential for trouble remains. "It's not that people in athletics are innately more homophobic than others," he concludes. "But athletics is an area in which they're given permission to dislike and exclude gays — even empowered to do so. That's where the problem lies."

Appendix: The Strategies

Why Physical Educators and Coaches Must Address Homophobia in Schools

• Athletes carry their fears and prejudices with them when they join teams. Coaches must help them unlearn their prejudices.

• Violence and hate crimes directed at gay people — and those perceived to be gay — are on the rise.

• Up to 30 percent of teen suicides are gay and lesbian youth who are so isolated and unhappy that they kill themselves. In addition, a high percentage of students drop out of school because of sexuality-related issues.

• High school and college-age young adults are beginning to explore their sexuality and sexual identities, whether heterosexual, homosexual, or bisexual.

• Coaches and physical education teachers are responsible for teaching more than just sports, fitness skills, and teamwork. They also bear the responsibility of setting examples for athletes and students in the areas of social justice and appreciation of social diversity.

• Discrimination against gay teachers, coaches, and administrators often goes unaddressed either because there is no legal protection or because victims are too afraid to protest unfair treatment.

• Because so many schools are silent about homosexuality and because few gay coaches and teachers feel they can reveal their identities without risking their careers, many educators and students have no accurate information to contradict destructive stereotypes of gay people.

• Unless coaches and teachers address homophobia, the next generation of young people will inherit the same prejudices and fears that have existed for decades.

• It is the right thing to speak out against injustice and prej- udice wherever it occurs.

Tips for All Coaches

• **Recognize that gay athletes exist.** Do not assume that everyone on a team is straight. Realize that every player does not dream about dating or marrying someone of the opposite sex; understand further that this may cause concern and worry. Watch your language; never use words like "faggot" or "queer" to demean anyone, even on the other team. Create an open and accepting atmosphere. By speaking neutrally about homosexuality, you communicate the idea that same-sex attraction is natural and normal.

• **Deal decisively with antigay slurs and actions.** Of course you do not permit bias based on race and ethnicity; do not permit bias based on sexual orientation either. Coaches are in a unique position to teach about human rights and diversity; do not be afraid to reprimand a player for antigay prejudice. Most athletes want to respect their coaches for being good, respectful people — and those who don't are in particular need of role models who are.

• **Understand that gay people are everywhere.** If they are not on your team, they're among the men and women who provide medical services, clean your uniforms and locker rooms, write about your games, and drive your buses. When you realize that most extended families include at least one gay or lesbian member — a brother, sister, parent, grandparent, cousin, aunt, uncle, niece, or nephew — you will realize that virtually everyone knows someone who is gay.

• **Remember that being lesbian or gay is natural.** Despite popular myth, sexuality is an orientation, not a choice. The American Psychiatric Association and American Psychological Association agree that homosexuality is neither a mental nor an emotional disorder. Most gay men and lesbians recognize their orientation at an early age; it is society's actions and values, not their own sexuality, that cause worry and anguish.

The Many Ways Straight Coaches Can Support Gay Colleagues and Athletes

• Wearing a button saying something like "I'm straight but not narrow" or a pink-triangle pin.

• Reading gay-themed books.

• Attending cultural or educational events about gay topics.

• Speaking up when someone tells a homophobic joke or makes an antigay comment.

• Not being afraid to say the words "gay," "lesbian," and "bisexual" out loud.

• Attending gay pride rallies and parades — if only to watch.

• Reading news articles and discussing current events about gay issues.

• Monitoring your own stereotypes about gay people and committing yourself to unlearning them.

• Asking gay friends and colleagues how you can be a straight ally.

• Respecting the rights of gay people to decide when and how to come out.

• Insisting that your sport's governing organization and coaches association take stands against homophobia and discrimination against gay athletes and coaches.

Four R's for Gay Coaches and Physical Education Teachers

• **Rights.** Know your rights *before* you are confronted. Find out what legal protection you have. Does your union contract prohibit employment discrimination based on sexual orientation? Do local or state laws prohibit it — and if so, are educators included? Do you have tenure? Does your school have a nondiscrimination policy that mentions sexual orientation? Does your school have a sexual harassment policy, and if so, are you protected under it? Does your school, community, or state have hate-speech or hate-crime policies that include sexual orientation as a protected category?

• **Resources.** Find out what resources are available if you believe you are being discriminated against or harassed because of your sexual orientation. Which colleagues and parents can you count on to help? Do you have a personal support network — family and friends — outside of school? What kind of support will your local and state union provide? What aid can you count on from your national professional teaching and coaching associations? What gay legal resource organizations and lawyers are available in your community? Is there a gay education organization nearby?

• **Responsibilities.** You are responsible for establishing and maintaining a sound professional reputation. Keep records of all formal evaluations of your teaching or coaching performances by administrators and students. Keep thank-you notes and other letters of appreciation from parents, students, athletes, colleagues, and administrators. Keep records of your participation in professional conferences and graduate course work. Maintain warm but professional relationships with athletes. Establish and maintain good working relationships with administrators, colleagues, and parents.

• **Resolve.** Believe in your right to teach and coach. Believe in your right to be as open about your sexual orientation as you choose to be. Know that gay educators have just as much to offer young people as heterosexuals. Learn to understand and change the ways that you have internalized negative feelings about yourself and other gay people. Learn to differentiate between situations that are genuinely unsafe and those in which your own fear is your biggest obstacle to speaking out against homophobia. Speak out against homophobia in your school and on your team. Ask for homophobia-awareness training for fellow coach-

236 es, faculty, and administrators. Check the library for available reference material for students and teachers; suggest additions. Come out whenever you can; silence will not protect you. If you are harassed or discriminated against because of your sexual orientation, stand up for your rights. If you have done nothing wrong, do not accept unfair treatment from anyone.

Source: Pat Griffin, Associate Professor, Social Justice Education Program, School of Education, University of Massachusetts, Amherst. Excerpted with permission.